Cognitive Therapy in Action

Cognitive Therapy in Action

A Practitioner's Casebook

Ivy-Marie Blackburn,
Vivien Twaddle
and Associates

A CONDOR BOOK
SOUVENIR PRESS (E&A) LTD

First published 1996 by
Souvenir Press (Educational & Academic) Ltd,
43 Great Russell Street, London WC1B 3PA

Reprinted 1999

ISBN 0 285 63282 5

Photoset by Rowland Phototypesetting Ltd
Bury St Edmunds, Suffolk
Printed in Great Britain by
Redwood Books, Trowbridge, Wiltshire

Contents

Preface		ix
Acknowledgements		xiii
1	The Evolution of Cognitive Therapy	1
	What is cognitive therapy?	1
	The first twenty years, 1960s–1970s	2
	The second twenty years, 1980s–1990s	10
2	The Empirical Status of Cognitive Therapy	22
	Experimental studies	22
	The efficacy of cognitive therapy	33
3	A Case of Depression	57
	Definition of depression	58
	The cognitive model	59
	The referral	62
	The assessment	63
	Suitability for short-term cognitive therapy	69
	Initial formulation	71
	Treatment	72
	Progress of therapy	75
	Final formulation	83
	Outcome	84
	Relapse-prevention	85
	Discussion	85
4	A Case of Generalised Anxiety Disorder	88
	Definition of generalised anxiety disorder	88
	The cognitive model	90
	The referral	92
	The assessment	92

Suitability for short-term cognitive therapy	98
Initial formulation	100
Treatment	100
Progress of therapy	102
Final formulation	116
Outcome	116
Relapse-prevention	118
Discussion	121
5 A Case of Panic Disorder	122
Definition of panic disorder	123
The cognitive model	123
The referral	126
The assessment	126
Suitability for short-term cognitive therapy	130
Initial formulation	131
Treatment	131
Progress of therapy	133
Final formulation	142
Outcome	142
Relapse-prevention	145
Discussion	145
6 A Case of Obsessional–compulsive Disorder	148
Definition of obsessional–compulsive disorder	148
The cognitive model	150
The referral	154
The assessment	154
Suitability for short-term cognitive therapy	157
Initial formulation	159
Treatment	159
Progress of therapy	162
Final formulation	170
Outcome	172
Relapse–prevention	173
Discussion	173
7 A Case of Bulimia Nervosa	176
Definition of bulimia nervosa	176
The cognitive model	178

The referral 180
The assessment 180
Suitability for short-term cognitive therapy 187
Initial formulation 189
Treatment 189
Progress of therapy 192
Final formulation 207
Outcome 207
Relapse–prevention 207
Discussion 209
8 A Case of Long-term Problems 213
Definition of personality disorders 214
The cognitive model 216
The referral 220
The assessment 221
Suitability for short-term cognitive therapy 225
Initial formulation 226
Treatment 228
Progress of therapy 230
Final formulation 243
Outcome 243
Relapse–prevention 247
Discussion 248
9 Epilogue 252
General principles 252
Areas not addressed in this book 254
Training in cognitive therapy 255
Future directions 257

References 261
Index of Subjects 298
Index of Authors 302

Preface

This book is for practitioners of cognitive therapy. It is about the therapeutic stories of six people referred to the Newcastle Cognitive Therapy Centre, each with a different emotional disorder. They represent the 'bread and butter' clinical work of the Centre. For the purposes of confidentiality, details have been changed so as to camouflage the identity of the individuals. In writing the book, we have assumed a fair degree of theoretical knowledge and clinical experience in the reader, and so we have not gone into detail about basic concepts or strategies (see pp. 252–4 for an overview of our aims). Instead, space has been devoted to illustrating how to develop cognitive formulations, and make therapeutic decisions based on them. Because we are writing about real-life case studies, we have presented them 'warts and all' and hope that our enjoyment of practising cognitive therapy has shone through.

The book begins with a chapter on the theoretical and on-going evolution of cognitive therapy. It reasserts the guiding principles of the approach, and pays particular attention to the emerging themes that are of central importance to the clinical practitioner: for example, the integration of cognitive therapy with other theoretical traditions, the developing emphasis on the therapeutic relationship, the role of unconscious processes, constructivist models and the expansion of therapeutic strategies.

In Chapter 2 we present the empirical basis of cognitive therapy across all the emotional disorders described here. Interested readers are referred to the expansive bibliography on pp. 268–86. A selection of experimental studies aims to give a flavour of basic research methodology, and outcome research is extensively examined.

Chapters 3–8 are the clinical case studies. Each covers the same format: an outline of the disorder is followed by an explication of the specific cognitive model, details of the referral, and a section on assessment which includes symptomatology, history and presentation; the question of suitability for cognitive therapy is accorded a section of its own. Next, an outline formulation leads on to the plan of treatment and a description of the progress of therapy; then, the final formulation is proposed, which leads to a discussion of outcome, post-intervention prognosis and other pertinent issues. The case of depression is described by Ivy Blackburn, and that of obsessive–compulsive disorder by Vivien Twaddle. Ian James, clinical psychologist, has written the chapter on panic disorder, and collaborated with Ivy Blackburn on the chapter on personality disorder. Anne Garland, clinical nurse specialist in cognitive therapy, has contributed the chapters on bulimia nervosa and general anxiety disorder.

The final chapter covers topics that are, strictly speaking, outside the scope of this book, but which are relevant to the ongoing development of cognitive therapy: that is, therapist training, some uncharted theoretical territory, the need for empirical validation of recent theoretical concepts, schematic measurement, and the mechanism of change.

Cognitive therapy continues to be an exciting and rapidly developing area within psychotherapy. We hope that our enthusiasm for the approach comes across to you.

The Newcastle Cognitive Therapy Centre, which came into existence in 1988, was one of the first centres of clinical excellence for cognitive therapy in the United Kingdom. Its remit is threefold: to carry out research which is at the forefront of the field, to train clinicians in cognitive therapy, and to provide a specialist cognitive therapy service to patients in Newcastle-upon-Tyne and Northern England. Vivien Twaddle, consultant clinical psychologist, is the Head of Clinical Service for the

Centre and, along with Steve Galvin and Jan Scott, was responsible for setting up the Newcastle post-qualification course – to
our knowledge, the first in the United Kingdom. She remains
responsible for the clinical aspects of the Centre and its strategic
direction within Newcastle City Health NHS Trust.

Ivy Blackburn, consultant clinical psychologist and visiting
Professor of Clinical Psychology at the University of Durham,
came to the centre from Edinburgh at the beginning of 1993 as
Head of Training and Research. She has been the course
director since the second year of the post-qualification course
and has initiated and fostered research at the Centre. Two main
areas of interest are outcome research and the investigation of
methods of evaluating therapist competencies, with implications for training. In 1995 the post-qualification course received
accreditation from Durham University in acknowledgement of
its academic and clinical calibre. In 1994 the centre received its
most important accolade when Professor A. T. Beck became its
Honorary President.

Acknowledgements

In addition to Anne Garland for the chapters on bulimia nervosa and general anxiety disorders, and Ian James for the chapter on panic disorder and his contributions to the chapter on personality disorders, we wish to thank a number of others for making this book possible: Katharina Reichelt and Eileen Wardle for their invaluable secretarial assistance and patient determination; Lionel Joyce, Chief Executive of Newcastle City Health, for his continued moral and financial support and the brave risk he took in backing the Centre's inception in 1988; Tim Beck, whose inspiration the book was in the first place; and last, but certainly not least, the patients.

I.-M. Blackburn
V. Twaddle

1

The Evolution of Cognitive Therapy

WHAT IS COGNITIVE THERAPY?

Cognitive therapy is the field of applied psychology that is unified by a belief in the central role played by mediating knowledge structures or thinking processes in explaining and changing human behaviour. While acknowledging a reciprocal interaction between cognition and emotion, the many diverse orientations within cognitive therapy tend towards viewing cognition from the point of view of its contributory role in influencing emotion, although a few have begun to explore emotion as a primary source of information and meaning in its own right. All orientations draw heavily on a broad repertoire of cognitive and behavioural techniques, and some are expanding into experiential methods.

This chapter attempts to explore some of the historical roots of this evolving field of psychotherapy. It splits the discussion into two main sections, which broadly represent the first and second twenty years of the lifespan of cognitive therapy to date. It attempts to illustrate the intrinsic and ongoing dialectical growth process that continues to enhance cognitive therapy's utility and range of application. And while considering what is quite unique about this type of psychotherapy, we address emergent integrating issues.

THE FIRST TWENTY YEARS, 1960s–1970s

The theoretical (and practical) underpinnings of cognitive therapy were shaped by a variety of sources both within the general field of psychology and within applied clinical observation and practice. From the general field, three major strands of thinking stand out: the phenomenological approach and its contention that the view of one's self and of the world is central to the determination of behaviour (Adler, 1936; Horney, 1950); structural theory, which expounds the concept of hierarchical structuring of knowledge to include primary- and secondary-process thinking (Piaget, 1972); and the academic field of cognitive psychology which, while integrating both assumptions, stresses the importance of cognition in information-processing and behavioural change (Williams *et al.*, 1988).

From the clinical field, a number of workers have been influential: George Kelly, whose model (1955) of personal constructs expounded the idiosyncratic ways of construing and interpreting the world in the context of behavioural change; Arnold (1960) and Lazarus (1966), whose theories of emotion attributed a primary role to cognition in emotional and behavioural change; Ellis (1962), whose Rational–Emotive Therapy encapsulated the principle of the primacy of cognition for clinical intervention and emphasised the control that can be brought to bear over patterns of thinking and behaviour. From the behavioural field, Bandura's Social Learning Theory (1977) was important in attempting to explain the development of new behavioural patterns in terms of the cognitive aspects of observational learning. In doing so, it shifted behaviour therapy into the cognitive domain, as did Meichenbaum's (1977) self-instructional learning model and Mahoney's early work on cognitive control of behaviour (1974).

But it was Beck's model that really took the clinical literature by storm. This heuristic cognitive model was developed as a reaction to the theoretical excesses and practice limitations of classical psychoanalysis and to the rigidly restrictive nature of radical behaviourism. The model became the cornerstone of cognitive methodology and conceptualisation in the 1970s and, indeed, it continues to have its place at the forefront of empirical and clinical endeavour today. Much of cognitive therapy's development since his 1967 thesis (Beck, 1967) uses this 'grandfather' of models as a benchmark. For this reason we use it as a main reference point for the rest of this section.

Early cognitive conceptualisations

Cognitive therapy's focus on phenomenology necessarily accorded the content of a patient's experience a position of central importance in clinical understanding and intervention. Indeed, content-focused frameworks, such as Meichenbaum's self-instructional training (1977) and Ellis's rational–emotive therapy (Ellis and Greiger, 1977), were some of the first to appear in the cognitive therapy literature. One of the prominent more recent examples is that proposed by Beck and Emery (1985), which focuses on content issues of danger and vulnerability in patients with anxiety disorders; the negative triad which appears in Beck's conceptualisation of depression is another.

The advantages of this type of clinical framework became clear very early on. Such frameworks provided a working understanding of the immediate cognitive phenomenology influencing affect and behaviour in a manner that patients could easily relate to. Their straightforward and concretely descriptive focus made them workable for less traditional clinical subjects such as those with personality disorders and psychotic presentations, children and people with learning disabilities. However, their weakness was that they did not address the non-accessible cognitive processes and structures indicated in emotional and behavioural disorders (Craik and Tulving, 1975; Goldfried et al., 1984). There was also an issue of parsimony: different content-based models were required for different emotional disorders and, apart from the problem that such disorders are not mutually exclusive, there was the additional difficulty that patients with the same disorders did not necessarily share a common content.

The limitations, therefore, led to tripartite cognitive models which attempted to embrace the idea of different 'levels' of cognition. Beck's was the clearest and most influential. His framework distinguished between automatic thoughts (content), faulty information-processing (process) and dysfunctional assumptions (structures, or schemata). In doing so it advanced the cognitive understanding of patients' problems beyond that of content. The model views informational content as the products of information-processing. Automatic thoughts represent that part of conscious knowledge which is not the result of directed (logical) thinking, but which occurs out of the blue. They are synonymous with Meichenbaum's 'self statements' and Ellis's irrational beliefs (Meichenbaum, 1977; Ellis and Greiger, 1977).

Schemata are the deep, relatively stable, cognitive structures which reflect fundamental beliefs about oneself, the world and others. They represent complex patterns of thoughts that determine how experiences are perceived and conceptualised. They operate as a type of transformation mechanism that shapes incoming data so as to fit and reinforce preconceived notions. This 'distortion', or manipulation, of experience is maintained through the operation of characteristic information-processing mechanisms: arbitrary inference, selective abstraction, overgeneralisation, magnification and minimisation, personalisation, labelling/mislabelling and dichotomous thinking (Beck et al., 1979).

The model encapsulated the idea of a cognitive diathesis, or vulnerability, which represented a major issue in the academic and clinical literature – for instance, Seligman's developing ideas of a vulnerable attributional style in the onset of depression (Alloy, 1988). Beck proposed that the idiosyncratic dysfunctional schemata form the basis of vulnerability to specific emotional disorders. When 'activated' by stressful events that reflect those in which they were originally laid down, the schemata produce the cognitive shift that leads to the systematic bias in how an individual notices, interprets, integrates and remembers data. Schemata are considered unconscious in the sense that they are 'ideas we are unaware of . . . because they are not in the focus of attention but in the fringe of consciousness' (Campbell, 1989).

The extent of the disruptive effect that a particular schema has on an individual is dependent on several factors: the strength with which the schema is held; how much the schema is essential to a person's sense of personal integrity and safety; the amount of disputation the individual engages in when a particular schema is activated; previous learning with regard to the importance and essential nature of the schema; and how early the schema has been internalised (see Freeman, 1992). Beck argued that the schema returns to its previous dormant state once the stressor is removed. This has been given as the reason why some patients can rapidly return to health at the beginning of therapy – it happens, presumably, because the therapist and his or her explication of a model that 'makes sense' has reduced the stress (Freeman, 1992). This return to a state of dormancy has also been used to account for the observation that previously depressed patients are no different in schematic profile from never depressed individuals, as measured by the Dysfunctional Attitude Scale (Weissman, 1979; Hamilton and Abramson, 1983; Silverman et al., 1984).

This observation led to more complex explanations of vulnerability: Teasdale addressed the issue with his differential activation hypothesis (Teasdale, 1988), by proposing that depressed affect increases the accessibility of negative interpretative categories and constructs associated with previous experiences of depressed mood. Teasdale incorporated ideas from extensive studies of the effect of mood on memory (Blaney, 1986; Fennell et al., 1987), and its relationship with a range of other cognitive processes such as interpretations of ambiguous situations, self-efficacy expectations, evaluations of self and future probability and negative events (Bower, 1981; 1983). In effect, Teasdale challenged Beck's view that dysfunctional schemata are activated as a result of a precise fit between an environmental stressor and the content domain of the particular schema. By contrast, Teasdale argued that this activation occurred as a result of the depressed affect *per se* reactivating negative constructs that had been most frequently and prototypically associated with previous experience of depression as a whole. The clinical implication of this is that a particular stressor should necessarily activate a wider range of constructs than those proposed by Beck. Biological and other psychological factors were also introduced, to complicate the picture further. So, paradoxically, in its attempt to embrace the complexities of cognitive operations, Beck's model was criticised for oversimplification.

Since Beck's model first appeared in the literature, a main avenue of investigation has been to discover which types of negative interpretative structure are most important in relation to the development of emotional disorders. It appears that they are those relating to the self. Individuals with pervasively dysfunctional self-referent schemata seem more likely to be vulnerable to developing non-transient depressive disorders (Teasdale, 1988). Several cognitive psychology paradigms have illustrated the importance of these self schemata: the Stroop test, incidental recall, colour-naming tasks (Kuiper and Derry, 1982; Segal *et al.*, 1988).

Methodological assumptions

Cognitive therapy soon came to be associated with a set of explicit assumptions, or guiding principles, which have become the defining characteristics of the approach. There are, broadly speaking, eight of them.

1 *The centrality of the cognitive conceptualisation* The models came to be conceptually driven in that, rather than being a shot-gun technique-orientated approach with no theme or focus – as the early myth had it – they stressed the importance of a clear treatment conceptualisation guiding a series of organised and focused treatment strategies.

2 *The phenomenological emphasis* The phenomenological

approach to psychopathology naturally led to the patient's idiosyncratic subjective experience becoming the central focus of the therapeutic exchange. And this became one of the most distinctive early aspects of cognitive therapy. Seeing the 'world through the patient's eyes' naturally meant relying heavily on his own reports of his experience, and taking it at face value; the point of variation across therapists and conceptual models was the focus that each put on the different aspects of that experience (content, process, structure).

3 *The collaborative nature of the therapeutic relationship* The emphasis on phenomenology required a context of collaboration: the patient and therapist working together in an atmosphere of negotiation – a direct descendant of Kelly's notion of patient and therapist as 'personal scientists' (Kelly, 1955). Beck and colleagues (1979) coined the phrase 'collaborative empiricism', which encapsulated the idea of a team approach in which the patient provides the raw data to be investigated with the therapist's guidance. The objective of such a relationship is to develop a milieu in which specific cognitive change techniques can be applied most efficiently (1979, p. 49). And for the most part this was the focus of the clinical relationship, which was considered primarily as the context for the execution of techniques. Only later was the relationship to be viewed as an intervention tool in itself.

Beck's model originally viewed difficulties in the therapeutic relationship, such as 'incapacitating transference', as technical problems to be identified and examined in the same fashion as any other cognitive behavioural data. The emphasis was on minimising its occurrence in therapy. This stance was common in all the models of the time, more attention being given then to technique than to the relationship between therapist and patient *per se* (Meichenbaum, 1985; Rehm, 1977). Documented prerequisite therapist characteristics for developing a collaborative therapeutic milieu include both non-specific ones such as non-possessive warmth, accurate empathy and genuineness (Beck *et al.*, 1979; Beck and Emery, 1985; D'Zurilla, 1988), and specific ones such as good educational skills in instructing, challenging and reinforcing patients' efforts at change in a reciprocal, non-superior fashion, along with openness and directness for fostering an atmosphere of equality and partnership (Dobson and Block, 1988; Beck and Emery, 1985; Rothstein and Robinson, 1991).

4 *Active involvement of the patient* With a collaborative type of relationship the process of therapy naturally evolved into a highly interactive one. The models heavily emphasised actively engaging the patient in devising and experimenting with strategies for cognitive and behavioural change. Both therapist and patient came to have a role in selecting therapeutic targets and negotiating how such targets should be approached. This was, and still is, a more or less unique aspect of cognitive therapy.

A study by Vallis *et al.* (1988) is of interest here. They compared therapist competency ratings of cognitive therapists and general non-specific therapists, using the Mattarazzo checklist of therapist behaviours (Mattarazzo *et al.*, 1965). They observed among the most competent cognitive therapists a greater frequency of brief questions necessitating 'yes/no' answers, and of interruptions. These are classed as 'errors' in communication on this scale, but in cognitive therapy such questions and interruptions are regarded not as errors but as a critical part of the active collaboration between patient and therapist. This nicely illustrates that what is deemed to be competent in one system of psychotherapy may not be so judged within another.

5 *The use of Socratic questioning and guided discovery* The type of questioning used within cognitive therapy became known as Socratic dialogue. Rather than interpreting the patient's thoughts and actions, the therapist's role was to raise questions about thoughts, feelings and actions, so encouraging the patient to discover things for herself: a process of guided discovery. This was in sharp contrast to communication via interpretations. Apart from running the risk of 'mind-reading' and of misunderstanding the patient, interpretations were considered to risk putting her in a compromising position – in that it

is simpler to agree than to disagree, or to seem ungrateful or difficult. The Socratic questioning format of cognitive therapy allowed the patient to maintain integrity and the therapist to gather the most accurate data – accuracy being an important prerequisite for developing hypotheses, the building blocks of cognitive conceptualisation.

6 *Explicitness of the therapist* From the idea of negotiation, or collaboration, followed the requirement that the therapist share explicitly the model, his or her own working hypotheses and ideas on conceptualisation. It also entailed admitting mistakes and agreeing to disagree, and so on. There was to be no place for 'private' therapist models within the cognitive therapy paradigm, as this would sabotage the collaborative stance.

7 *The emphasis on empiricism* The models have always been heavily empirical: creating and testing out the working hypotheses emerging from the collaborative guided-discovery process via a number of techniques, broadly categorised as cognitive (focused primarily on modifying thoughts, images and beliefs) and behavioural (focused primarily on modifying overt behaviours). The categories are not, of course, mutually exclusive. For instance, a behavioural technique such as assertiveness-training has cognitive components to it: it can be used to accomplish cognitive changes, such as adjustment in expectancies regarding the consequences of assertion, as well as changes in interpersonal behaviour itself.

8 *The 'outward' focus* The empirical active aspect of cognitive therapy was designed to facilitate the generalisation of in-session therapeutic change: the so-called 'homework' of cognitive therapy. Different models vary in the extent to which such generalisation activities are explicitly determined, monitored and evaluated. But it has become a general rule that cognitive therapy does not focus selectively and entirely on the in-session interaction. On the contrary, much attention is given to functioning outside of the therapy context. Indeed, there are several studies suggesting that compliance with homework assignments is related to better outcome

(Neimeyer *et al.*, 1985; Persons *et al.*, 1985; Primakoff *et al.*, 1989).

THE SECOND TWENTY YEARS, 1980s–1990s

Emerging themes

The major changes that have been occurring in the field of cognitive therapy since the 1970s, in terms both of theory and of practice, are due to two factors. The first is the integrative force within applied psychology. What we have seen over the last twenty years is the emergence of 'broader' models which have been concerned with integrating non-cognitive theoretical models with cognitive ones. Illustrations include Neimeyer and his colleagues and their interest in Kelly's Personal Construct Theory (1955); Guidano and Liotti (1983) and their considerations of Bowlby's Attachment Theory; and Safran and Segal (1990) with their incorporation of Sullivan's Interpersonal Theory. The second factor responsible for theoretical and practical changes in cognitive therapy is the integration of cognitive psychology into the mainstream of cognitive therapy. This is best illustrated by the growing body of research on the role of schemata in cognition (Hollon and Kriss, 1984; Kuiper and Olinger, 1986; Williams *et al.*, 1988; Segal, 1990), and not least by the contribution of recent theoretical developments in the field of cognitive psychology itself (Teasdale and Barnard, 1993; Bower, 1981, 1983).

The emergent themes in the literature have been broad and varied, reflecting this process of change. Constructivism, development, relationship, emotion, unconscious processes, metacognition, change mechanisms, deep structures and experiential methods are just some of the ongoing considerations (Rosen, 1993). The result has been new models that have shifted ideas on therapeutic targets and strategies. The best-articulated are the constructivist developmental models, first expounded in the 1980s by Guidano and Liotti (1983) and Mahoney (1988), then the development in the 90s of the cognitive interpersonal model by Safran and Segal (1990). These neatly encapsulate the majority of the issues above, and will therefore take up most of the rest of this section.

Constructivist/developmental perspectives

This perspective relies heavily on developmental theory and structural models of knowledge (Piaget, 1977). Here, the notion of thought developing through a process of structural differentiation and integration is central – a process that moves in a hierarchical direction towards more advanced and adaptive ways of 'knowing the world'. It is held that an individual knows the world by assimilating conceptual data into existing structures, which, in turn, can be accommodated to the external structure of the world that the individual encounters. This is called the equilibration model. 'Objective relativism' is the optimum goal: here an individual develops from one stage to another through a process that takes him from disequilibration to re-equilibration, brought about by cognitive disturbances generated by the incongruity, discrepancy or contradiction between incoming data with *a priori* internal structures. The process entails the creation of a new cognitive organisation, which leads to a new and improved balance of knowledge.

Piaget's ideas fit well into the central aim and philosophy of a cognitive therapy approach to psychopathology. Cognitive strategies and techniques are designed to bring about disequilibrating experiences and subsequent re-equilibration in a bid to advance an individual's understanding through the reordering or modification of his assumptions, beliefs and expectations.

The idea of the active construction by the individual of his knowing structures is the central premise of the constructivist philosophy, which embraces a conceptualisation of ontology (the nature of reality) and epistemological assumptions (the nature of knowledge and the process of change). This philosophy reflects practical changes in the cognitive models during the second half of cognitive therapy's lifespan hitherto. Mahoney (1988) contrasted the constructivist viewpoint with its ontological and epistemological alternative, rationalism. The latter is concerned with truth and logic, adopting the position that one's thoughts and feelings should correspond directly to external reality. In contrast, the constructivist viewpoint holds that an individual creates knowledge and that such knowledge corresponds to his idiosyncratic internal and independently existing reality. The emphasis is not on whether knowledge is accurate and true, but whether it is viable and adaptive.

Over the last two decades there has been an increasing tendency towards constructivist thinking and, in turn, an emphasis on different techniques within a therapeutic relationship which, in the process of change, has taken on a new and heightened significance in its own right. But it would be an unfair reflection of the developments in the field to date constructivist models only to the last twenty years. Ellis (1990) has argued that even models like Rational–Emotive Therapy have never been truly rationalistic; and Beck's model fits somewhere in the middle of the constructivist–rationalist continuum.   Some aspects of Beck's framework are clearly based on the rationalist conviction of a separate external world, for example, subjecting cognitions to logical analysis and behavioural experiments for hypothesis-testing. Other aspects reflect more of a constructivist philosophy: for instance, techniques like listing the advantages and disadvantages of holding specific beliefs; techniques designed to consider the usefulness of the cognitions and to reconstruct them in the direction of greater viability. Furthermore, the model espouses the use of inductive questions that reflect both traditions: 'Where is the evidence?' and 'How could you test that?' are examples of rationalist questions; 'What is the impact that thinking has on you?' and 'How does that way of thinking help you?' are constructivist ones. Indeed, the maladaptive assumptions within the model itself are 'constructions' made by the individual. So Beck's model embraces both philosophical traditions. He did not make this explicit because this philosophical debate was not a pertinent one at the time the model was being developed.

Guidano's systems/process-orientated model of change exemplifies a mainly constructivist standpoint (Guidano, 1987; 1991; Guidano and Liotti, 1983). It combines ideas from Piaget's genetic epistemology (Piaget, 1972) and Bowlby's Attachment Theory (Bowlby, 1969, 1973, 1980) with the guiding principles and underlying assumptions of a cognitive model of change. In general terms, although cognitive techniques are used, they are accorded second place to the modification and transformation of deep 'tacit' structures in the human knowing system. Emotion is given a more primary role in both an ontogenetic and an evolutionary perspective. Emotion and cognition are indistinguishable in the sense that they are integral to each other, and, unlike the rationalists' view of emotion as disturbance, it is considered here as a vital reflection of changing structures over the course of therapy.

The approach differentiates tacit from explicit knowing, and highlights the central role of self-knowledge in emotional dysfunction and well-being. Attachment is seen as playing a major role in the development of this self-knowledge. Emphasis is placed on therapeutic interventions that are designed to alter deep core structures and that require in-depth examination of the developmental stages leading to the formation of self-knowledge. Thus, more time is spent on historical and process-focused issues than was hitherto apparent in the cognitive field, where more attention was given to problem-solving and symptom-resolution. The aim of the constructivist approach is the same as that in precedent models – to help illuminate the obsolescence of particular knowing structures and behaving in the world, and to help modify and reorganise key schemata into a more functional status.

It is fair to say that the model has received a mixed reaction: Mahoney (1991) welcomes the attention to complex processes of development and change; Ellis (1990) sees it as embracing some of the less desirable (non-empirical) features of psychoanalysis. Paradoxically, constructivist ideas are now receiving their most powerful empirical support from the field of academic cognitive psychology itself. Teasdale (1993) welcomes greater attention to emotion and the requisite focus on more experiential change techniques and therapeutic processes. He describes emotion as a 'higher-order' knowing process. Its implicational, as opposed to propositional, level of knowing and construing demands the use of a less rationalist stance. He has accorded the constructivist models a new academic status, which undoubtedly adds weight to their central position in the developing field of cognitive therapy (Teasdale and Barnard, 1993; Teasdale, 1993; Barnard and Teasdale, 1991). And the introduction of experiential techniques has expanded the cognitive therapist's repertoire considerably (Beck *et al.*, 1990; Edwards, 1989; Young, 1990). The goal, however, remains primarily a cognitive one, in the sense that experimental techniques are used to access existing cognitions, generate new ones, reach 'hot' (implicational) knowledge and facilitate structural change.

Cognitive–interpersonal perspectives

A second major developmental thrust within cognitive therapy is the interpersonally based frameworks which bring with them the whole debate about the changing emphasis on the therapist–patient relationship within cognitive therapy. Safran is the main figure involved in this development (Safran, 1990; Safran and Greenberg, 1988; Safran and Segal, 1990). The model views the therapeutic relationship as a central vehicle for revealing core dysfunctional interpersonal schemata – which are considered to be the most central structures. These ideas are shared by Liotti (1991), who articulated similar connections between dysfunctional types of early attachment patterns and their significance for developing interpersonal schemata as manifested in the therapeutic relationship. An interpersonal schema is 'a generic cognitive representation of interpersonal events . . . that is abstracted on the basis of interactions with attachment figures . . . and permits the individual to predict interactions in a way that increases the probability of maintaining relatedness with these figures' (Safran, 1988).

An important aspect of Safran's model is the distinction

between the information-processing model and the ecological model of cognitive functioning. The former position holds that an individual receives and transforms information. The latter views the individual in terms of interaction with the environment, which is, by and large, interpersonal. Safran's framework is associated more with this latter position, in which knowing and acting are seen from a socio-functional perspective (Safran and Segal, 1990). Of central importance is the interaction between patient and therapist, so as to understand how this might reflect the patient's interpersonal schemata and distress. This is not to say that the model is akin to a psychoanalytic relationship; the same guiding methodological principles of cognitive therapy, described earlier, apply just as much in this model as in previous ones. The model views the therapeutic relationship rather like a training ground for developing healthier interpersonal relationships, where attention is given to patient behaviours, cognitions and emotion within the session in the context of the feelings and responses that the patient evokes in her therapist (Jacobson, 1989).

The interpersonal perspective has much to offer in cognitive therapy's extension into the field of personality disorders (Beck *et al.*, 1990; Freeman, Pretzer *et al.*, 1990; Young, 1990). Recent developments attempt to conceptualise the more characterological nature of personality disorders and the core interpersonal problems that are involved. These are necessarily evident in the relationship with the therapist. A major implication of theoretical expansions of this nature within cognitive therapy has been the parallel expansion of experiential techniques. This has been accompanied by the elaboration of emotion theory with a view to illuminating its relationship to cognitive therapy, the unconscious and the construction of meaning (Safran and Greenberg, 1987, 1991; Greenberg and Safran, 1984, 1987). Wessler's cognitive appraisal therapy (Wessler, 1993) is an example of a cognitive therapy which embraces this shift into emotional frameworks.

The changing emphasis within the therapeutic relationship

The traditional view of the therapeutic relationship within cognitive therapy was that it was the context within which the technical intervention occurred (Lambert, 1983). However, as the previous section has intimated, this is changing, and greater stress is being laid on interpersonal mechanisms and core schemata. Arnkoff (1981) was one of the first clinicians to challenge the traditional view, talking in terms of using the therapeutic relationship to understand wider relationships; and Jacobson (1989) described how the relationship itself could be used as a vehicle to produce change in depressive patients. Currently, frameworks such as those already described are being considered more explicitly in the debate about the objective of the therapeutic relationship, the required therapist characteristics and the process of change.

Guidano and Liotti (1983) and Guidano (1987) talk in terms of the relationship providing the context in which the patient's developmental history is uncovered as it relates to the dysfunctional attachment patterns that have prevented the integration of self-knowledge. Issues such as trust, dependency, aggression, over-compliance and avoidance are classed as integral information which serves to guide exploration. This is in sharp contrast with Beck's earlier writings, which consider these intra-sessional phenomena as 'technical problems' requiring a problem-solving approach. Models like that of Guidano and Liotti highlight additional therapist characteristics which are not covered explicitly on the Cognitive Therapy rating Scale (Beck and Young, 1988). Helping a patient to understand the meaning of his obstructive behaviour towards the therapist requires the therapist to be in tune with how the patient is feeling in the relationship, before making it a focus of attention. The therapist's skill is more than rapport-building – it necessitates being in tune with one's own responses during the session, as well as with the patient's. Less emphasis is placed on challenging old beliefs or helping to build up new ones; instead, the focus is on acknowledging current self structures and looking at the advantages, problems and contra-indications within them.

Consider the following example of the difference in approach: a patient says, 'People don't understand me.' The traditional line would be for the therapist to ask confirming and disconfirming questions, such as 'Where is the evidence that leads you to this belief?', 'Can you give me some examples?', and to look for practical solutions such as helping the patient to communicate more skilfully with people. In comparison, more recent orientations would tend towards an exploration of the personal meaning of the patient–therapist relationship in order to probe for core self-knowledge. This leads to a different set of questions: for instance, 'Do you feel misunderstood by me?' or 'What does it mean for you to have people misunderstand you?' Notice that both sets of questions employ Socratic dialogue and are aimed at guided discovery. The choice of content of the questions depends on the cognitive framework being employed in the therapy.

Padesky (1993) has looked in detail at the issue of choice of question. She discusses the complex process of Socratic questioning and stresses the importance of listening beyond the answers to specific questions and being open to discovering the unexpected. She urges cognitive therapists to listen for idiosyncratic words, emotional reactions, metaphors, words oddly placed in a sentence, and for incongruous elements in a story. She argues that reflecting this phenomenology back to the patient will intensify affect and create new and faster inroads into core structures. She separates the process of guided discovery into four stages: asking informational questions, listening, summarising, and synthesising. The last stage is most critical. It involves applying to the old structure the new information gained from the Socratic questioning process. In the case of the example above, a synthesising question would be 'How does all this information fit in with your idea that people don't understand you?' Safran and Segal (1990) have much to say about the therapeutic relationship; they encourage testing out the patient's expectations of it. They consider that the patient's subjective experience in therapy and the therapist's feelings and behavioural tendencies are equally important in pinpointing clinical problems.

The issue of resistance

With the increased attention devoted to relationship issues within cognitive therapy has evolved a parallel interest in the issue of resistance. Typically, cognitive therapists have taken a problem-solving approach to this, viewing resistance as an unwelcome phenomenon. But newer, alternative, concep-tualisations portray resistance as a normal process which provides a valuable opportunity to explore fundamental cognitive processes.

The traditional models conclude that resistance is due to several factors involving the patient, the therapist and/or the patient–therapist relationship (Beck *et al.*, 1979; Ellis, 1983a, 1983b; Lazarus, 1987; Lazarus and Fay, 1982). Patient factors include failure to do homework, failure to use self-disputation consistently, failure to accept personal responsibility for in-appropriate emotions, excessive deficits in functioning, and undervaluing treatment outcome. Therapist factors include mis-application or inflexible use of techniques, and a mistaken focus on secondary rather than central problems. Relationship factors include poor therapist–patient attributional match (Jack and Williams, 1991) and patient–therapist collusion – for example, when both have a low tolerance of anxiety.

The constructivist models place a different emphasis on resist-ance. Neimeyer (1986) argues that therapeutic impasse may be due to shortcomings in the patient's existing construct system, so that it does not support the insights that the therapist thinks the patient should be able to achieve. When this is the case, anxiety and a sense of threat may be manifested by the patient. Liotti (1987) addresses the issue by arguing that the manifesta-tion of so-called resistance reflects the patient's attempts to preserve his meaning structures. The preservation of meaning is thought to be the primary aim of human mental functioning.

Old structures of meaning will naturally be resistant to change because of the individual's innate need to predict and attribute meaning and because of the stability afforded by the established meaning structures. Mental processes are ordered hierachically, according to level of organisation. The higher-order ones, which are related to the sense of personal integrity and identity and provide coherence and consistency, are the most resistant to change.

Although cognitive therapy's ideas on resistance have broadened over the last twenty years, they remain very distinct from those of other schools of thought. The psychoanalytic explanation of resistance, for instance, is that of defence against unconscious drives and repressed memories. Within cognitive therapy resistance is seen as an expected phenomenon because of its natural and healthy self-protective function, which guards against changing structures too much or too quickly.

The conceptualisation of the mechanism of change

The increasing amount of literature pertaining to the differential outcome in cognitive therapy, particularly in terms of relapse-prevention (see pp. 33–56), has fuelled the whole debate over the change process *per se*. A variety of models has been proposed. The most eloquent is that of Freeman, who describes schematic change as four points on a continuum from least to most change (Freeman and Leaf, 1989; Beck *et al.*, 1990).

The first point on the continuum is referred to as schematic camouflage. This involves teaching an individual to do the 'right' thing despite her schema-driven behavioural tendencies – for example, teaching the schizoid person to act in a more socially appropriate fashion. This is related to Persons' and Miranda's ideas on a coping-skills model of change (Persons, 1993). The second point on the continuum is that of schematic reinterpretation, which involves using the schema in a more adaptive and effective manner; for instance, a medically trained person who is uncomfortable with relating to patients may be better off going into a specialty such as pathology rather than psychiatry. The third point is that of schematic modification, which involves helping an individual move from an absolute position to a more relative one – for example, from that of needing to be loved by everyone in order to be a worthwhile person to the more adaptive position of needing to be loved by nearly everyone or by certain people. The final point on the continuum, representing most schematic change, is that of schematic reconstruction. This involves removing, rebuilding or reconstructing old schemata. The data supporting this type of 'cure' is sparse (Beck *et al.*, 1990).

Hollon *et al.* (1987) describe three models of change: accommodation – that is, changing the basic schema either in content or in process terms; activation–de-activation – that is, de-activating rather than changing the schema, while making another one available; compensatory skills – that is, inculcating a set of skills to deal with the negative thoughts when they occur. In investigating the evidence, Barber and DeRubeis (1989) have pointed to a number of methodological issues, but appear to come down on the side of the third model from an empirical viewpoint. Persons (1993) points to the fact that different frameworks emphasise differences in the forms of change, and suggests that Beck and his colleagues adhere to the compensatory-skills model whereas the constructivists align themselves with the schema-change model.

The debate continues. And given the need to explain the efficacious results of cognitive therapy in both the short and the long term (see Chapter 2), it is an essential one. Relapse prevention requires a more empirical understanding of the type of change required and the mechanism by which it is to be achieved. More research is required to look into these issues, which will necessarily have implications for focus and technique in the practice of cognitive therapy.

SUMMARY

This chapter has attempted to offer the reader a glimpse of the main theoretical and practice issues within the field of cognitive therapy. It is a rapidly expanding field, both in terms of the depth of understanding of cognitive systems and in terms of its range of application.

It represents an applied field, with diverse frameworks, which is highly satisfying to the clinician who combines the need for empiricism with a creative flexibility of working – that is, a focused overt 'here and now' phenomenology with a more constructivist developmental analysis of tacit-meaning structures. But although diverse, the approach is specific and identifiable at both a theoretical and a practical level. In theoretical terms, it remains primarily focused on changing the cognitive aspects of psychological dysfunction. All the orientations are cognitive in conceptualisation. In practice terms, there are explicit assumptions encapsulated in the specific and unique type of therapeutic relationship and in the method of discovery and change. Especially in the light of the new integrative models, it is important for cognitive therapists to understand and value these distinctive aspects of the approach, for it is these that appear to account for its efficacy.

Every new development brings with it new questions and new opportunities for research. Much more work needs to be done in investigating the understanding of mechanisms of change. Cognitive therapy needs to continue to foster close links with academic cognitive psychology if it is to continue to grow and develop as it has over the last 40 years.

2

The Empirical Status of Cognitive Therapy

Cognitive therapy originated from empirical findings in the 1950s, and the strong empirical tradition continues to flourish. Several new journals accommodate the wealth of experimental and treatment studies, such as *Cognitive Therapy and Research*, the *Journal of Cognitive Psychotherapy: An international quarterly*, and *Behavioural and Cognitive Psychotherapy*, while other well known clinical psychology and psychiatry journals also regularly publish articles relevant to cognitive theory and therapy.

A full review of the experimental literature underpinning cognitive therapy is outside the scope of this book, and so we shall attempt to give only a general overview while pointing the interested reader towards the relevant writings. More emphasis will be given to treatment studies, in particular, in the areas relevant to the case studies described in the later chapters.

EXPERIMENTAL STUDIES

The link between products of thought and emotion

A large number of studies attest to the role of cognition in the emotional disorders, although the exact relationship between thinking and feeling is still controversial: for instance, in terms of the primacy of one over the other (Zajonc, 1980; Rachman, 1981, 1984) or of the actual cognitive processes involved in the experience of emotion and in the treatment of the emotional disorders (Barnard and Teasdale, 1991).

Beck's early clinical findings (Beck and Ward, 1961; Beck, 1963), from the analysis of the dreams of depressed patients and of psychotherapeutic interviews, set the tone for the cognitive theory of the emotional disorders. He was struck by the negative content common in both the dreams and the conscious thoughts of these patients, and the processing errors which maintained the negative bias in the content of thought. Since these early observations were made, the various aspects of *information-processing* have been studied in both depression and the anxiety disorders.

The cognitive aspects of depression have been by far the most studied. Haaga *et al.* (1991) provide an excellent review of studies relating to the descriptive and causative aspects of the theory. At a descriptive level, it is well established that depressed patients, relative to other clinical groups or relative to normal controls, show greater negativity of thinking. On scales such as the Automatic Thoughts Questionnaire (ATQ) (Hollon and Kendall, 1980), the Cognitive Style Test (CST) Blackburn *et al.*, 1986a) and the Crandell Cognitions Inventory (CCI) (Crandell and Chambless, 1986), depressed patients have been found to score higher than normal controls (Eaves and Rush, 1984; Hollon *et al.*, 1986; Blackburn *et al.*, 1986a; Lam *et al.*, 1987), higher than remitted depressed patients (Blackburn *et al.*, 1986a; Hollon *et al.*, 1986) and higher than themselves when remitted (Eaves and Rush, 1984; Dohr *et al.*, 1989; Dobson and Shaw, 1987).

Nonetheless, many studies also indicate that depressed patients do not have exclusively negative thoughts – for example, Clifford and Hemsley (1987) and Derry and Kuiper (1981) showed that depressed subjects rate as many positive as negative adjectives when asked to choose self-descriptors. The ideal proportion of positive to negative thoughts for personal well-being is, according to Schwartz (1986), 1.7 to 1.0. This has been compared with the 'golden' proportion of classical architecture. The 'golden section' in Greco-Roman aesthetics is the division of a line in which the relation between the smaller part of the line to the larger part is equal to the relation between the larger part and the whole.

The negative content of thought described above has been shown to relate to elements of the cognitive triad – that is, the view of self, of the world and of the future as described by Beck (1967). However, it is not clear whether every element of the triad is equally important or necessary in the syndrome of depression. Nekanda-Trepka et al. (1983) found that a substantial proportion of depressed patients (13 per cent) showed no negative view of the future as assessed by the Hopelessness Scale (Beck et al., 1974a). The three elements of the triad are conceptually very close and not easily discriminated (Bebbington, 1985). Blackburn and Eunson (1989), in a content analysis of depressed patients' records of their thoughts, confirmed this observation, finding that 47 per cent of a sample of two hundred automatic thoughts obtained from fifty depressed patients, when rated for content, represented combinations of two or three of the elements of the negative cognitive triad. Moreover, they found that 66 per cent of the thoughts related to the self – alone or in combination with the other two elements. It is likely that the negative view of self is the predominant and necessary element of the triad in depression, and that the negative view of the world and the negative view of the future are important only in so far as they relate to the self.

In contrast to the negative content of thought in depression, in anxiety and panic disorder common themes relate to personal danger and threat and inability to cope with that danger. Beck et al. (1974b), Hibbert (1984), and Beck and Emery (1985) have described these themes in detail. They involve thoughts and, in particular, images of vulnerability, inadequacy, loss of control, social ridicule, disease, physical harm and death. Butler and Mathews (1983) found that anxious patients are more likely than non-anxious control subjects to interpret ambiguous situations as personally threatening and to overestimate the degree of subjective risk to themselves. They do not view the world as necessarily universally threatening but, rather, they tend to regard themselves as especially at risk. Similarly, it is with regard to themselves that the future is unpredictable and dangerous. Thus, as in the negative triad found in depression, in the anxiogenic triad of the self as vulnerable, the world as threatening and the future as uncertain, it is the view of self as vulnerable and as lacking in coping ability which appears to be the predominant and necessary component.

Information-processing

The cognitive theory of the emotional disorders stresses that particular biases in information-processing will lead to congruent emotions (Beck *et al.*, 1979; Bower, 1981, 1987). A number of studies have examined biases at several stages of information-processing in depressive and anxiety disorders. In general, studies support an attentional bias in anxiety and a memory bias in depression (for example, Williams *et al.*, 1988; Dalgleish and Watts, 1990; Mogg *et al.*, 1991), although some inconsistent results have also been reported.

An attentional bias for fear-relevant words demonstrated by faster rate, higher frequency and/or lower threshold of recognition has been recorded in auditory tasks (Parkinson and Rachman, 1981; Burgess *et al.*, 1981; Mathews and MacLeod, 1986); by longer latencies in the Stroop colour-naming test (Ray, 1979; Watts *et al.*, 1986a; Mathews and MacLeod, 1985; Carter *et al.*, 1992); by attention shift in a probe detection task (MacLeod *et al.*, 1986; Mogg *et al.*, 1995).

Mogg *et al.* (1995), though, reported an attentional bias towards the spatial location of negative stimuli in their probe detection task in depressed patients, relative to normal controls. Depressed patients showed an attentional bias for negative words presented supraliminally, in contrast with anxious patients who showed an attentional bias for negative words presented both subliminally and supraliminally. Indications are that the bias seen in anxious patients when processing stimuli at a subliminal level is a preconscious one which, the authors suggest, may render them unconsciously sensitive to unpleasant cues in the environment and perhaps explain the attentional and concentration problems which are characteristic of anxiety states. Depressed patients, relative to controls, have also been reported as showing more self-focused attention and more negative thoughts when attending to themselves (Ingram *et al.*, 1987). Several studies have commented on the phenomenon of 'even-handedness' in depression (Coyne and Gotlib, 1983; Mogg *et al.*, 1991), indicating that depressed subjects attend to negative and positive stimuli equally, while non-depressed subjects are biased towards positive stimuli.

There is substantial evidence of a negative bias in retrieval processs in depression (Blaney, 1986; Williams *et al.*, 1988; Teasdale and Barnard, 1993). One of the first experiments in this area, by Lloyd and Lishman (1975), found that in a group of clinically depressed patients the more depressed took longer to retrieve pleasant memories associated with neutral words than unpleasant memories. Thus depression appears to decrease the accessibility of positive memories. This study was influential in stimulating better-designed studies, as two problems in its methodology could have affected the results. Firstly, the more depressed patients could genuinely have experienced more negative events, which would have rendered negative memories more accessible; secondly, they could have been interpreting neutral or ambiguous memories negatively as an effect of depression. A series of studies by Teasdale and his colleagues using more adequate methodology has confirmed the finding of Lloyd and Lishman. Using normal volunteers in induced sad or happy mood, Teasdale and Fogarty (1979) found that induced sad mood, relative to induced happy mood, lengthened the latency for happy memories to neutral cue words. There was no difference in the retrieval of unhappy memories. Teasdale *et al.* (1980) and Teasdale and Taylor (1981) found that depressed mood decreased the probability of retrieving positive memories and increased the accessibility of negative ones. Using more traditional memory experiments, involving recall from lists of words, consistent results have been found in several studies (*inter alia*, Isen *et al.*, 1978; Teasdale and Russell, 1983; Breslow *et al.*, 1991; Zuroff *et al.*, 1983; McDowell, 1984). Moreover, Zuroff *et al.* (1983), Hammen *et al.* (1986) and Bradley and Mathews (1988) found the same negative bias in memory function in recovered depressed patients, which may indicate a stable characteristic in vulnerable individuals, regardless of mood state.

An ingenious variation on the induced-mood studies was the study by Clark and Teasdale (1982), who used naturally occurring changes in mood in patients with diurnal mood variation to demonstrate differential retrieval of happy and unhappy memories. Substantially the same results were obtained as in studies which manipulated mood artificially.

In contrast, anxious patients have not been found to show the same consistent pattern of facilitated recall for threat-related stimuli. Williams *et al.* (1988) proposed that 'anxiety involves biased allocation of attention at the pre-attentive stage, and depression involves biased use of mnemonic cueing at the elaborative stage' (p. 181). Thus, it is predicted that anxiety is associated with facilitated integrative processing of threat-related stimuli, but not with facilitated elaborative processing of such stimuli. Indeed, several studies have found no bias in memory for threat words in anxious subjects (*inter alia*, Mac-Leod 1990, 1991; MacLeod and Mathews, 1991; Mineka, 1992; Mogg *et al.*, 1987; Watts *et al.*, 1986b). These experiments require subjects to recall or recognise previously presented stimulus items in an *explicit* memory task. The proposition of Williams *et al.* (1988) leads to the prediction that it is *implicit* and not explicit memory that would be affected by selective processing in anxiety. Implicit memory tasks do not require subjects to consciously recall previously presented stimuli, but assess retention by 'examining the degree to which previous exposure to stimulus items passively serves to facilitate the subsequent processing of these same stimuli' (MacLeod and McLaughlin, 1995).

Implicit memory has been tested in anxious patients by word-stem completion tasks after the presentation of threat- and non-threat-related words (Mathews *et al.*, 1989; Zeitlin and McNally, 1991; Richards and French, 1991), with conflicting results. Recently MacLeod and McLaughlin (1995) have criticised word-stem completion tasks as an inadequate test of implicit memory. Instead, they used a tachistoscopic task after a word and colour-naming task adapted from the Stroop test. They did find a bias in implicit memory for threat words in anxious patients relative to normal controls, but no difference in explicit memory.

Thus, it appears that the bias in information-processing differs in depression as compared with the anxiety disorders (general anxiety, panic disorder, phobias, post-traumatic stress disorder and obsessive–compulsive disorder). More studies of implicit memory in depression are needed, however, before firm conclusions can be reached, as most studies in this area have addressed explicit memory only. The cognitive theories underlying the bias in information-processing have been addressed in Chapter 1 – these include Beck's cognitive theory (Beck, 1967), Bower's associative network theory (Bower, 1981), Teasdale's differential activation hypothesis (Teasdale, 1988) and his more recent Interacting Cognitive Subsystems (ICS) theory (Teasdale and Barnard, 1993).

Schemata, attitudes and beliefs

The structural aspect of the cognitive model of the emotional disorders is the most abstract and hypothetical of its components. Research in this area has been confounded by two important factors: different authors have used the term 'schema' in different ways, and the methodology for assessing and measuring schemata is, to this day, not well established.

In Beck's terminology (Beck, 1976; Beck *et al.*, 1979; Beck and Emery, 1985) the word 'schema' appears to be used interchangeably to mean basic attitudes, basic assumptions, personal rules or personal equations. Kovacs and Beck (1978) stated:

'We postulate that the schemata that are active in depression are previously latent cognitive structures. They are re-activated when the patient is confronted with certain internal or external stimuli.' Thus defined, schemata have been measured by a particular scale, the Dysfunctional Attitude Scale (DAS) (Weissman and Beck, 1978).

Several studies have found that depressed subjects score significantly higher than controls on this scale (*inter alia*, Hamilton and Abramson, 1983; Blackburn *et al.*, 1986b). However, not surprisingly according to Beck's theory, the level of depressogenic attitudes decreases markedly with remission and becomes indistinguishable from normal level (*inter alia*, Blackburn *et al.*, 1990; Hamilton and Abramson, 1983; Simons *et al.*, 1984). Eaves and Rush (1984) and Peselow *et al.* (1990) found that recently remitted depressed patients still showed raised levels of dysfunctional attitudes on the DAS, although these were lower than during the acute episode of depression. Reda *et al.* (1985), in a one-year follow-up of sixty depressed patients treated with antidepressant medication, found that although DAS scores decreased significantly in parallel with level of depression, some beliefs did not change over time. These related to a need to please others and to compulsive self-reliance.

The level of dysfunctional attitudes has been found to predict future levels of depression (Rush *et al.*, 1986; Simons *et al.*, 1986), although negative thinking assessed by different questionnaires (measures of locus of control, of expectation of negative and positive outcomes, of irrational beliefs, of perception of control and of self-esteem) in a large prospective study by Lewinsohn *et al.* (1981) failed to discriminate between subjects who did and did not become depressed a year later.

The endorsement of self-referent adjectives is another method of assessing the self schema (Segal, 1988). In support of his *differential activation hypothesis*, Teasdale (1988) cites several studies which indicate a specific self schema activated in mild depressed mood (induced) in recovered depressed subjects as compared to never depressed individuals. For example,

Teasdale and Dent (1987) found that subjects vulnerable to depression recalled more global self-referent negative adjectives (such as 'pathetic', 'stupid', 'worthless') than the never depressed subjects, who recalled more of the milder self-referent adjectives (such as 'thoughtless', 'rude', 'inconsiderate'). Teasdale and Dent (1987) also found that the number of global negative words endorsed by mildly depressed women at time 1 predicted the level of depression at time 2, five months later. The general hypothesis from Teasdale's (1988) review is that the type of thinking activated in mild dysphoric states (which incorporate a globally negative view of self), in combination with high neuroticism (which is known to have the same effect as mild depressed mood on selective recall), activates and maintains higher levels of depression, possibly by activating more depressogenic schemata.

In summary of this section, when global scores on questionnaires measuring attitudes are being used, depressogenic attitudes appear to be state-related and therefore unstable. Better prediction can be made from the analysis of individual items of such questionnaires. Teasdale's approach of examining the self schema in mild dysphoric mood (induced, or naturally occurring) appears to be a more promising method of tapping into the cognitive structures which render some people vulnerable to the onset and persistence of depression. It remains to be shown that the same processes apply in the anxiety disorders.

Recent developments in schema studies

Two recent developments in the concept of schemata have been, firstly, the delineation of higher-order, possibly more stable, personality characteristics which may act as vulnerability factors in the emotional disorders. These have been described as sociotropy and autonomy (Beck et al., 1983; Beck, 1983). The second innovation has been the differentiation between core beliefs or unconditional schemata, and conditional beliefs or basic assumptions, particularly in the personality disorders.

Sociotropy and autonomy

A great deal of evidence has already accumulated regarding the validity of these constructs in depression. They have not yet been investigated in other disorders. A sixty-item scale, the Sociotropy–Autonomy Scale (SAS), was developed by Beck *et al.* (1983) to measure the two constructs. The sociotropy scale has usually been shown to have high internal consistency, and the three subscales based on the factor structure (concern about disapproval, about attachment/separation and about pleasing others) have been shown to be highly intercorrelated (Clark and Beck, 1991). Moreover, sociotropy has been found to be related to vulnerability to interpersonal life events (Hammen *et al.*, 1989; Segal *et al.*, 1989; Robins and Block, 1988; Robins, 1990); to level of depressive symptoms (Barnett and Gotlib, 1988; Gilbert and Reynolds, 1990; Moore and Blackburn, 1994); to level of neuroticism (Gilbert and Reynolds, 1990; Moore and Blackburn, 1994); to level of dysfunctional attitudes as measured by the DAS, and to the subscale of the DAS which measures the need for social approval (Moore and Blackburn, 1994); and to various measures of interpersonal dependency (Barnett and Gotlib, 1988).

The autonomy scale, on the other hand, reported by Beck *et al.* (1983) as consisting of three factors (individualistic achievement, freedom from control by others and preference for solitude), has not shown the same degree of conceptual and concurrent validity. Although internally consistent (Moore and Blackburn, 1994), the scale has been found to be only minimally related to level of depression (Clark and Beck, 1991; Gilbert and Reynolds, 1990; Moore and Blackburn, 1994). It has yielded poor correlations with other measures of independence, and mixed results have been obtained regarding the interaction of autonomy and negative achievement events in producing depression (Hammen *et al.*, 1989; Robins and Block, 1988; Clark *et al.*, 1992).

These indifferent results have led to doubt about the validity of the scale and/or of the relevance of the concept of autonomy in depression. Consequently, Clark and Beck (1991) have attempted to improve on the measurement of autonomy by adding items to the original questionnaire. In a recent study involving 2,041 undergraduate subjects, Clark *et al.* (1995) found that fifty-nine items of the 93-item expanded version were sufficient 'to establish the generalisability' of one dimension of sociotropy and two dimensions of autonomy – namely, solitude and independence. By using a large number of measures, the convergent and discriminant validities of the subscales of autonomy were satisfactorily established. Solitude was positively correlated with dysphoria, perfectionism, self-criticism and loneliness. Independence, on the other hand, was positively correlated with perfectionism and self-efficacy and negatively related to concern about approval from others. More research in clinical populations is needed to support the validity of the new autonomy scale.

Importantly for the concept of a vulnerability factor, Moore and Blackburn (in press), in a large clinical sample, have demonstrated the stability of sociotropy in pre- and post-treatment comparisons.

Core schemata

The differentiation of conditional and unconditional schemata remains a relatively untested clinical hypothesis deriving from recent interest in cognitive therapy for personality disorders (Beck *et al.*, 1990). Conditional beliefs such as 'If I don't do what others demand of me, they will reject me' may well derive from a core unconditional belief about the self, such as 'I am unworthy' or 'I am unlovable.' These core beliefs, or Early Maladaptive Schemata (EMS) (Young, 1990), are derived from clinical formulations and, to date, no adequate measurement exists. Young (1990) has developed a schema questionnaire consisting of 123 items, which has now been expanded to 205. The psychometric properties and validity of the scale have not yet been established.

Conclusion

This short review of experimental studies in the cognitive theory of the emotional disorders, as indicated earlier, is not intended to be exhaustive. It aims primarily to give a sample of the type of experimental studies that have been undertaken to test the cognitive models of the emotional disorders. The references provided at the end of the book will help interested readers to pursue more detailed accounts of work on empirical investigations into cognitive variables which may be associated with the onset of depressive and anxiety disorders.

Note that it is Beck's cognitive theory that has been the most tested empirically, while the rational–emotive theory of Ellis and the constructivist theories have, in general, been little tested.

THE EFFICACY OF COGNITIVE THERAPY

Since the first controlled outcome study of the efficacy of cognitive therapy compared with antidepressant medication in depression (Rush *et al.*, 1977) nearly twenty years ago, a large number of controlled studies have now been published, primarily in unipolar non-psychotic depression. The outcome literature in general anxiety disorder (GAD), panic disorder (PD), bulimia, social phobia and obsessive–compulsive disorder (OCD) is also accruing gradually. Cognitive therapy for personality disorders, psychosis, post-traumatic stress disorder and other disorders is still mostly tested only in single-case studies, but the results for larger controlled studies are expected soon.

Depression

Treatment outcome

The evidence for the efficacy of cognitive therapy in depression is well established, as can be attested in several outcome studies, reviews (Williams, 1992; Blackburn, 1995, 1988; Stravynski and Greenberg, 1992) and meta-analytic studies (Dobson, 1989; Robinson *et al.*, 1990). Most studies have included out-patients satisfying criteria for major unipolar depression, although some have concentrated on in-patients (Miller *et al.*, 1985).

COGNITIVE THERAPY AND PHARMACOTHERAPY

Fifteen studies were identified recently, comparing cognitive therapy with medication, either alone or in combination, in depressed out-patients. These are summarised in Table 2.1.

Table 2.1 Comparisons of cognitive therapy with pharmacotherapy in unipolar major depression – out-patients

Study	Outcome
Rush *et al.* (1977) (N: 41)	CT > imipramine
Beck *et al.* (1979) (N: 26)	CT = CT + amitriptyline
Dunn (1979) (N: 20)	CT + imipramine > supportive therapy and imipramine
McLean & Hakstian (1979) (N: 154)	CT > amitriptyline = relaxation > insight therapy
Blackburn *et al.* (1981) (N: 64)	Hospital clinic: COM > CT = antidepressants General practice: CT = COM > antidepressants
Rush & Watkins (1981) (N: 38)	Individual CT = individual CT + antidepressants > group CT
Murphy *et al.* (1984) (N: 70)	CT = nortriptyline = CT + nortriptyline = CT = placebo
Teasdale *et al.* (1984) (N: 34) (GP)	CT + treatment as usual > treatment as usual
Beck *et al.* (1985) (N: 33)	CT = CT + amitriptyline
Ross & Scott (1985) (N: 51) (GP)	CT (individual) = CT (group) > treatment as usual
Beutler *et al.* (1987) (N: 56 elderly patients)	Group CT = CT + alprazolam = group CT + placebo = placebo
Covi & Lipman (1987) (N: 90)	Group CT = group CT + imipramine > psychodynamic
Elkin *et al.* (1989) (N: 239)	Imipramine + clin. management = CT = IPT Imipramine + clin. management > placebo + clin. management

	For HRSD > 20, GAS < 50 imipramine + clin. management > IPT > CT > placebo + clin. management
Scott & Freeman (1992) (N: 121) (GP)	CT = counselling = amitriptyline = treatment as usual
Hollon *et al.* (1992) (N: 154)	CT + imipramine = Ct = imipramine

COM	combination of antidepressant medication and cognitive therapy
CT	cognitive therapy
GAS	Global Assessment Scale (Endicott *et al.*, 1976)
HRSD	Hamilton Rating Scale for Depression (Hamilton, 1960)
IPT	interpersonal psychotherapy

All the studies in the table used random allocation and standard measures of assessment, by independent raters, although the blindness of raters was attempted in only a few of these studies. The *main points* that emerge are as follows.

1   Cognitive therapy is at least as effective as antidepressant medication in the treatment of depressed out-patients.
2   There is disagreement over the status of cognitive therapy for the most severe depressive disorders. In the large National Institute of Mental Health study of Elkin *et al.* (1989), where severity of depression was defined as scores of 20 or more on the Hamilton Rating Scale for Depression (HRSD), 17-item version (Hamilton, 1960), although medication was significantly superior to placebo and clinical management, cognitive therapy was not significantly differentiated from placebo and clinical management. The conclusion drawn (Freedman, 1989; Gelder, 1990) was that drug treatment is indicated for the most severe depressive disorders. This was contested by McLean and Taylor (1992), Hollon *et al.* (1992) and Thase *et al.* (1991), who found no negative interaction between severity of depression and response to cognitive therapy. Hollon *et al.* (1993) also note that of the three research sites in the NIMH study, only one actually found medication to be superior to cognitive therapy.
3   Studies which have compared the response of endogenous and of non-endogenous depression to cognitive therapy (Rush

et al., 1977; Blackburn *et al.*, 1981; Teasdale *et al.*, 1984) have found that endogenicity is not a negative predictor of treatment. These studies have used research diagnostic criteria (RDC) (Spitzer *et al.*, 1978), which are recognised as not stringent. Stricter criteria, such as the Newcastle depression index (Carney *et al.*, 1965) or *DSM*-IV melancholia subtype (American Psychiatric Association, 1994), may offer more discrimination.

4   The combination of cognitive therapy and medication may be more effective than either treatment on its own for depressed hospital out-patients (Blackburn *et al.*, 1981; Hollon *et al.*, 1992; Murphy *et al.*, 1984). However, in depressed in-patients the combination of cognitive therapy and antidepressants, although not superior to medication alone at the time of discharge, was superior following a few months of out-patient treatment (Miller *et al.*, 1989).

5   Two methodological points may decrease the validity of the promising results described above. Firstly, most studies (except for Murphy *et al.*, 1984, and Elkin *et al.*, 1989) did not include a placebo pill condition. Hollon *et al.* (1993) comment that 'in the absence of such controls, it is not possible to determine whether the sample selected was indeed pharmacologically responsive (Klein, 1989) or whether pharmacotherapy was adequately operationalised (Meterissian and Bradwejn, 1989)'. In addition, the lack of a placebo psychotherapy condition in these studies may also prevent us from making definitive statements about the specific effect of cognitive therapy. Blackburn (1995), though, argues against the validity of including a placebo psychotherapy condition in outcome research.

The second methodological issue concerns the lack of statistical power to detect real differences because of the relatively small groups of subjects in the studies described in Table 2.1. Meta-analytic studies can circumvent this problem to a large extent. Dobson (1989) analysed the results of twenty-eight studies and concluded that cognitive therapy patients, on average, did better than 70 per cent of pharmacotherapy patients.

COGNITIVE THERAPY FOR DEPRESSION, AND OTHER THERAPIES

Comparisons of cognitive therapy with other psychological treatments control not only for time with the therapist (attention effect) but also for the so-called non-specific effects of therapy – structure, encouragement of hope, warmth, genuineness, understanding, unconditional acceptance and the provision of a plausible rationale for the patient's symptoms. Some of the studies in this category were not as methodologically sound as the studies comparing cognitive therapy and pharmacotherapy, as subjects were sometimes media-recruited or distressed rather than depressed, and undergraduates were included on the basis of scores on self-rating measures of severity of depression. Moreover, the treatment administered was not always the classical package of Beckian cognitive therapy, but included an *ad hoc* combination of cognitive and behavioural techniques (Table 2.2, overleaf).

As can be seen from Table 2.2, cognitive therapy, across different populations ranging from self-referred students to elderly hospital out-patients, has been shown to be as effective as or superior to some other systematised treatments (behaviour therapy, brief psychodynamic therapy or group psychodynamic therapy), and superior to waiting-list controls or supportive and non-directive therapies. The combination of cognitive therapy and behaviour therapy is usually not superior to either treatment on its own. In the case of Beckian cognitive therapy, at least, this would not be surprising as cognitive therapy involves both cognitive and behavioural methods of treatment, administered within the cognitive theory underlying the treatment.

Long-term effects

The previous section indicated that cognitive therapy is an effective method of treatment in major depression, and specifically in non-psychotic out-patients. Thus, it provides a viable treatment for patients who cannot or will not take medication, or for those who do not respond to antidepressants. However, the major problem of depression is its recurrent nature, which has been well documented in pharmacotherapy treatment

Table 2.2 Comparisons of cognitive therapy (CT) with other
psychological treatments

Study	Outcome
Shaw (1977) (N: 32 undergraduates)	CT > BT = non-directive therapy > waiting-list
Taylor & Marshall (1977) (N: 28 undergraduates)	CT + BT > CT = BT > waiting-list
Zeiss et al. (1979) (N: 44 media-recruited)	CT = social skills training = pleasant activities > waiting-list
Shipley & Fazio (1973) (N: 28 undergraduates)	CT > supportive therapy
Wilson et al. (1983) (N: 25 media-recruited)	CT = BT > waiting-list
Gallagher & Thompson (1982) (N: 30 elderly patients)	CT = BT = brief psychodynamic therapy
Steuer et al. (1984) (N: 33 elderly patients)	Group CT = group psychodynamic therapy (observer rating scale) Group CT > group psychodynamic therapy (self-rating scale)
Thompson et al. (1987) (N: 91 elderly patients)	CT = BT = brief psychodynamic therapy

BT   behaviour therapy
CT   cognitive therapy

trials (Glen *et al.*, 1984; Prien *et al.*, 1984; Kupfer *et al.*, 1992).

Antidepressant medication, especially the longer-established kinds such as the tricyclics, is much cheaper than cognitive therapy in the short term, especially if it is prescribed by general practitioners and not by consultant psychiatrists (Scott and Freeman, 1992). But when cost and efficacy are put in the balance, the long-term or prophylactic effect of different treatments has to be taken into consideration. The cost of depression to the nation involves not only costs of treatment, but also the human cost of suffering and indirect costs due to lost social and economic productivity (West, 1992). The maintenance of medication after the treatment of the acute episode of depression is known to reduce both relapse (six to nine months after remission) and recurrence (nine months, and over, after remission) (for example, Glen *et al.*, 1984; Prien *et al.*, 1984). Nonetheless, these two studies showed that even patients on active medication had less than 50 per cent probability of remaining well for two to three years. More recent studies report much better results with maintenance on high doses of tricyclic medication for three years (Frank *et al.*, 1990) and five years (Kupfer *et al.*, 1992). However, the problem of long-term compliance with medication is evident and its desirability may be questionable.

According to its theoretical underpinnings, cognitive therapy would be expected to reduce relapse and recurrence because of its educational nature and because it aims to reduce psychological vulnerability to depression by modifying the underlying schemata of the individual which may lead him or her to process information in a global negative way. Although the process through which cognitive therapy works is not well understood (DeRubeis *et al.*, 1990; Miranda and Persons, 1988; Whisman, 1993; Teasdale, Segal and Williams, 1995), its prophylactic effect holds promise, as shown in Table 2.3, overleaf. The studies in Table 2.3 are naturalistic rather than controlled (except for Evans *et al.*, 1992), and the numbers of subjects are generally small. However, the fact that all the data indicate the same outcome tends to reduce the likelihood of false positives (Type I error), although the likelihood of false negatives (Type II error) cannot be ruled out.

Gallagher and Thompson (1982) also indicated that in older adults with major depression, although there was no difference in response after twelve weeks of treatment with brief psychodynamic psychotherapy, cognitive or behavioural therapy (as shown in Table 2.2), at one-year follow-up improvement was maintained more effectively with cognitive and behavioural therapy. In in-patients given standard hospital treatment alone (tricyclic antidepressants *plus* hospital milieu) and standard treatment in combination with cognitive–behavioural therapy, Miller *et al.* (1989) found that at twelve-months follow-up more

Table 2.3 Percentage recurrence of depression: a comparison of medication and other psychological therapies with cognitive therapy

Study	12 months	18 months	24 months
	%	%	%
Kovacs et al. (1981) (N: 35)			
CT	33	—	—
TCA	59	—	—
Beck et al. (1985) (N: 79)			
CT	42	—	—
CT + TCA	9	—	—
Simons et al. (1986) (N: 36)			
CT	20	—	—
TCA	66	—	—
CT + TCA	43	—	—
CT + P	18	—	—
Blackburn et al. (1986b) (N: 36)			
CT			23
TCA			78
CT + TCA			21
Shea et al. (1992) (N: 61)			
CT	—	41	—
TCA + CM	—	61	—
IPT	—	57	—
Evans et al. (1992) (N: 44)			
TCA (no continuation)	—	—	50
TCA (continuation)	—	—	32
CT	—	—	21
CT + TCA	—	—	15

CM   clinical management
CT   cognitive therapy
IPT   interpersonal psychotherapy
P   psychotherapy
TCA tricyclic antidepressants

patients in the combined treatment group had remained well (54 per cent as compared with 18 per cent in the standard treatment group).

Conclusion

These studies indicate that cognitive–behavioural therapy may indeed prevent the recurrence of depression, although better-controlled studies are awaited to confirm these tantalising results.

General anxiety disorder and panic disorder

Treatment outcome

Several recent reviews of cognitive therapy in general anxiety disorder (GAD) have indicated that cognitive therapy (CT) or cognitive–behavioural therapy (CBT) is an effective method of treatment (Durham and Allan, 1993); Chambless and Gillis, 1993; Blackburn and Davidson, 1995). Since the early case studies (Hollon, 1982; Last *et al.*, 1983; Waddell *et al.*, 1984) indicating that modifying the cognitive components in general anxiety can be effective, several controlled trials have been published. These are summarised in Table 2.4, overleaf.

These studies generally show that CBT in GAD is at least of equal efficacy as anxiolytic medication, and superior to waiting-list control and placebo. In their meta-analytic examination of five studies where CBT was compared with one of several conditions, and in two further studies, Chambless and Gillis (1993) reach essentially the same conclusions – which is not surprising, considering that the seven studies they quote are included in Table 2.4. They found an average effect size of 1.54 for CBT compared with an effect size of 0.7 for control/waiting-list or non-directive therapy or pill placebo.

The efficacy of CBT relative to behaviour therapy (BT) is less well established, studies indicating different outcomes. Borkovec *et al.* (1987) found CBT in combination with relaxation superior to non-directive therapy combined with relaxation in college students, while Borkovec and Mathews

Table 2.4 Controlled trials of cognitive therapy for generalised anxiety

Study	Outcome
Durham & Turvey (1987) (N: 41)	CBT = BT
Lindsay et al. (1987) (N: 40)	CBT = anxiety-management training = benzodiazepine > waiting-list
Butler et al. (1987) (N: 45)	CBT > waiting-list
Blowers et al. (1987)	CBT = non-directive therapy > waiting-list
Borkovec et al. (1987) (N: 30 – college students)	CBT + relaxation > non-directive therapy + relaxation
Borkovec & Mathews (1988) (N: 30 – community sample)	CBT + relaxation = non-directive therapy + relaxation
Butler et al. (1991) (N: 38)	CBT = behaviour therapy > waiting-list
Power et al. (1989) (N: 31)	CBT > placebo CBT = diazepam
Power et al. (1990) (N: 101)	CBT = CBT + diazepam CBT + placebo > diazepam = placebo
Borkovec & Costello (1993) (N: 55)	CBT = applied relaxation > non-directive therapy
Durham et al. (1994) (N: 80)	CBT > analytic psychotherapy

BT   behaviour therapy
CBT   cognitive–behavioural therapy

(1988) found no difference between the two modes of treatment in a community sample. However, the superiority of CBT over non-directive therapy in the student sample was found only on a self-report measure of anxiety, while no significant difference was found on an observer rating scale of anxiety in either study. Borkovec and Costello (1993) compared CBT with applied relaxation and found no difference between the two treatments. Butler et al. (1991) compared a pure version of cognitive therapy with a complex and fuller package of behaviour therapy/ progressive relaxation, exposure, graded-task assignments and pleasurable activities. Cognitive therapy was superior to behaviour therapy on the most validated measures of anxiety (the Hamilton Anxiety Scale (Hamilton, 1959); the Beck Anxiety Inventory (Beck and Steer, 1990), but not on all measures.

Long-term effects
The few uncontrolled follow-up studies indicate that treatment gains are maintained at six- to twelve-months follow-up. Chambless and Gillis (1993) quote a follow-up effect of 1.95 for CBT. Blowers *et al.* (1987) found no difference between CBT and non-directive therapy at six months, while Borkovec and Costello (1993) found that at twelve months 57.9 per cent of CBT patients, 33.3 per cent of applied-relaxation patients and 22.2 per cent of non-directive therapy patients had maintained their improvement.

Butler *et al.* (1991) also found a net superiority of CBT over behaviour therapy at six-months follow-up: 42 per cent of CBT and 5 per cent of behaviour therapy patients met criteria for recovery.

Conclusion
As in the case of depression, controlled follow-up studies are needed. The general findings indicate that for GAD a combination of cognitive and behavioural techniques is indicated. However, cognitive therapy in its pure form has not been well tested. The best studies using cognitive therapy are those of Butler *et al.* (1991) and Durham *et al.* (1994), and both obtained very promising results. Hollon and Beck (1994) comment that more recent studies of cognitive therapy in GAD have shown better results, probably reflecting a higher level of expertise in the cognitive therapists.

Panic disorder with or without agoraphobia

Treatment outcome

Cognitive therapy for panic disorder is based on the cognitive therapy of panic (Clark, 1986), which is based on Beck and Emery's (1985) model of cognitive therapy for anxiety disorder and phobia which emphasises the catastrophic interpretation of bodily sensations in panic disorder patients and the avoidance and safety behaviours engaged in by them to prevent or deal with potential panic attacks. Several cognitive–behavioural approaches have been developed to help patients identify and modify their misinterpretations of bodily sensations. The best-tested approaches are those of Barlow and colleagues (Barlow and Craske, 1989; Barlow and Cerny, 1988) and those of Clark, Salkovskis, Beck and colleagues (Clark, 1989; Gelder *et al.*, 1993; Clark, 1986; Clark *et al.*, 1985). While Barlow's panic-control treatment (PCT) uses a wide range of behavioural and cognitive techniques (including coping techniques, exposure to interoceptive stimuli and relaxation training), Clark's cognitive therapy emphasises cognitive restructuring of the misinterpretations of bodily sensation, some exposure to interoceptive stimuli and no relaxation training.

Since the mid-1980s, treatment evaluation of cognitive therapy in panic disorder has been accumulating. At the beginning, several uncontrolled case studies indicated the efficacy of cognitive–behavioural methods (Barlow *et al.*, 1984; Clark *et al.*, 1985; Salkovskis *et al.*, 1986; Shear *et al.*, 1991; Welkowitz *et al.*, 1991). More recently, several controlled studies have been published or reported at conferences. Table 2.5 provides a summary of the published studies. All six studies attest to the efficacy of cognitive therapy, either alone or in combination with behavioural techniques, as effective in the treatment of panic disorder with or without agoraphobia. Cognitive therapy has been found to be superior to supportive therapy, relaxation training and waiting-list/minimum-control groups, but Shear *et al.* (1994) found no difference between cognitive–behavioural therapy and focused non-prescriptive treatment. The authors

Table 2.5 Efficacy of cognitive therapy for panic attacks

Study	Outcome
Barlow et al. (1989) (N: 46)	PCT = cognitive restructuring + exposure > relaxation > waiting-list
Klosko et al. (1990) (N: 57)	PCT > placebo; waiting-list Alprazolam = CT = waiting-list
Beck et al. (1992) (N: 33)	CT > supportive therapy
Shear et al. (1994) (N: 65)	CBT = non-prescriptive treatment
Clark et al. (1994) (N: 64)	CT > relaxation; imipramine > waiting-list
Beck et al. (1994) (N: 64)	CT > relaxation > minimal contact

CBT cognitive–behavioural therapy
CT cognitive therapy
PCT panic-control treatment

called in question the specificity of cognitive–behavioural treatment.

Long-term effects

Clark et al. (1994) reported that at six-months follow-up cognitive therapy did not differ from imipramine, both treatments being superior to applied relaxation (Ost, 1987). However, at fifteen months, cognitive therapy was superior to both imipramine and relaxation. Shear et al. (1994) reported that at six months after treatment, the cognitive–behavioural therapy group continued to improve, while subjects who had received focused non-prescriptive therapy showed slight worsening. Craske et al. (1991) reported a two-year follow-up of the Barlow et al. (1989) study: they found that 81 per cent of patients in the panic control treatment (PCT) were panic-free, 43 per cent of the PCT in combination with relaxation group, and only 36 per cent of the relaxation group.

Conclusion

Thus, as with depression and general anxiety, the effect of cognitive therapy in panic disorder appears to be long-lasting. The Craske *et al.* (1991) study indicated that, for long-term effect in panic disorder with agoraphobic avoidance, other treatment techniques than cognitive therapy may be necessary.

Obsessive–compulsive disorder (OCD)

Treatment outcome

Until recently, the two most widely accepted treatments for OCD have been pharmacotherapy (for example, clomipramine or, more recently, fluoxamine) and behaviour therapy including modelling, exposure and response-prevention. Behavioural interventions have been reported as highly successful, with a success rate of 60–85 per cent (Rachman and Hodgson, 1980), and as having an efficacy equivalent to fluoxamine (Cottraux *et al.*, 1990). Thoren *et al.* (1980) also found clomipramine effective in obsessional symptoms, although they found a recurrence of symptoms after medication was stopped. However, Foa (1979) noted that non-responders to behaviour therapy tended to have overvalued ideas, that is to believe that their obsessional fears were realistic. In such patients, a number of cognitive processes have been found to be important – concern about responsibility, perfectionism, and fear of punishment or of catastrophic outcomes if obsessive rituals are not followed.

Consequently, Beck (1976) and Salkovskis (1985) have developed the cognitive model of OCD and particular cognitive therapy techniques have evolved (van Oppen and Arutz, 1994). Beck explained the overdeveloped sense of responsibility of the obsessional patients as due to concerns related to actions they believed they should have taken or to outcomes they should not have caused. Salkovskis suggests that normal intrusive thoughts may become obsessions when the intrusion is perceived as potentially harmful and the patient assumes responsibility for that potential harm. The appraisal of the intrusion leads to increased anxiety, and the patient then develops overt or covert neutralising responses (rituals) to reduce the anxiety.

James and Blackburn (1995) published an up-to-date review of outcome studies using cognitive therapy techniques. In addition to single-case studies (Ownby, 1983; Salkovskis and Warwick, 1985; Blue *et al.*, 1987; Ellis, 1987; Willmuth, 1988; Moore and Burrows, 1991; Gandev, 1992; Dupont, 1992; Gandev, 1993), they found one uncontrolled group study (Enright, 1991) and five controlled studies. Since this review, one more controlled study has been published (van Oppen *et al.*, 1995). Table 2.6 summarises the controlled studies.

Table 2.6 Controlled studies of cognitive therapy in obsessive–compulsive disorder

Study	Outcome
Emmelkamp *et al.* (1980) (N: 15)	CT + BT = BT
Jaremko (1982) (N: 1; A–B design)	CT + BT > BT
Emmelkamp *et al.* (1988) (N: 18)	CT = BT
Kearney & Silverman (1990) (N: 1; A–B design)	CT + BT (alternatively) > CT + CT, BT + BT (alternatively)
Emmelkamp & Beens (1991) (N: 21)	CT = BT = CT + BT
van Oppen *et al.* (1995) (N: 71)	CT > BT

BT behaviour therapy
CT cognitive therapy

Note that a variety of cognitive therapy approaches have been used in those studies, including cognitive restructuring, self-instructional training and rational–emotive therapy. Only the van Oppen *et al.* (1995) controlled study and the single-case study of Salkovskis and Warwick (1985) have evaluated cognitive therapy as described by Beck (1976) and Salkovskis (1985).

Conclusion

Cognitive therapy in OCD promises to be a useful adjunct to exposure and prevention of response, particularly in the case of ruminators, non-responders to behavioural therapy and in-patients who are convinced of the rationality of their obsessions and compulsions. More controlled studies are necessary for both short- and long-term outcome before the role of cognitive therapy in OCD can be fully appreciated.

Bulimia nervosa

Treatment outcome

Of the eating disorders listed in *DSM*-IV (American Psychiatric Association, 1994) – bulimia nervosa, anorexia nervosa and obesity – it is generally agreed that the evidence for the efficacy of cognitive therapy is best-established in bulimia nervosa. For this reason and because a case of bulimia nervosa will be described in Chapter 7, only this particular disorder will be reviewed here.

Cognitive approaches to bulimia nervosa (Fairburn, 1985; Fairburn and Cooper, 1989) stress cognitive factors in the maintenance of the disorder. Chronic low self-esteem leads to over-concern about shape and weight. The individual, who is usually female, invests her self-esteem in dietary control which, in turn, triggers binge eating through both physiological and psychological processes. A vicious cycle is initiated as binge eating leads to compensatory behaviours such as vomiting, excessive use of laxatives or of diuretics and excessive exercising. This further decreases self-esteem, triggering a number of self-critical negative automatic thoughts. Cognitive-behavioural therapy involves presenting the cognitive rationale to the patient, providing education regarding the negative physiological effects of the compensatory behaviours, monitoring and changing attitudes towards shape and weight, and monitoring and changing basic dysfunctional attitudes relating to the self. Thus treatment consists of both behavioural and cognitive techniques aimed at establishing normal patterns of eating, and at cognitive restructuring.

Several studies have indicated that cognitive–behavioural therapy is superior to waiting-list control and minimal intervention (*inter alia* Lee and Rush, 1986; Freeman *et al.*, 1988; Agras *et al.*, 1989; Ordman and Kirschenbaum, 1985; Leitenberg *et al.*, 1988). In a review of outcome studies in bulimia nervosa, Fairburn (1988) concluded that the levels of specific and general pathology of patients allocated to waiting-list control groups do not decrease, whereas improvement occurs with active treatment.

Table 2.7 summarises studies comparing cognitive–behavioural therapy with other psychological treatments.

Table 2.7   Outcome studies comparing cognitive–behavioural therapy with other psychological therapies in the treatment of bulimia nervosa

Study	Outcome
Fairburn *et al.* (1986) (N: 24)	CBT > brief psychodynamic therapy (on some measures only)
Wilson *et al.* (1986) (N: 17)	Cognitive restructuring + BT > cognitive restructuring
Freeman *et al.* (1988) (N: 122)	CBT = BT = group psychotherapy > waiting-list
Agras *et al.* (1989) (N: 77)	CBT > self-monitoring; CBT + vomiting-prevention; waiting list
Fairburn *et al.* (1991) (N: 75)	CBT = BT > IPT (on some measures only)
Garner *et al.* (1993) (N: 66)	CBT > supportive expressive therapy (on most measures)
Wilfrey *et al.* (1993) (N: 56)	Group CBT = group IPT > waiting-list

BT   behaviour therapy
CBT   cognitive–behavioural therapy
IPT   interpersonal psychotherapy

The studies in this table indicate that, in the short term on some measures, CBT is at least as effective as other therapies – for example, behaviour therapy and interpersonal psychotherapy. Craighead and Agras (1991) reviewed ten studies of CBT in bulimia nervosa. They found a mean reduction of 79 per cent in binge eating and purging, and 59 per cent of patients were in remission. Mitchell (1991), in his review, found a mean decrease of 69.9 per cent in binge-eating frequency and only 32.8 per cent of the patients were in remission.

Wilson and Fairburn (1993) found comparable rates for reduction in binge eating (73–93 per cent) and in purging (77–94 per cent), but, like Mitchell (1991), they found much lower rates of remission (51–71 per cent for binge eating and 36 per cent for purging). Harmann et al. (1992), in a meta-analytic study of eighteen treatment trials, found no statistical differences in effect for different treatment modalities.

Antidepressant medication has been shown to be effective in the treatment of bulimia nervosa (Mitchell et al., 1990; Agras et al., 1992). Fairburn and Cooper (1989, p. 304) comment: 'Few patients . . . make a complete recovery and the disturbed attitudes to shape and weight tend to persist.' These authors suggest that antidepressant drugs are indicated only when there is a co-existing depressive disorder, and even in such cases CBT should be given in combination.

Long-term effects

Follow-up studies indicate that treatment gains with CBT are maintained over periods of one to three years (Luka et al., 1986). In the Fairburn et al. (1991) study, behaviour therapy patients showed a significantly higher rate of relapse over periods of four, eight and twelve months than CBT or interpersonal psychotherapy (IPT) patients. On the other hand, IPT patients continued to improve over follow-up, so that at twelve months 44 per cent of IPT and 35 per cent of CBT patients met criteria for recovery (Fairburn et al., 1993). Agras et al. (1992) reported that CBT had a preventive effect on relapse at a 32-week follow-up, and Freeman et al. (1988) found CBT to be superior to group therapy at six-months follow-up.

Conclusion

Although CBT has been described as the treatment of choice in bulimia nervosa, its specificity may be questionable. Many of the studies described above may have used more eclectic treatment packages than well defined cognitive–behavioural therapy. In general, a combination of educational, cognitive and behavioural methods seems to be superior, although IPT also appears promising, as it has been in depressive illness. Fairburn *et al.* (1955) concluded that longer-term outcome with cognitive therapy or focal interpersonal therapy was superior to behaviour therapy, which appears to have only a short-lived effect.

Two long-term problems

Two areas of psychopathology usually associated with long-term or chronic problems have recently attracted growing interest from cognitive therapists: these are the psychoses and the personality disorders. Outcome studies in both areas are still primarily based on single-case studies or on single-case methodology, and are therefore suggestive rather than convincing.

Psychoses

The modification of delusional beliefs with cognitive therapy is based on the assumption that delusional beliefs develop as a result of normal attempts to make sense of abnormal perceptual experience (Chadwick and Lowe, 1994). People with delusions have biased reasoning (Bentall *et al.*, 1994) and show bias in their attributional style, in their associations between events and in their probabilistic reasoning (Garety, 1991). Chadwick and Lowe (1994) state that 'an integral part of our approach to challenging delusions [has been] that the person be encouraged to construe his or her delusion as a reaction to, and an attempt to make sense of, particular events, and that an alternative perspective from which to understand these events be supplied and evaluated'. Thus, a person who is deluded constructs his or her delusional belief from external events through faulty reasoning.

Studies which have indicated positive effects for cognitive therapy in single cases or uncontrolled trials include Fowler and Morley, 1989; Chadwick and Lowe, 1990; Kingdon and Turkington, 1991; Perris and Skagerlind, 1994; Chadwick and Birchwood, 1994; Alford and Correia, 1994.

Chadwick and Lowe (1994) described the outcome of cognitive therapy in twelve out-patients maintained on neuroleptic medication, using multiple-baseline design. Cognitive therapy involved challenging the evidence for the beliefs starting with the least important bits of evidence and explaining the influence of beliefs on behaviours and interpretations; highlighting inconsistent features of the beliefs in order to reduce their plausibility; offering the rationale that the belief was developed in response to, and to make sense of, specific experience; and, finally, assessing the delusion and the therapist's alternative in the light of available information. The results indicated that ten out of the twelve participants (83 per cent) reported reduced conviction as a result of the interventions. Six of these ten subjects also obtained reduced anxiety and preoccupation ratings. In addition, depression scores were considerably reduced in all ten responders.

A few controlled studies have already been reported. Tarrier *et al.* (1993a) compared coping-strategy enhancement (CSE) with problem-solving therapy in twenty-seven patients. Both treatments included cognitive and behavioural methods. At the end of the five-week treatments, both were equally effective for delusions and anxiety. Hallucinations, general functioning and negative symptoms were not affected. At six-months follow-up, CSE was marginally better than problem-solving (Tarrier *et al.*, 1993b).

Garety *et al.* (1994) treated thirteen patients showing persistent drug-resistant psychotic symptoms with cognitive–behavioural therapy, and assigned seven subsequent patients to a waiting-list control. Active treatment brought about significant changes in the conviction with which delusional beliefs were held, in measures of distress and in preoccupation with beliefs, but not in general functioning.

In conclusion it can be said that the results across case studies and controlled studies are quite consistent. Cognitive–behavioural methods can be effective for the degree of belief in delusions, for the preoccupation with delusions and for associated anxiety and depression, but not for general functioning and negative symptoms. Many more controlled studies are currently being conducted, and future results should shed more light on both the applicability and the limits of cognitive therapy in this challenging group of patients.

Personality disorders

The development of clear diagnostic criteria for the personality disorders (Axis II, *DSM*-III-R and *DSM*-IV, American Psychiatric Association, 1987, 1994) has helped in bringing about a degree of consensus and of systematisation in their description and diagnosis, so that it is now easier to develop specific treatment methods and carry out treatment outcome studies.

The cognitive model of the personality disorders (Beck *et al.*, 1990), as described on pp. 216–20, is a natural evolution of the cognitive theories for the emotional disorders. Because of the long-standing problems associated with personality disorders, particular emphasis is placed on modifying early maladaptive schemata (Young, 1990), and specific methods of treatment have been developed. In particular, therapy typically extends over a longer period than for an Axis I disorder, and follows after the alleviation of the acute symptoms. Although therapy may last for one to two years, treatment sessions are more widely spaced, possibly taking place once a month, and involve greater use of the therapeutic relationship, as described on pp. 16–19.

The main influences on the development of cognitive therapy for the personality disorders have been the therapeutical work of Beck *et al.* (1990), Young (1990), Linehan (1993a, 1993b) and Layden *et al.* (1993), the last two volumes being dedicated to the treatment of borderline personality disorder. Pretzer and Fleming (1989) also present a detailed guide of recommended cognitive therapy treatment methods.

The cognitive theory of personality disorders and the practical treatment methods which it inspires have been encouraging. They empower the therapist and engender hope for these long-term patients, who are known to be poor responders to treatment (Sullivan *et al.*, 1994; Tyrer *et al.*, 1994; Burns and Nolen-Hoeksema, 1992). However, to date the only evidence of efficacy relies primarily on single-case reports. A number of case descriptions, with good outcome, are described in the edited volumes of Freeman and Dattilo (1992) and Dattilo and Freeman (1994). Turkat and his colleagues (Turkat and Carlson, 1984; Turkat and Levin, 1984; Turkat and Maisto, 1985) have used single-case methodology based on detailed formulation of individual cases, from which they derive hypotheses that are tested through treatment. Successful outcome confirms the formulation made by the therapist, while a negative outcome leads to a new formulation and new hypotheses. Turkat and Maisto (1985) report a positive outcome for avoidant, dependent, narcissistic and paranoid personality disorders. But they obtained negative outcome for antisocial, borderline, obsessive–compulsive, histrionic, passive–aggressive and schizoid patients. They attribute bad outcomes to lack of cooperation, dropping out of treatment or wrong case formulation.

Few controlled studies have been reported. Woody *et al.* (1985) reported a controlled study of brief cognitive therapy and psychodynamically orientated supportive therapy in drug addicts with symptoms of major depression and antisocial personality. Significant improvement was obtained with both treatments in patients presenting with these symptoms, but not in non-dependent patients with antisocial personality. Linehan *et al.* (1991) contrasted dialectical behaviour therapy (DBT) – a specific type of cognitive behaviour therapy package, fully described in Linehan (1993b) – with treatment as usual (any type of therapy available in the community, including psychotherapy or group therapy) in forty-four parasuicidal patients with borderline personality disorder. Assessments were carried out at the end of treatment and at one-year follow-up (Linehan *et al.*, 1993). During treatment 6.8 per cent of patients receiving

DBT attempted suicide, as compared with 33–35 per cent in the control groups; DBT patients spent less time in hospital (8.5 days as compared with 38.8 days). Drop-out rates also differed markedly (16.7 per cent for DBT and 50 per cent for the control group). At the end of the one-year naturalistic follow-up, most assessment measures of adjustment favoured DBT; the difference in parasuicides was not significant, but the DBT patients had had fewer days as in-patients.

CONCLUSION
Cognitive therapy for personality disorders is in its infancy, its empirical status being still mostly at the stage of case description and single-case studies. However, research in this area has reached an exciting point; the cognitive conceptualisation and detailed therapy methods described in manuals allow for optimism – which only future data can justify.

OVERALL SUMMARY

This chapter has given an overview of the empirical evidence underlying cognitive therapy. Experimental studies support the information-processing model of the cognitive theory of the emotional disorders, implicating attentional, perceptual, interpretative and memory biases. These appear to differentiate depressive and anxiety disorders. The methodology for the assessment of schemata remains unsatisfactory, so that this important aspect of the theory is still inferential and clinically based rather than empirically demonstrated.

Treatment outcome studies have indicated the efficacy of cognitive therapy in depression, generalised anxiety disorder, panic disorder and bulimia nervosa. The other areas reviewed, obsessive–compulsive disorder, and delusions and hallucinations in psychotic illness and personality disorders, still need better-controlled treatment trials to establish their validity, but the results so far are promising.

Several other areas of application – for example, health anxiety, hypochondriasis, pain management, social phobia and marital problems – have not been reviewed, but it must be noted that a vast experimental and treatment outcome literature is rapidly growing for these psychopathological conditions as well.

Two areas of research in cognitive therapy remain largely unaddressed: the process of change during treatment (Whisman, 1993) and the prediction of response. In view of the equivalence effect often found in controlled treatment trials, it is essential to be able to predict with a degree of certainty who will respond best to cognitive therapy, or to some other treatment such as pharmacotherapy, short-term focused psychodynamic therapy or interpersonal psychotherapy.

3

A Case of Depression

Frances – a Superwoman Who Cannot Control Her Tears

We indicated in Chapter 2 that cognitive therapy has been shown to be effective in unipolar depression, and that most outcome treatment trials have been in out-patients presenting with non-psychotic major depression.

Depression is the most common psychiatric condition encountered both in primary care settings and in hospital settings. It has been estimated that the lifetime prevalence of major depression is about 20 per cent, the rate in women being double that in men. It is estimated that at any one time 4.5–9.3 per cent of women and 2.3–3.2 per cent of men suffer from depression. Several studies have indicated that approximately 5 per cent of consecutive patients in general practice meet diagnostic criteria for major depression, and a further 5 per cent meet criteria for minor depression. In addition, a further 10 per cent have some depressive symptoms (Blacker and Clare, 1987; Clinical Resource and Audit Group, the Scottish Office, 1993). It is also suggested that as many as 25 per cent of individuals with symptoms of major depression do not seek treatment, and that of those who do the diagnosis may be missed in 50 per cent (Freeling and Tylee, 1992). Most depressed patients are treated by their general practitioners, who refer only around 10 per cent of such cases to psychiatric services. Nonetheless, about a quarter of out-patient referrals at psychiatric clinics are for depression, and about a quarter of hospital beds are occupied by depressed patients.

An estimate in 1989 showed that 71 million working days were lost in Britain because of mental illness, and that half of this may have been due to depressive illness. West (1992) estimated that the cost of depression in the UK runs to £333,000,000 per year, including treatment costs, direct hospital costs and GP consultations. This estimate is deemed to cover only 25 per cent of the total costs of depression to society, the other 75 per cent comprising indirect costs such as lost social and economic productivity. Moreover, the risk of suicide in depression is very high. Of some four thousand reported in the UK each year, depression is thought to be responsible for at least 70 per cent (Wilkinson, 1989). Suicide occurs frequently in individuals with undiagnosed or inadequately treated depressive illness (Schou and Weeke, 1988; Isacsson et al., 1992).

DEFINITION OF DEPRESSION

The short introduction above indicates clearly that depressive illness is a common, serious and costly illness. Diagnosis is now made easier by the use of standard diagnostic criteria (DSM-IV, American Psychiatric Association, 1994; ICD-10, World Health Organisation, 1993). The application of these criteria has helped resolve many of the old controversies regarding the classification of depressive illness and, if used routinely by general practitioners, psychiatrists, psychologists and other mental health workers, they would guard against misdiagnosis, non-recognition and inappropriate or inadequate treatment. The cardinal symptoms of a major depressive illness are summarised in Table 3.1.

Several subcategories of depressive illness are differentiated by DSM-IV, such as mild, moderate, severe without psychotic features, severe with psychotic features, with melancholic features, with atypical features and with post-partum onset. ICD-10 includes very similar categories, using the term 'somatic syndrome' instead of 'melancholic features'.

Table 3.1 Diagnostic criteria for major depressive illness (summarised from *DSM*-IV)

Five or more of the following symptoms have been present during the same 2-week period (symptoms 1 or 2 must be present)

1 Depressed mood
2 Loss of interest or pleasure
3 Weight loss or weight gain; decreased or increased appetite
4 Insomnia or hypersomnia
5 Psychomotor retardation or agitation
6 Fatigue or loss of energy
7 Feeling of worthlessness or excessive or inappropriate guilt
8 Diminished concentration/indecisiveness
9 Suicidal ideation or behaviour

THE COGNITIVE MODEL

The diagnostic criteria described above stress the importance of changes in mood (depressed mood) and/or motivation (loss of interest and pleasure) as central features of depression. These changes are considered in biological psychiatry to reflect functional abnormalities in brain neurotransmitters – in particular, noradrenaline and serotonin – and consequently the treatment of choice is antidepressant medication to regulate the levels of these transmitters.

The cognitive model of depression (Beck, 1967; Beck *et al.*, 1979; Blackburn and Davidson, 1995; Fennell, 1989; Williams, 1992), on the other hand, stresses the changes which occur in the depressed person's thinking. According to Beck (1967, 1976), the most salient psychological symptom in clinical observation is the profoundly altered thinking pattern. This was described in the studies detailed in Chapter 2, and the model has been amply discussed in the references cited above. So only a brief reminder will be given here.

The negative content of thought, described as the negative cognitive triad – referring to the negative view of the self, of one's world and of one's future – is seen as the psychological cornerstone of depression. The negative content of thought does not cause depression, but is an essential feature of it (Beck, 1983). A psychological formulation of depression, without negating the importance of biological factors and without ascribing primacy to one category of factors over another, would attempt to understand the symptoms as resulting from the negative cognitive triad. This is presented schematically in Figure 3.1.

Figure 3.1 Psychological formulation of depressive symptoms

Content of thought	Symptoms

Negative view of self

Thinking that one is
inadequate, unworthy, etc.
and lacking the necessary
qualities to obtain one's goals

*Negative view of the
environment*

Seeing one's world as
unfulfilling, punishing and
obstructive

Negative view of the future

Seeing one's future as bleak
and as continuously
unfulfilling, empty and painful

Mood
sadness, despair, anxiety, guilt

Cognition
self-derogation, self-blame,
negative predictions, negative
memories, seeing life as a
burden, feeling others don't
understand

Motivation
loss of interest, loss of
enjoyment, indecision, suicidal
wishes/gestures

Somatic
loss of appetite, libido, sleep

Behaviour
inactivity, crying, pacing

Physiology
tension, somatic anxiety

As a patient remarked to me recently: 'I feel trapped in an empty mind, empty body and empty life.' This may sound like poetic hyperbole, but this man of sixty-three said it with total conviction, and, as he observed with some surprise on questioning, he had not even rehearsed this comment before coming to his therapy session. It is understandable that his mood was extremely low: he felt anxious; he isolated himself, engaged in progressively fewer activities, had suicidal thoughts, had difficulty falling asleep and woke up early; he was no longer interested in food, had difficulty concentrating on reading or television, though that he was a burden on others and that the future would be even worse than the present.

The negative products of thoughts described above result from various biases in information-processing, as described on p. 4 and pp. 25–8. Thus, by *selective attention and abstraction*; by making *arbitrary inferences* with a negative bias; by *magnifying* the negative and minimising the positive aspects; by *overgeneralising* from the negative information that has been abstracted and by making internal, stable and global attributions (*personalisation*) for negative outcomes, the depressed person astonishes her friends and relatives by the consistency of her negative interpretations and her pessimism. Some may think that she is 'putting it on' and is not genuine, and they may get impatient – in particular when encouragement or reasoning do not appear to make any difference. Burns (1980) commented that, unlike the alchemists of old who thought that they could turn base metal into gold, the depressed person appears to be able to turn gold into base metal. The content of the processing style described above used to be labelled 'logical errors', but with recent studies demonstrating that normal subjects use non-logical 'heuristics' in their thinking (Kahneman *et al.*, 1982; Nisbett and Ross, 1980), it now seems more appropriate to use the term 'bias' when systematic and consistent negative judgements are being made (these can lead to accurate or inaccurate inferences), and the term 'distortion' when the judgement or conclusion does not agree with a commonly accepted measure of reality (Alloy and Abramson, 1988).

Finally, and importantly, the cognitive model implicates the presence of *attitudes, beliefs, assumptions, rules and core schemata* which explain why, for a particular individual, certain situations, which may appear insignificant to some or which may cause only transient distress in others, may act as triggers to more lasting depression (see pages 4–5; 28–32). These core structures may relate to love, approval, achievement, autonomy, entitlement, omnipotence and perfectionism and are deemed to have been learned in early childhood, then reinforced through life by the process of attaching importance to validating experiences and disqualifying invalidating experiences. This is, of course, a process to which none of us, including – alas – scientists, are immune. The difference is that in emotional disorders the schemata, rules or assumptions are extremely dysfunctional, rigid and over-generalised. An example might be: 'Unless I do everything that people ask of me, they will not want to know me.' This conditional schema may point to a core belief such as 'I am unlovable' or 'I am worthless' and, therefore, 'The only way of making myself acceptable is by pleasing others at all times.'

The various elements of the model are exemplified in the case of Frances.

FRANCES

THE REFERRAL

Frances was referred by her general practitioner for cognitive therapy, at her own request. The referral letter said very little, except that Frances was a 38-year-old married woman who had been depressed for one year. She had not responded to various antidepressants; she had read *Coping with Depression* (Blackburn, 1987), a self-help book intended to help people with mild depression to use cognitive therapy techniques to manage their condition and, perhaps, prevent it from developing into a major depression. The letter also said that she had had to resign from her post as an accountant with a major bank, because of illness. She had a son aged six.

THE ASSESSMENT

Symptom profile

Frances reported her low mood both verbally and non-verbally. Her mood was low most of the time, but she was able to brighten up in certain circumstances – for example, if a good friend called or her son said something funny. In the session she cried throughout the interview, using a boxful of tissues, and made poor eye contact. She felt that she had let everybody down, including her colleagues, her clients at the bank, her husband, her son, her friends and her parents. She felt helpless and hopeless, and thought that everybody would be better off if she were dead, as there was little hope of her ever being able to cope again. However, she had never considered or attempted suicide.

Although she had no difficulty falling asleep, as she felt totally exhausted, and she slept through the night for an average of five hours, she regularly woke up at about 3 to 4 am and lay awake, ruminating about worrying and depressing thoughts. She had let her appearance go, and could not concentrate enough even to read a newspaper article. But she continued doing housework and looking after her husband and son quite dutifully. She had given up all her leisure and social activities, such as playing the violin in an amateur band, aerobics, hill walking, entertaining friends and going out for meals and to the theatre. She worried continually about her health, about her marital relationship, about being a bad mother and about the future. She suffered few somatic symptoms of anxiety, experiencing butterflies in the stomach and palpitations only if she met somebody she knew while out shopping. General somatic symptoms included frequent headaches and backache and loss of energy. She was eating more than usual and had put on half a stone in the last three months. Her libido was mildly impaired.

Frances avoided all social situations, as she felt ashamed of not being at work. She felt totally lacking in self-confidence, useless and pathetic. There were no phobic, obsessive–compulsive or psychotic symptoms.

Her symptom profile satisfied criteria for major depressive

illness. The anxiety symptoms were part of the depressive syndrome and did not satisfy criteria for a concurrent generalised anxiety disorder. There was no indication of an Axis II disorder.

Psychometric assessment showed a moderate level of depression:

- Hamilton Rating Scale for Depression (HRSD), 17-item version (Hamilton, 1960): 17 (non-depressed score ≤ 6)
- Beck Depression Inventory (BDI) (Beck *et al.*, 1961): 24 (non-depressed score ≤ 9)
- State-Trait Anxiety Inventory, state version (STAI-S) (Speilberger *et al.*, 1970): 52 (normal population score: 36)

On scales of cognitive biases and distortion, the following scores were obtained:

- Automatic Thoughts Questionnaire (ATQ) (Hollon and Kendall, 1980): 111 (normal population score ≤ 42)
- Hopelessness Scale (HS) (Beck *et al.*, 1974): 19 (normal population score ≤ 3)
- Dysfunctional Attitude Scale (DAS) (Weissman and Beck, 1978): 195 (normal population score ≤ 113)
- Cognitive Style Test (CST) (Blackburn *et al.*, 1986): 84 (normal population score ≤ 59)

History of the disorder

At the age of eighteen   When she was taking school-leaving examinations, Frances felt extremely anxious and somewhat depressed. She did not seek treatment, but recognises now that she felt very miserable at the time.

At twenty-one   Having enjoyed her three years at university, she again felt anxious and depressed at the time of the final examinations. This lasted for about six months. No treatment was sought.

At twenty-six   At the time of the break-up of a long-standing relationship, Frances felt extremely depressed. She had to stay off work and was prescribed antidepressant medication by her GP. The depression lasted three months; the medication was continued for six months.

At thirty-three   After a move to a new job and a different town she experienced interpersonal difficulties at work; she felt de-skilled and devalued. She developed depressive symptoms, but not full-blown depression. Improvement was related to a change in personnel and a better working situation.

At thirty-six   After another move to a different town, Frances learned that the job she had shaped and had done well in the previous employment had been more or less abolished after she left. She began to feel depressed. She started a new job, which was chaotic and where she felt she would not cope.

At thirty-seven   The illness intensified. After four months of increasing depression she consulted her GP, who put her on medication. The depression improved, and after three months' absence she went back to work after the Christmas break.

At thirty-eight   Frances had only been at work for a week when she felt totally out of her depth. She suffered a relapse and was advised by her employers to resign. Six months later she was referred by her GP for cognitive therapy, as she was showing no improvement on medication.

Personal background

Frances had been married for nine years to Denis, who is a university lecturer. Their one child, Marc, was aged six. The couple wanted another child and were hoping that Frances would get pregnant 'before the time runs out'.

Before marrying Denis in 1985, Frances had had a long-standing relationship with Philip, which broke up in 1982 when she was twenty-six. She had met Philip at university and they lived together for financial reasons, as Philip was still studying for a postgraduate degree and Frances was already working and could support him financially. They began to grow apart, and she realised at Philip's graduation party that she no longer knew him or any of his friends. She felt that his friends looked down on her as intellectually inferior and that Philip considered her a social embarrassment; also, he was having an affair with a fellow student. The couple separated bitterly. This was a difficult period, accompanied by a short-lived depression for Frances.

Both her parents were still alive and living in a village some two hundred miles away. Her father was a retired businessman who spent a lot of time away from home, having worked very hard all his life and risen to the position of manager in a local firm based in the village. He was well known there and highly thought of. People still came to consult him about their financial affairs, although he had been retired for eight years. Her mother was seen as fragile; she had worked as an office clerk before her marriage and after the children had gone to full-time school. She suffered from occasional depression, which was treated by her GP with mild antidepressants. Frances felt close to her mother and felt that her mother could understand her problems. However, she did not like burdening her with them, as she would worry excessively and might get depressed again. She did get on well with her father, but did not feel close to him, as he had been a distant figure when she was growing up.

There was an older sister by two years, Madeline, who had been happily married for twenty years to a personnel manager and had three teenage children. Frances had never been close to her, as Madeline was seen as very different. She was bright, but had never been interested in school. Consequently, she had gone to a different school from Frances and left at sixteen to get married shortly after. There was a younger sister by four years, who had been brilliant at school and university and now held a prestigious post in industry. She had married recently and was in frequent communication with Frances.

Frances had worked hard at school and was always at or near the top of the class. After leaving school, she obtained a good university degree in history and immediately afterwards, at twenty-two, started working in a bank in a trainee managerial post. Encouraged by her employers, she studied accountancy at the same time, and obtained her accountancy qualifications two years later. She felt that there was an expectation at home that she should do well and better herself.

Since her marriage to Denis in 1985 she had changed jobs twice, against her will but to suit her husband who, in the process of furthering his university career, had applied for and obtained more prestigious posts.

Presentation

First sight of Frances in the waiting-room was of a young woman sobbing her heart out, crumpled up in a chair and dressed as if she wanted to be incognito – hat pulled right down over her face, large winter coat, boots and gloves.

The first thing she said when the therapist noted how distressed she seemed was that she did not like being 'a patient', being seen in the hospital grounds and sitting with other 'patients' in the waiting-room. She thought it was shameful and that it somehow diminished her.

These initial comments, as well as the way the patient presents herself, are often very illuminating for the therapist to begin to form ideas and hypotheses which will lead to a preliminary conceptualisation.

During the two assessment sessions, in spite of her evident distress and continuous crying, Frances was able to give a good account of herself, her life situation and her history. She related well to the therapist, appearing to trust her and to want to communicate as openly as she could. She apologised frequently: 'I'm sorry. I can't stop crying.' 'This is terrible – I am totally out of control.' When asked whether she often felt so tearful, she said: 'No, it's only when I talk about myself. Normally, I can keep a good grip on myself.' Apart from being ashamed of not being at work, she avoided meeting her friends or even talking to them on the telephone because she might break down in tears and 'they would think that I'm totally past it'. The themes that often came up when Frances was describing difficult situations are exemplified by the following comments:

- 'I felt totally out of control.'
- 'Changes of job were not under my control. I just had to follow where Denis wanted to go.'
- 'I felt diminished.'
- 'I don't want to be just a housewife.'
- 'All the efforts I've put in over the years, all for nothing.'

Summary of the assessment

Frances was suffering from recurrent major depressive illness. She came across as an able, determined and ambitious young woman who had worked hard during her school, university and professional education and who had put a lot of effort into her job as a banking accountant, where she had been successful in spite of it being a predominantly male-dominated environment.

She had also been fully in charge in the home, arranging her work schedule around her husband and her son. Life had been a whirlwind: making breakfast, dropping her son off at school, picking him up, stopping at the supermarket on her way from work to be sure that she could prepare a good supper for her husband, preparing work in the evening for the next day, as well as putting in a hard day's work at the office. She had been excellent at organising all this, as well as the couple's social life and arranging for the home-help and babysitters when necessary.

At this point the therapist is asking herself: 'Why has this person been depressed in the past, and why is she depressed now?' The clues lie in past events associated with the onset of depression, and in recent triggers. The following factors are of note:

1   The short early episodes of depression were associated with evaluation of performance – namely, examinations.
2   The break-up of a relationship was seen as a failure, particularly since she perceived the cause as her own intellectual inferiority.

3   She had invested a lot in her personal relationships, sub-jugating her profession to that of her husband's, which she also perceived as superior.

4   New job situations were perceived as threatening and she was sensitive to negative evaluation at work. For example, when the post she left changed into a more junior one, she interpreted this as meaning that what she had been doing was not important enough. If a job did not go well, she attributed the cause to herself – it was because she was not good enough.

5   Finally, she had tried to be superwoman: top job, best of wives, best of mothers and best of housewives. She now wanted to have another baby – to have a perfect family.

The triggers for the current episode were a 'disastrous' new job where she felt inadequate and out of control; regret and anger at having had to leave a job she loved; and being trapped in the current job, because she was not succeeding in getting pregnant again.

SUITABILITY FOR SHORT-TERM COGNITIVE THERAPY

The Suitability for Short-term Cognitive Therapy Rating Scale (Safran and Segal, 1990) was used to assess suitability formally. Frances was highly suitable for cognitive therapy. The items on this scale are rated 0 to 5, where highest scores indicate greatest suitability.

1   *Accessibility of automatic thoughts*   She could report core negative automatic thoughts spontaneously (5).

2   *Awareness and differentiation of emotions*   She had access to her emotions both in and out of session and could differentiate between them, except that anger was not well differentiated and was not reported without guiding questions from the therapist (4).

3   *Acceptance of personal responsibility*   She accepted personal responsibility for change, having sought cognitive therapy and wanting to do something for herself in addition to taking medication.

4   *Compatibility with cognitive rationale*   She knew the

cognitive model because she had read a self-help cognitive therapy book; she accepted the model as a valid approach and welcomed the use of homework (5).

5 *Alliance potential (in-session evidence)* From the start of the therapy she showed good alliance potential in session. Nevertheless, the therapist had some reservations: firstly, to do with the patient's apparent high autonomy, which might lead to resistance to help; and secondly, to do with the fact that Frances compared herself with the therapist in a negative light, seeing her as having achieved everything that she, Frances, had not – which was, of course, a misperception (3.5).

6 *Alliance potential (out-of-session evidence)* Her alliance potential out of session was excellent. Frances had had close relationships at work and socially. She had good friends and was the member of the family in whom everybody else confided (5).

7 *Chronicity of problems* The long duration of the current episode of depression, over one year, could have been a negative predictor. However, the present problems were not chronic and were seen within the context of current unresolved situations and of psychological issues amenable to cognitive therapy (4).

8 *Security operations* On the whole, there was no reason to believe that she would engage in security operations or avoidance behaviours which would interfere with collaboration and participation in therapy. It was feared that her sense of shame in being in the role of patient might lead either to early termination of therapy or to missing appointments (4).

9 *Focality* Frances was able to remain focused on the problems being discussed, and scarcely ever had to be prompted to come back to the issue at hand (5).

10 *Patient optimism/pessimism regarding therapy* Finally, she laid great hope in cognitive therapy. She knew that she had responded to medication in the past, but she thought that cognitive therapy would help both in the short and long term (5).

The total score adds up to 44.5 out of a total maximum score of 50, which made Frances highly suitable for short-term cognitive therapy.

INITIAL FORMULATION

An initial formulation was arrived at tentatively after the two assessment sessions and two treatment sessions. This formulation utilises the information gleaned from the history of the patient, from the main themes of her communication, from her typical automatic thoughts, from her affective responses and from her non-verbal behaviour. This is presented schematically in Figure 3.2.

Figure 3.2   Initial formulation

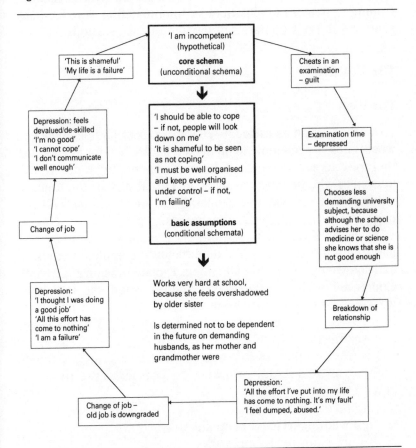

The formulation was not shared with Frances until the eighth session, when she was already showing good progress and a good therapeutic relationship has been firmly established. (Some therapists prefer to share the preliminary formulation with their patients earlier in therapy – say by the third or fourth session. This may be appropriate in some cases, but often it is better to wait until the seventh or eighth in order to ensure collaboration and understanding.) By that time, the therapist and the patient had gathered enough information both in session and in homework assignments to begin to be able to put together the pieces of the jigsaw and get an overall picture. Common themes in the patient's communication were fed back routinely in the summaries at the end of each session.

TREATMENT

The Plan

After the second assessment session, Frances had been given a weekly activity schedule to fill in (see Table 3.2), for her and the therapist to get an idea of how she spent her time. It was uncertain whether she was inactive a great deal of the time, as she asserted, or was in fact doing too many chores and not engaging in enough pleasant activities.

At the third treatment session, Frances came in weeping. She had found the activity schedule difficult to complete because it had confirmed to her that 'the things I spend time on are trivial'. Compared with her complex activities when she had been working, what she was doing now was 'repetitive and what anybody can do – probably better than myself'. This made her feel worthless.

The rest of the session was spent drawing up a detailed problem list and setting priorities. Frances listed two problems at the outset:

1 'not wanting to meet people';
2 'future plans regarding work'.

Table 3.2 Weekly activity schedule

Time	Monday	Tuesday	Wednesday	Thursday	Friday	Saturday	Sunday
9–10	prepared breakfast, took Marc to school, shopped	prepared breakfast, took Marc to school	prepared breakfast, took Marc to school	prepared breakfast, took Marc to school	prepared breakfast, took Marc to school	prepared breakfast, took Marc to Cubs	prepared breakfast
10–11	cleaning and washing	car to garage for service	changed beds, tidied up	sanded 3 doors	big supermarket shopping	more shopping	prepared food for barbecue
11–12	cleaning and washing	walked home	friends called for coffee	cleaned up	"	cleaning	row with Denis
12–1	sat around	mended clothes	"	washing	put shopping away	picked Marc up	two of his colleagues whom I don't like came for barbecue
1–2	post-office, bank	did the accounts	took curtains down for washing	tidying	collapsed in chair and read the paper	helped Denis with decorating	"
2–3	shopped, picked Marc up from school	walked to garage to pick up car and then Marc	picked Marc up from school	picked Marc up from school	picked Marc up	"	"
3–4	helped Marc with homework	Marc's homework	Marc's homework	sat in garden while Marc in paddling pool	called at friend's house to let Marc play with his friend	"	tidied up
4–5	watered the garden	more accounts	ironing	put washing away	"	tidied up	played with Marc
5–6	prepared meal for Marc	Marc's supper	Marc's supper	Marc's supper	Marc's supper	Marc's supper	Marc's supper
6–7	bathed Marc	bath-time	bath-time and playing with Marc	bath-time	bath-time	bath-time	bath-time
7–8	bedtime stories	bedtime stories	bedtime stories	bedtime stories	bedtime stories	bedtime stories	bedtime stories
8–12	Denis back from work, had supper, bed at 10	Denis back, supper, row with Denis at 11	ironing, Denis back at 9, supper, bed at 11	typed some work for Denis, prepared supper, Denis back, supper, TV, bed at 11	Denis back at 7, had a chat about Marc's school, supper, bed at 11	early supper, TV, bed at 10	read Sunday papers, supper, TV, bed at 11

Note: Grade activities M for Mastery and P for Pleasure

Further discussions led to three more problem areas:

3 'Accepting the role of patient'.

The therapist thought that if Frances continued to feel embarrassed and ashamed about coming to therapy, this would be a severe hindrance to working on the problems which had led to her seeking therapy, and simply create an additional problem.

4 Problems with her husband, which had arisen since she had been off work.

In fact, the therapist had detected some resentment in Frances' tone when she emphasised that she always changed jobs, against her wishes, to accommodate her husband's career.

5 Creating time to engage in pleasant activities for herself.

This arose from examination of the activity schedule she had brought back and her negative reaction to it.

When asked which of the problems listed above needed most urgent attention, Frances was surprised that she considered the situation with her husband to be the most pressing. She described him as self-absorbed and not involved enough with the family. He was very busy at work and came back late in the evening in a bad mood. He hid behind the newspaper, and she could not discuss anything with him. He went about with a long face – in fact, 'behaving just like my father'.

The therapist thought that this was a good starting-point, as it was an immediate situation and some resolution would bring about assertive behaviour in Frances – it was suspected that some of the problems at work could have been due to excessive compliance and lack of assertion – establish a sense of control, and decrease resentment.

France's *homework assignments* were:

1 to list problem situations with Denis;
2 to introduce some pleasant activities into the activity schedule – reinstate some hobbies, such as playing the violin, gardening.

PROGRESS OF THERAPY

Sessions 4–5

These two sessions related to the marital situation and to improving the quality of activities.

A review of homework indicated that Frances felt somewhat happier with her activities, as she had done 'more constructive things with her time' – for example, home decorating – and she had played the violin at home on two occasions and was surprised that she had enjoyed it.

The problems she listed regarding Denis were that he was selfish and inconsiderate, that he did not pay enough attention to details, and that Frances invested a lot of time in helping him and he did not reciprocate. Therapist and patient agreed to focus on the marital situation and, in addition, on a new problem that had arisen – a request from her former workplace that she produce a letter about a client she had dealt with a year earlier, and who was now complaining about the advice he had been given.

The main problems regarding the marital relationship were 1) lack of communication; 2) consequently, a great deal of mind-reading; 3) Frances' need to be seen as coping on all fronts and, therefore, her unwillingness to ask for help; 4) differences in personality, Denis being more carefree and impulsive and Frances more concerned with detailed advance planning and organisation.

Socratic questioning aimed to facilitate communication, by helping Frances discover that she was reacting to what she *thought* her husband was thinking, without checking out whether she was right or not.

Therapist: You say that Denis came back from work, asked you what sort of day you'd had and never even waited for an answer from you?

Frances: That's right – he doesn't care, he knows I lead a boring life anyway. He must be fed up with me.

T: This is what you said to yourself? How did that make you feel?

F: Hurt.

T: Did you feel resentful as well, even angry?

F: Yes, I guess so.

T: What did you do then?

F: I said nothing for the rest of the evening. I hid in the kitchen, cried a bit and sulked.

T: How did you know that's what Denis thought of your day?

F: What else? He doesn't want to know that all I did was hoovering and washing the bathroom. It's so trivial.

T: When you say that he didn't wait for an answer, what did he do?

F: He went upstairs to change his clothes and shouted: 'What's for supper?'

T: You've said to me before that your marriage was good. What would you have done in the past, if Denis had done exactly the same thing?

F: I guess I would have followed him upstairs and talked to him about my day and his day.

T: Right. Would you have thought that he thinks you lead a boring life and that he is fed up with you?

F: No, of course not. My life was not boring then.

T: Well, you were not depressed then and, in any case, we don't know that Denis thinks that your life is boring now. Has he ever said so?

F: No, in fact I think he quite likes it that I am at home. I can spend more time on him, on Marc and on the house.

T: Has he said so?

F: Yes, a few months ago he made such comments.

T: You see, Frances, there is some inconsistency here. You're putting thoughts that are derogating to you in his mind and reacting to them as if they were true. In fact, it is you who think of your current condition in derogatory terms. He seems to have said something quite different – at least on one occasion. What about him? What sort of thoughts to you think he may be attributing to you, since you didn't talk all evening?

F: I don't know.

T: Could he be thinking: 'She doesn't love me any more', 'I'm making her depressed', or whatever?

F: Um . . .

T: Maybe there's a vicious circle here. You react to the thoughts you attribute to him and he may be reacting to the thoughts he infers you have. How might we try and break this vicious circle?

They then engaged in role plays of various situations, with patient and therapist alternately playing the role of Denis, then of Frances. The differences in approach to life – easygoing and impulsive in the case of Denis and organised and cautious in the case of Frances – were reconstrued as differences in personality traits, which could be seen as complementary. Frances agreed that this was probably so, as they had got on well in the past and had had a lot of fun because of Denis' zest for life.

In order to change her current focus on the negative aspects of the marriage, Frances was asked to list all the occasions she could remember when Denis had been considerate to her and to their son, and when and how he had been of help to her.

This discussion was also used to check her automatic thoughts when she asked for help. It transpired that she had difficulties asking for help at any time – hence the shame about coming to therapy. Questions asked included: What did she feel when others solicited her help? What did she think of them? What might others, including Denis, make of the fact that she never asked for help? Would they feel left out? Did she want to be thought of as superwoman? What would happen if she did ask for help? The term 'superwoman' became a catchphrase in therapy, and was often used in a humorous fashion.

Two *behavioural tasks* were set up as homework assignments:

1   to tell Denis when she felt he was ignoring her because she thought her life was too boring, and find out more about what he really thought instead of mind-reading;

2   to ask him to help with taking Marc to the gym on Saturday,

while she went out shopping. To involve him more with house-hold decisions.

She would make predictions of outcome, check the results and see whether her mind-reading was correct. Regarding the letter requested from her former workplace, again a problem-solving approach was taken:

Therapist: What do you consider as a problem with this?

Frances: I can't write this letter as I don't have the file, and I can't remember the details.

T: Could you telephone and ask for the file?

F: I'm afraid that I'll burst out crying on the telephone. They'll think that I'm really pathetic – the little crying woman.

T: You've made two negative predictions there. Is there anything else you could do?

F: I could write and ask them to send the file by post?

T: Yes, you could do that. However, you would have lost a good opportunity to test out your negative predictions. Do you think that they expect you to remember the details of all the clients you dealt with a year ago? And if they do, would that be reasonable?

F: Maybe I can write and ask for the young man who is replacing me to come and see me with the file. If I prepare myself in advance, I won't cry.

T: This sounds good. Would you be able to write the letter if you see the file?

F: I really think it is not for me to do that. I don't work there any more, after all.

T: That's true. Would this young man be able to do it, if you briefed him?

F: I should think so.

T: OK. That's something else to try, then.

Again, a full rehearsal ensued of how she would behave when the young man from the bank came to the house. This was set as another *behavioural experiment* and included her predictions, as well as the recording of her automatic thoughts and of the results. During this phase of therapy, homework assignments involved the three behavioural tasks (above, and p. 77), the recording of automatic thoughts and the introduction of pleasurable activities in her weekly routine.

Sessions 6–9

These sessions involved recording automatic thoughts, challenging them in session, and then Frances challenging them herself. Some examples are given in Table 3.3, overleaf. At first she experienced difficulties with the dysfunctional thoughts records. Because the therapist was helping her in session to record the main 'hot' cognitions and to challenge them in a more helpful fashion, she concluded: 'I can't do this exercise, therefore I won't get better.' Again, this indicated her need to get things right and to succeed without asking for help.

This was discussed at length, using the following rationale: it is not easy to record one's automatic thoughts and to challenge them; it is not something that anybody does normally.

So why should she be good at it right away? Every new skill needs practice. Was she able to play the violin right away? Did she need help when she was learning? The reason for engaging in the 'abnormal' behaviour of recording automatic thoughts when one is depressed is that these thoughts maintain depression, and recording them, noting the common themes in them and challenging them, will help in recognising them. The common themes will lead to understanding what basic attitudes have made the patient vulnerable to particular situations.

Frances continued to do homework regularly, but she preferred doing it in her own way rather than use the therapist's forms. A special notebook was bought, and she did the homework in it.

This was also the occasion to discuss the 'shame about being a patient'. The line of reasoning was: Who are patients?, What does it mean to be a patient? This is a recurring theme in therapy, so a reconstructed excerpt is given here.

Table 3.3 Daily record of dysfunctional thoughts

Date	Situation Describe: 1 actual event leading to unpleasant emotion, or 2 stream of thoughts, daydream or recollection, leading to unpleasant emotion	Emotion(s) 1 Specify sad/anxious/angry, etc. 2 Rate degree of emotion 1–100%	Automatic thought(s) 1 Write automatic thought(s) that preceded emotion(s) 2 Rate belief in automatic thought(s) 0–100%	Alternative responses 1 Write alternatives to automatic thought(s) 2 Rate belief in alternative response 0–100%	Outcome 1 Re-rate belief in automatic thought(s) 0–100% 2 Specify and rate subsequent emotions 1–100%
	Wake up tired	empty 80% low 80%	I don't want to get up. Another pointless day ahead. I don't want to do more chores. 100%	I don't need to fill my day with chores. I could do something that interests me – play some music, visit my friend. 60%	1 50% 2 empty 50% low 50%
	At supermarket see somebody from work	anxious 100%	They will think that I'm skiving. If I was really ill, I wouldn't go shopping when everybody else is working. 100%	They know at work that I resigned because of depression. If they don't understand depression, that's their problem. I'm not doing anything illegal. If I want to shop, that's my business. 50%	1 50% 2 anxious 50%
	Denis has accepted invitation to dinner with work colleague and people I don't know	angry 100% anxious 100%	He should be more thoughtful. Where am I going to find a babysitter at such short notice? 100% They will ask awkward questions and I will feel ashamed of myself. 100%	There are a few people I can ring to babysit. If the worst came to the worst, we could cancel. I don't need to answer awkward questions. I can practise some answers and how to kick the ball back into their court. 70%	1 40% 2 angry 40% anxious 30%
	Denis is looking fed up and depressed	sad 100% irritated 60%	It's my fault. I make him miserable because I have been depressed such a long time. 100% He is selfish. 100%	Maybe it's not me. He is having problems at work. His job is on the line as departments are making staff redundant. He is very tired and needs a holiday. 90%	1 30% 2 sad 40% irritated 0%

Explanation: When you experience an unpleasant emotion, note the situation that seemed to stimulate it. (If the emotion occurred while you were thinking, daydreaming, etc., please note this.) Then note automatic thought associated with the emotion. Record the degree to which you believe this thought: 0% = not at all; 100% = completely. In rating degree of emotion: 1% = a trace: 100% = the most intense possible.

Therapist: What do you find shameful about being a patient?

Frances: It means one is not coping. I don't want to be like these people who have lots of problems.

T: So, everybody who comes to this clinic cannot cope and has lots of problems. What does this make them?

F: I don't know about everybody else – but it makes me a weak person, a failure.

T: The other side of the coin appears to be: strong and successful people do not have problems and do not seek help for depression or anxiety or whatever?

F: Yeah, that's what everybody thinks.

T: Do you consider A to be a weak person or a failure? And B, and C, and D?

[The therapist names a number of eminent people in the media, in politics and in academia who have openly talked or written about their depressions and their therapy.]

F: I didn't know about C. Is that right?

T: I see lots of people here, from all walks of life. I don't see them as weaklings or failures, because they evidently are not. What I see is people with problems, often associated with a depressive illness. Do you know how common depression is?

[The therapist then provides some data.]

Do you know anybody who has been depressed and had treatment?

The answer to this question is inevitably 'yes', and the patient realises that he or she does not think badly of them. Frances was encouraged to engage in some self-disclosure with some of her friends and to see what their reaction was. The results were very gratifying in that one friend who was highly thought of as a teacher had been treated for depression, and the other friend talked about another friend of hers who had been treated.

The situation with Denis was resolved in her own way and very satisfactorily. She had a heart-to-heart discussion with him and, to her surprise, he was eager to make changes, having been aware that their relationship was deteriorating. They decided to discuss crises as soon as they arose, rather than for each to go his or her own way feeling miserable and bitter.

By this time Frances' mood was much improved, and she was engaging in many more social and pleasurable activities. She had started looking at possible alternative careers.

Mid-treatment assessment   Hamilton Rating Scale for Depression: 10; Beck Depression Inventory: 14.

Sessions 10–14

The recording and challenging of negative thoughts and various behavioural experiments continued. The initial formulation (p. 71) was reviewed, and this involved filling in more details and discussing the origin of her core self schema. It was decided that 'incompetent' did not fit her beliefs about herself as well as 'inadequate'. 'Inadequate' was better because her sense of personal failure applied to both professional and personal domains, although the professional one had caused more problems. At that time she talked more of her childhood: of her mother's unhappiness; of her father, who generally felt inferior to his fellow managers in the firm because he was not university-trained, and who was distant and critical at home; of her older sister, who was much prettier and got on better with everybody; and of her younger sister, who always won all the prizes. Her sense of inadequacy, therefore, went back a long way, and Frances had compensated by hard work and by being the perfect wife, mother and professional woman. Any threat to these roles activated the badly camouflaged schema, and depression ensued.

Two sessions and a homework assignment related to 'I am inadequate' followed. She listed all the contra-indications, which were not difficult to elicit through Socratic questioning, and all the confirming evidence, which she then challenged. The aim of this part of the work was to increase and consolidate her sense of adequacy and to decrease her need for perfection and autonomy. By this point in the therapy the schema was already much less active and was partly modified, so that the schema-focused work did not have to be protracted. It must be noted that Frances had functioned well throughout most of her life and had no personality disorder, so that this part of the work was not as slow as it might have been with an Axis II patient.

The main technique she used in the homework was the *continuum method*, rating her sense of adequacy from 0 to 100 in her various roles. Adequacy was defined as: being a good mother, where 0 = child battering and 100 = never losing patience, always being there when the child needed her; being a good wife, where 0 = having extramarital affairs, never doing what husband wanted, and 100 = always being understanding and patient with husband, always being there for him; being a good professional woman, where 0 = never getting anything right and 100 = getting everything right all the time, never asking for help. This work continued over three weeks, both in session and as homework, and at the end Frances came to the conclusion that 100 on all these scales would denote an intolerable *superwoman*, who she did not really want to be.

When reviewing the course of therapy she made a list of her achievements, which went as follows:

- 'I have accepted that I have been depressed and that being ill is not a personal failure.'
- 'I have accepted being a patient.'
- 'I have learned to catch dysfunctional thoughts and to challenge them.'
- 'I have rebuilt my relationship with my husband.'
- 'I have learned to self-disclose and to accept help.'
- 'I have developed and sustained new interests – there is more to life than work.'
- 'I have learned to stop trying to be superwoman.'

FINAL FORMULATION

This was very similar to the initial formulation shown in Figure 3.2, except for the core schema, an additional conditional schema and additional critical events and incidents (see Figure 3.3).

Figure 3.3   Final formulation

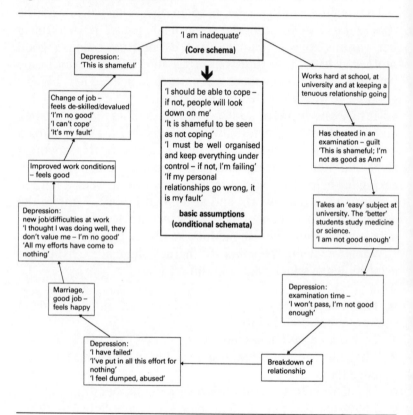

OUTCOME

At the end of fourteen sessions over four months, Frances had made a good recovery which was maintained at the three- and six-months follow-up.

At the end of treatment, her scores on severity measures were HRSD: 4; BDI: 5; STAI-S: 40. On measures of cognitive style, her scores were ATQ: 50; HS:4; CST: 60; DAS: 114. Figure 3.4 illustrates progress over the course of treatment (see p. 86).

RELAPSE-PREVENTION

This was dealt with in the final session and reviewed at follow-up, three and six months later. Frances made a list of the critical incidents related to her depressive episodes: breakdown of relationship; not confiding in anybody; loss of control in relationship and at work; new job situations; uncertainty about future job prospects.

Possible hazards in the future were related to past events, and relapse-prevention methods were discussed in the 'What if?' format:

- 'What if Denis wants to change job again?'
- 'What if, in your new job, you feel that you don't know as much as your colleagues?'
- 'What if you need to ask for help?'
- 'What if your son is sick, and you need to be off work?'
- 'What if you begin to feel depressed again?'
- 'What if you begin to feel out of control?'

All these 'What ifs?' were carefully discussed. Frances knew that she had to pay particular attention to not taking on too much, allowing for a degree of disorganisation, and making time for herself.

DISCUSSION

Frances responded well to cognitive therapy, as had been predicted from the Suitability for Short-term Cognitive Therapy Scale. She had been on antidepressant medication for one year when she came to therapy, and had not responded to any significant degree except that she fell asleep more easily. She continued to be on medication throughout therapy, and only

Figure 3.4 Progress through treatment

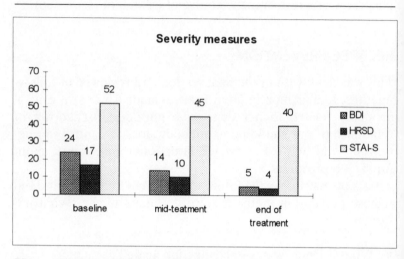

BDI   Back Depression Inventory
HRSD   Hamilton Rating Scale for Depression
STAI-S State-Trait Anxiety Inventory – State Version

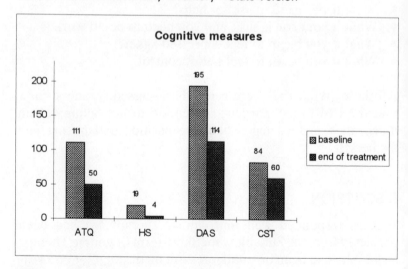

ATQ   Automatic Thoughts Questionnaire
HS   Hopelessness Scale
DAS   Dysfunctional Attitude Scale
CST   Cognitive Style Test

stopped it three months after therapy had stopped. There was no recurrence of symptoms.

The prognosis for Frances is thought to be good, both in the short and the long term. Her core early maladaptive schema – 'I am inadequate' – was not extremely rigid, and she did not have a pattern of avoidant or dependent behaviour. On the contrary, she had developed counter-dependent patterns of behaviour (though not extreme) to compensate for her sense of inadequacy. This compensation had worked mostly *for* her, but had left her vulnerable to interpersonal and professional situations which she perceived as personal failures. During therapy, she addressed key issues which should serve her well in the future.

In therapy, her degree of autonomy facilitated the use of cognitive methods in that she was eager to do homework assignments and to try things out for herself. The therapist allowed for this by nurturing her sense of control over the form of homework, over frequency of appointments and over decision-making regarding her future. Her thoroughness, persistence and personal honesty all helped the process of therapy to be focused, short-term and successful.

4

A Case of Generalised Anxiety Disorder

Gill – Looking for a Safe Footing on Shifting Sand

In recent years several research studies have sought to ascertain the epidemiology of generalised anxiety disorder (GAD). Breslau and Davis (1985) surveyed 375 women in the general population and identified a prevalence rate of 2.4 per cent and 11.5 per cent for one month and six months respectively. A number of researchers have investigated prevalence rates over one year, and report varied estimates of 6.4 per cent (Uhlenhuth et al., 1983), 2.3 per cent (Angst et al., 1985) and 2.6 per cent (Dean et al., 1983). Meanwhile, an American study by Blazer et al. (1991) demonstrates a prevalence rate of 3.5 per cent.

DEFINITION OF GENERALISED ANXIETY DISORDER

The diagnostic criteria for GAD as defined in the fourth *Diagnostic and Statistical Manual* of the American Psychiatric Association (*DSM*-IV, American Psychiatric Association, 1994) are summarised in Table 4.1. The defining feature of GAD, both within the *DSM*-IV diagnostic criteria and the research and clinical literature, is that it is characterised by the process of worry, and worry is a cognitive activity.

Table 4.1   Diagnostic criteria for generalised anxiety disorder
(summarised from *DSM*-IV)

---

1   Excessive anxiety and worry, which occur on at least 4 days out of
    7 for at least 6 months, about a number of events and activities
2   Difficulty in controlling the worry
3   The anxiety and worry are associated with at least three of the
    following symptoms:
    • restlessness, feeling keyed up or on edge
    • being easily fatigued
    • difficulty concentrating or mind going blank
    • irritability
    • muscle tension
    • sleep disturbance

Borkovec and Inz (1990) define GAD as 'An excessive or
unrealistic anxiety and worry over multiple life circumstances,
with accompanying symptoms of autonomic hyperactivity, motor tension, vigilance and scanning.' In addition, Barlow (1988)
observes that anxiety and worry are future-orientated states, in
which the individual predicts that something dangerous and
distressing is about to happen which he or she is unable to
control. Thus, the disorder is characterised by negative affect
with accompanying negative predictions about the unpredictable and uncontrollable nature of events. Barlow also notes that
the attentional focus in GAD is inward-looking, and the client
makes continual negative evaluations concerning his or her
ability to deal with the situation at hand. This in turn increases
arousal, narrowing the focus of attention further. The result
is apprehensive and hypervigilant cognitive schemata which
produce worry, subtle avoidance and reassurance-seeking
behaviour.

Barlow also suggests that individuals who develop anxiety
disorders probably have a biological predisposition to be anxious. Disorders such as GAD may emerge when a biologically
prone person experiences an early environment characterised
by unpredictability and lack of control. This creates a psychological vulnerability within him, increasing his susceptibility to

developing an anxiety disorder. It is important to note that while it is accepted that the cognitive activity of worry is a central theme in GAD, it has never been assumed that cognitions are primary in the disorder, and there is still debate surrounding this issue. Figure 4.1 illustrates the cognitive themes in anxiety and worry, adapted from Beck *et al.* (1985).

Figure 4.1   Cognitive themes in anxiety and worry

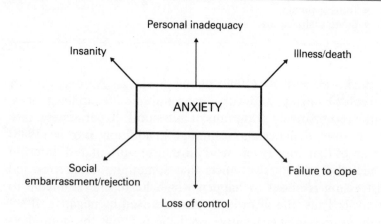

THE COGNITIVE MODEL

While there exists no one unifying model of GAD, a number of authors highlight salient features that define the disorder and require intervention as part of treatment. The following description draws on the work of Butler (1992), Barlow (1988), Borkovec and Costello (1993) and Blackburn and Davidson (1990). The cognitive model of GAD posits that the anxious individual possesses an increased perception of threat or danger, combined with a decreased perception of his ability to cope. Thus, he overestimates the probability and severity of an anticipated event going wrong, as well as underestimating both internal and external coping resources. In this context GAD consists of:

- threat-cue detection;
- somatic activation and inhibition;
- thought activity characterised by the worry process, which has verbal and imagery content;
- negative predictions about future events.

In addition, Barlow (1988) emphasises the key focuses of GAD as uncertainty, unpredictability and uncontrollability. Blackburn and Davidson (1990) offer a slightly different emphasis, summarised in Figure 4.2.

Figure 4.2   Anxious content of thoughts, and anxiety symptoms

Content of thoughts	Symptoms
	• Anxiety
	• Depression
View of self as vulnerable	• Lack of self-confidence
	• Increasing dependency
View of world as threatening	• Autonomic symptoms
	• Disturbed sleep
View of future as unpredictable	• Loss of initiative
	• Poor concentration
	• Excessive alertness

In discussing the overall aim of treatment, Butler (1992) uses the metaphor 'to bring order out of chaos'. Thus the aim is to mobilise the patient's resources and change his coping balance, by decreasing his perception of threat and increasing his perception of coping. Butler (1992) asks whether therapy is more profitable if interventions are focused on the activity of worry itself, rather than its content. She advises the therapist to avoid the application of numerous techniques, and to concentrate on formulation of the problem as a means to understanding its development and maintenance. This is done while at the same time modifying conditional assumptions as a way of under-mining the patient's psychological vulnerability.

There is much debate in the literature about the function of the worry process in GAD. Borkovec and Inz (1990) hypoth-esise that, while patients report worry as a verbal activity, this represents a form of cognitive avoidance of distressing imagery. If their hypothesis is correct, the modification of core schemata encapsulated in catastrophic imagery would be indicated.

GILL

THE REFERRAL

Gill was referred to the Cognitive Therapy Centre by a com-munity psychiatric nurse (CPN) who described her main prob-lem as anxiety and panic attacks, with some depressive features. The CPN had engaged Gill in a course of non-directive counsell-ing; this had given her insight into her problem, but her symp-toms had persisted. The referrer identified a number of negative cognitive biases that might be amenable to cognitive therapy.

THE ASSESSMENT

Assessment of Gill's problem took place over three sessions, using interview, psychometric measures and baseline self-monitoring to gather information regarding three specific areas:

1 symptom profile;
2 history of the disorder;
3 personal background.

Symptom profile

Gill, a 38-year-old woman, described a problem of generalised anxiety. She reported feeling 'tense, irritable and on edge', as well as experiencing symptoms of autonomic arousal in the form of palpitations, gastro-intestinal disturbances, hot flushes and tingling sensations in her arms and fingers. These symptoms were of variable duration and intensity. Baseline self-monitoring revealed that on three to five days per week she would feel tense and on edge. She rated the intensity of these feelings at 6 on a 0–8 (minimum–maximum) scale. On such days the feelings would persist for between four and twelve hours. Approximately once a week the symptoms would intensify, and Gill would experience a panic attack lasting two to three minutes. She reported that she started feeling uncomfortable as soon as she got out of bed, describing an 'almost overwhelming sense of fear and dread'. Accompanying automatic thoughts focused on pervasive anxiety about what the day would bring – for example, worrying about the safety of her family or catastrophising about potential difficulties in her husband's business. Gill also worried about her own well-being, and expressed particular concern that she was 'going mad', reporting catastrophic imagery of herself collapsing and flailing her arms and legs uncontrollably until she was taken away and incarcerated in the local 'asylum'.

Her chief strategies for coping with her anxiety were to keep busy in order to distract herself, and to seek constant verbal reassurance from her husband, daughter, mother and health professionals that she was mentally well. She also carried two temazepam tablets in her handbag at all times in case she needed to calm herself in an emergency. In addition, she would repeatedly read literature about anxiety and listen to relaxation tapes, to try and 'ward it off'. All of these strategies offered only temporary relief, and indeed in the long term exacerbated rather than alleviating the problem.

Gill also engaged in subtle avoidance behaviour – she avoided:

- dealing with problems, for fear of making herself feel worse;
- any activities that increased her symptoms;
- thinking ahead and planning;
- changing her routine.

She described her mood as demoralised. Her concentration and memory were as normal, but she did describe some sleep disturbance characterised by early-morning wakening. This generally occurred approximately once a week, when she would wake at 5 am and be unable to get back to sleep. On the Beck Depression Inventory (BDI) (Beck *et al.*, 1961) she obtained a score of 11, indicative of a normal mood state. When her problem first began she had experienced thoughts of self-harm over a period of three days. However, these had not occurred for over eight months, and at assessment she did not report any suicidal ideation.

Gill was not taking any prescribed medication at the time of assessment. She did not use alcohol to manage her anxiety symptoms – and, indeed, tended to avoid it as it accentuated her feelings of being out of control. Her caffeine intake was within acceptable limits and was deemed not to be exacerbating her symptoms.

She described a mixed presentation of symptoms, which raised the issue of differential diagnosis. But while the anxiety symptoms she described did, on occasion, meet *DSM*-IV criteria for a panic attack, a diagnosis of panic disorder was ruled out in accordance with the exclusion criterion that the panic attacks could be better accounted for by another disorder – in this instance, the worry aspect of generalised anxiety disorder. Similarly, the intrusive imagery and reassurance-seeking behaviour could have indicated a diagnosis of obsessive–compulsive disorder. But this too was ruled out on the ground that the intrusive imagery was restricted to the worry aspect of the generalised anxiety and she did not describe any overt or covert compulsions. Gill's description of her difficulties did not meet criteria for major depression, nor was the presence of an Axis II disorder indicated.

It is worth noting that Barlow (1988) suggests that a presentation of GAD alone is rare, and that 90 per cent of clients would meet criteria for an additional anxiety disorder. Barlow suggests that this may be accounted for in part by personality characteristics and by the presence of an Axis II disorder.

However, he concludes that this is a conceptually difficult area to investigate.

Baseline psychometric measures scored as follows:

- Beck Depression Inventory (BDI) (Beck *et al.*, 1961): 11
- Hopelessness Scale (HS) (Beck *et al.*, 1974): 9
- Dysfunctional Attitude Scale (DAS) (Weissman and Beck, 1978): 130
- Hamilton Rating Scale for Depression (HRSD), 17-item version (Hamilton, 1960): 7
- Beck Anxiety Inventory (BAI) (Beck and Steer, 1990): 45.

(For an interpretation of these measures see pp. 64 and 142.)

History of the disorder

Gill reported a year-long history of anxiety symptoms. She recalled waking up one day and experiencing a numbness in her big toe. Her immediate thought was 'This is the start of a stroke.' She visited her GP, who offered some reassurance. But she became vigilant with regard to bodily sensations, and the problem generalised to the extent that she became preoccupied with worries that she had breast cancer. She started going to see her GP approximately once every three weeks for reassurance, as well as paying privately to have two mammograms. In addition, she was checking for breast lumps three or four times a day.

An associated stressor at the time centred on the financial difficulties of her husband's business. Over a period of six months she took responsibility for dealing with the bank manager, and largely shielded her husband from the problems. Once these were alleviated, Gill's anxiety symptoms receded and her worries regarding ill-health dissipated.

Eight months later, she experienced a recurrence of her difficulties when she became very anxious and agitated, unable to sleep or engage in any purposeful activity. On this occasion the anxiety was more diffuse and did not focus on concerns about physical health, but on worries about her mental well-being. During this time she was unable to be left alone; she was very tearful and would physically cling to her husband and mother for security. Once more, triggers focused on financial worries within the family business. On next visiting her GP, Gill was referred to a consultant psychiatrist who prescribed anti-depressant and anxiolytic medication. This was of limited value in ameliorating her anxiety symptoms, and she was referred to a CPN.

Over the six months before assessment, Gill's anxiety state waxed and waned. During this time she sought additional help from a number of sources to try and solve her problem. These included hypnotherapy, reflexology and private psychotherapy, as well as reading copious amounts of self-help literature. Maintaining factors to Gill's anxiety state appeared to be a belief in the need for control combined with reassurance-seeking behaviour and subtle forms of avoidance.

Personal background

An only child brought up by her mother and maternal grand-mother, Gill was born and spent her childhood in a Kent village. Her father left home when she was six weeks old, and she never knew him. Two uncles also lived in the same house. As her mother went out to work in order to support her, she recalled always feeling much closer to her grandmother. She remembered her mother as 'unhappy' most of the time and 'very bitter' about the fact that her husband had left her for another woman. No one was allowed to mention her father in the family home. Gill described herself as a 'shy' and 'anxious' child. In particular, she remembered her two uncles drinking to excess every weekend. As a result there would be frequent arguments and she would worry in anticipation of their returning home at the end of their drinking sprees.

She stated that she neither liked nor disliked school, having plenty of friends and actively socialising. However, she reported feeling 'stigmatised' because she did not have a father, and had felt that she was in some way different from other children. Despite her own perception, she was never teased or bullied about her father not being at home.

Gill left school at sixteen with two O levels, and got a job in a local department store. This was not something she enjoyed, and at nineteen she married her only boyfriend, David, and left work. She described her marriage as 'basically happy', although her husband had always been self-employed and over their eighteen years of marriage the business had brought numerous stressors, including bankruptcy and house repossession.

Throughout this time Gill had taken responsibility for dealing with David's distress, and recalled feeling particularly sensitive to his mood changes if the business was not going well. He would become bad-tempered and withdrawn, and she would feel compelled to try and placate him. The couple had one daughter, Ellen, aged thirteen. Gill described herself as striving to be a perfect mother and wanting to protect Ellen as much as possible from any unpleasant aspects of life.

She helped with her husband's business and had a part-time job in a local supermarket.

Presentation

Gill presented as a very anxious woman who was searching with increasing desperation for a solution to her difficulties. She spoke at speed and was over-inclusive in her answers to most questions. She would repeatedly ask for reassurance, with questions such as 'Can you guarantee my anxiety will go away?', 'Have you ever met anyone with problems as severe as mine, and did they get better?', 'How long will it take to get better?' At times, it was quite difficult to shift her away from this focus. But she did respond to immediate limit-setting, and with direction could focus on and discuss a given topic to a reasonable depth. She was able to identify and label thoughts and feelings, and had begun to make some links between these aspects of her problem and her behaviour.

Summary of the assessment

Gill described symptoms of generalised anxiety disorder. Subjectively she reported her problem as very disabling. On days when she experienced high levels of anxiety her self-perception was of 'not being able to cope', with an accompanying sense that a total loss of control was imminent. While there appeared to be concordance between the precipitating event in terms of the financial difficulties within the business (which she perceived as unpredictable and beyond her control) and her reported automatic thoughts, this did not seem to account entirely for the level of distress she displayed. It was as if some vital piece of information was missing. Equally, her almost constant reassurance-seeking suggested that one of her main forms of coping was avoidance. She also appeared to have an exaggerated sense of responsibility, particularly in relation to her husband and daughter, and spent a good deal of time trying to protect them from upsetting events. Her previous help-seeking behaviour suggested that she could become dependent on the therapy if the sessions were not structured so as to prevent it.

SUITABILITY FOR SHORT-TERM COGNITIVE THERAPY

Suitability for treatment was formally measured using the Safran and Segal (1990) Suitability for Short-term Cognitive Therapy Rating Scale (as described on pp. 69–70). High ratings indicate a good prognosis and low ratings indicate a poor one. The total maximum possible score is 50.

1   *Accessibility of automatic thoughts*   Gill spontaneously reported automatic thoughts, and on questioning was able to articulate imagery with relative ease (5).
2   *Awareness and differentiation of emotions*   She was able to recognise and label emotions upon questioning, but demonstrated some reluctance to focus on them for any length of time (3.5).

3 *Acceptance of personal responsibility* She repeatedly stated that she 'accepted she was the only person who could solve her difficulties'. However, her compulsive use of self-help literature and alternative therapies suggested that she was, at one level, looking for a 'magic cure' to her problem (2).

4 *Compatibility with cognitive rationale* When the therapist shared the cognitive rationale with Gill, she was able to readily identify links between her thoughts, emotions and behaviour. She understood the rationale for homework assignments and was keen to understand her problems and develop coping strategies (4).

5 *Alliance potential (in-session evidence)* Gill appeared to be somewhat emotionally detached, did not readily display warmth and at times appeared a little guarded. However, feedback indicated that she felt listened to and understood (3.5).

6 *Alliance potential (out-of-session evidence)* In describing relationships with others, Gill indicated that she had a number of female friends whom she socialised with, but she did not regard these as confiding relationships. She described a close relationship with her daughter, but some barriers between herself and her husband. There was some tendency to avoid conflict (3.5).

7 *Chronicity of problems* Gill described a one-year history of anxiety symptoms (4).

8 *Security operations* This refers to psychological and/or behavioural activities that are aimed at reducing anxiety and increasing self-esteem. It is assumed that these will act as obstacles to the process of therapy. In this respect Gill demonstrated some avoidance of certain topics, but, in discussing this, she was able to acknowledge that she engaged in this strategy and accepted that it would need to be addressed as part of treatment (4).

9 *Focality* With guidance, she was able to remain focused on a specific topic. There was some tendency for her to shift from issue to issue, but with prompting she was able to re-focus (2).

10 *Patient optimism/pessimism regarding therapy* Gill did report feeling demoralised, and expressed some concern that

treatment might not help. However, she also remained open to trying cognitive therapy and reported that she felt she had nothing to lose by engaging in treatment (3).

A total score of 34.5 on this scale indicates that the patient's problem was moderately suited to being treated with short-term cognitive therapy.

INITIAL FORMULATION

The initial formulation of Gill's problem is shown in Figure 4.3. This was developed using Beck's (1976) cognitive model for the development and maintenance of emotional disorders.

TREATMENT

The Plan

Initially, ten to twelve sessions of cognitive therapy were negotiated. Through a process of discussion four specific treatment goals were identified and prioritised as follows:

1   to be able to deal more effectively with feelings of apprehension and anxiety;
2   to stop asking David, Ellen and the therapist for reassurance about problems;
3   to stop engaging in subtle avoidance behaviour;
4   to be able to take less responsibility for David's worries regarding the business.

It is usual in cognitive therapy for the first step in treatment to be education about the problem. But Gill had a wealth of knowledge on the subject of anxiety and the physiological mechanisms that produce its symptoms. She also already used a range of strategies including relaxation, visualisation techniques, meditation and positive self-statements to try to deal with her anxiety. All of these had little impact on the problem.

Figure 4.3   Initial formulation

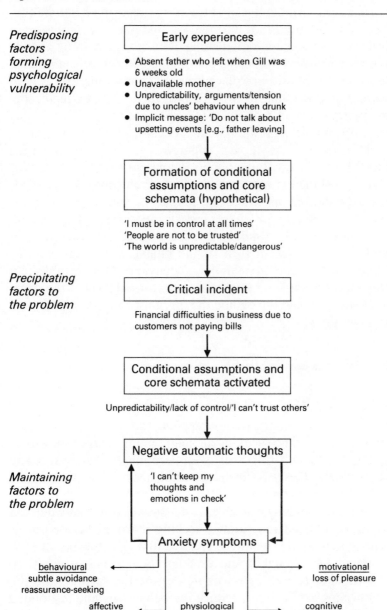

Thus, treatment needed to be modified in a way that could engage Gill productively. Following assessment, there appeared to be important information that had to be accessed in order to gain some understanding of what triggered the anxiety symptoms and what specific beliefs and behaviours maintained them. So emphasis was placed on self-monitoring as a way of gathering the data. It was hypothesised that a specific behavioural test would be the most expedient means of obtaining the information, and the obvious focus was Gill's reassurance-seeking behaviour. It was apparent that this was a strong maintaining factor, but since its whole purpose was to reduce anxiety, asking her not to engage in this behaviour and instructing individuals from whom she sought reassurance not to meet the request would lead to an increase in anxiety. This should, hopefully, allow Gill and the therapist to access salient emotions and beliefs, which in turn should enable her to identify the idiosyncratic meaning behind the behaviour. Once established, this would provide a more immediate formulation of the problem, which would then guide the therapist towards appropriate interventions.

PROGRESS OF THERAPY

Sessions 1–4

In accordance with the treatment plan, a written rationale of the role of reassurance-seeking in maintaining anxiety disorders was given to Gill (for a detailed account see Salkovskis and Kirk, 1989). This was illustrated using her reassurance-seeking behaviour in the session. Then the rationale for eliminating reassurance-seeking was given, and she was told that when the therapist noticed reassurance-seeking it would be identified, and no reassurance would be given. Gill would then be asked to examine her thoughts and feelings. She was also asked to monitor her reassurance-seeking outside the session, and the following week to try to reduce the behaviour. She responded well to the written rationale and readily engaged in the activity of self-monitoring. This yielded useful information. Initially she identified a number of forms of reassurance-seeking:

- when she felt anxious, asking David or Ellen if she was going to be all right;
- carrying anxyolitic medication in her handbag;
- ritualistically reading anxiety literature three times over;
- making copious notes about how she was feeling.

From this, a behavioural test was devised regarding the consequences of throwing away her anxyolitic medication; her prediction was an increase in her anxiety levels. She did so after the third session and reported no adverse effects, but she was unable to identify any reasons for this result. A second behavioural test was to put the anxiety literature away and not refer to it. Again, Gill predicted an increase in her symptoms. However, she carried out the test, without any ill effects. Once more she was unable to identify any reasons for the invalidation of her predictions.

This enabled the therapist to introduce the cognitive model of anxiety in the context of negative predictive cognitions based on an increased perception of risk and danger and a decreased perception of ability to cope. Gill readily acknowledged that often events were not as bad as she anticipated, and asked: 'Why do I never learn from this?' This was highlighted as an important question to answer, and homework focused on monitoring negative predictive cognitions.

This exercise revealed an important piece of information. When Gill accessed negative predictive imagery, the content of which focused on the time when her problems first began, she would pace the house at night clinging on to her mother and David, crying and pleading for help. In exploring the meaning behind this, she identified the following automatic thoughts:

- 'I should be able to control my thoughts.'
- 'I should keep my mind in check at all times.'

Her perception that she could not control her thoughts was indicative of being out of control, the implication of which was that she was going mad. She then predicted that if she were to go mad she would lose her home, her husband and her daughter and be taken away to the local psychiatric hospital where she would stay for ever. During this discussion, Gill became very tearful and observed how much she hated being alone – something she avoided at all costs. She was unable to articulate what it was about being alone that she found so distressing.

Returning to the question she had posed – 'Why do I never learn from the fact that often events are not as bad as I anticipate?' – she was asked to examine unpredictable events in her life. Recalling her childhood, she remembered that she had always been anxious and had always worried that 'things were going to go wrong'. She recalled again the unpredictable behaviour of her uncles when they had been drinking, and stated that most of her eighteen years of marriage had consisted of unpredictable events, on account of the business. She also identified David as an unpredictable person, describing him as volatile and impulsive.

A second point that emerged during this early stage of treatment was Gill's tendency to be self-critical about not doing things properly. As a result, she reported feelings of sadness and guilt.

From these first four sessions it had been ascertained that:

- Gill predicted the future negatively and underestimated her ability to cope with the predicted impending disaster;
- she tended to discount things that went well and be self-critical, which made her vulnerable to periods of low mood;
- new information, shown in Figure 4.4, was now available to the formulation.

Sessions 5–8

From the information gathered in the first four sessions an intervention was made to evaluate how realistic Gill's negative predictions were. This involved following six steps:

Figure 4.4   Formulation of relationship between current events and
underlying beliefs

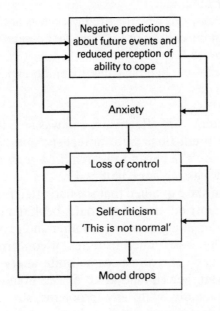

Hypothesised core schemata

'I am a failure'
'I am vulnerable/weak'
'People are unpredictable'
'The world is dangerous'

Hypothesised basic assumption

? 'If I can't keep control of my
thoughts, I will lose everything'

1   identifying the negative prediction;
2   estimating the percentage likelihood of its being realised;
3   engaging in the activity;
4   evaluating the outcome;
5   identifying the reasons why the prediction was not realised –
e.g., that it was an unrealistic prediction, that coping strategies
had been implemented.
6   considering what had been learned from the experience.

Gill used this strategy very effectively, and was able to observe
that her negative predictions were unrealistic and largely un-
founded. Once more she began to search for a reason for this,
and returned to discussing her childhood.

On this occasion she explained that she had often felt 'unsafe'
as a child, and worried that she would be left alone. She
remembered praying at night that her mother and grandmother
would not die. This was framed in terms of concern that she
would be abandoned. She also became quite angry while re-
counting that during her childhood no one at home had sup-
ported her emotionally with any problems she had. She
described the family attitude as 'Life is hard and the world is a
difficult place'. Thus the family maxim was 'You can't give in,
you've got to fight, pull yourself together – once you give in,
you've had it.' From this Gill identified how insecure she had
always felt and how important it was for her to know that she
was wanted and needed. This highlighted the possibility of
dependency underlying her problem.

A further intervention at this stage was to continue to try to
reduce reassurance-seeking behaviour. This time the behavioural test was to resist asking David for reassurance (see
Figure 4.5). Gill was able to identify that the time she frequently
sought reassurance from David was when she got up in the
morning. Not engaging in this behaviour revealed vital information about triggers to her anxiety on a day-to-day basis. This was
added to the formulation.

By the end of session 8 she reported a reduction in the

Figure 4.5   Information gathered from behavioural test of resisting asking David for reassurance

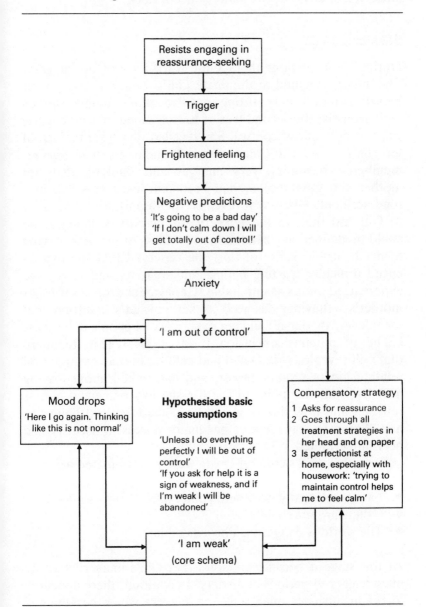

intensity of her anxiety symptoms, and began to experience anxiety-free days approximately once a week.

Sessions 9–12

During these sessions therapeutic work focused on imagery. Two images seemed to dominate Gill's thoughts: one was of herself as an old lady, sitting in a flat, all alone and crippled with arthritis; the second was of herself alone in a psychiatric ward, totally out of control. She recalled that from the age of ten she had been left alone every Monday evening. She remembered becoming very anxious and thinking that her mother and grandmother had been murdered or killed in a road accident. Discussion revealed the importance of security to Gill and that, in the imagery she described, being alone could be defined as abandonment and loss of security. Trying to make further sense of this, she observed that she experienced difficulty trusting people and that, by and large, she experienced others as unreliable. Her evidence for this was her mother's behaviour, as well as her mother's assertion that 'people let you down'; and her experience of people in business led her to the same conclusion. It was at this stage in treatment that Gill revealed that David had entered into an extramarital relationship two years earlier, and had talked about leaving her. Up until this point in her life she had perceived him as reliable, and now this view had been shattered. Although he had chosen to stay, one of her main sources of security had been undermined.

From this, Gill's core schemata were re-formulated as:

- 'I am emotionally weak and vulnerable.'
- 'Others are unreliable.'
- 'The world is dangerous/unpredictable.'

At this stage it became apparent that Gill's imagery was the main trigger to periods of anxiety. In addition, there appeared to be an intrusive quality to her imagery which perpetuated her anxiety symptoms. This process of intrusive thinking and resultant anxiety is shown in Figure 4.6.

Figure 4.6   Cognitive model of intrusive thoughts

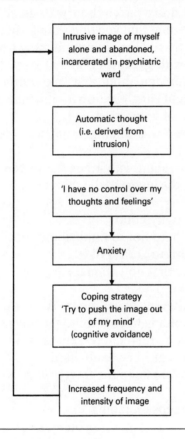

A rationale for this phenomenon, in accordance with Sal-kovskis' (1989) model of intrusive thoughts, was given to Gill. A behavioural test was carried out in the session:

Therapist: Gill, I want to try an experiment, to test this thought – 'I have no control over my thoughts.' In a moment I'm going to ask you to carry out a specific task. Please listen carefully to what I'm going to say, and try to carry it out. Are you with me so far?

Gill: Yes.

T: Over the next two minutes I want you to think about anything other than a large fluffy pink rabbit with green fluorescent ears. It is very important that you don't think about the rabbit at all and that you try to take your mind away from the large fluffy pink rabbit with green fluorescent ears. I hope very much you're not thinking about that large fluffy pink rabbit with green fluorescent ears, because it's imperative you try to keep the rabbit out of your mind.

Now, Gill, while I was talking, what was going through your mind?

G: A large fluffy pink rabbit with green fluorescent ears.

T: What happened to the image of the rabbit when you tried not to think about it?

G: It kept coming into my mind.

T: Did you try really hard not to think about the rabbit?

G: Yes, but it was hard to get rid of it.

T: That's interesting, what do you make of that?

G: I'm not sure really.

T: OK, let's try a different experiment. What I'd like you to concentrate on is holding in your mind the image of the large fluffy pink rabbit with green fluorescent ears. Try and keep it there as long as you can. Try really hard.

Gill, how easy is it to keep the image of the rabbit in your mind?

G: Not that easy, it keeps on fading.

T: That's interesting, too – what do you make of that?

G: I'm not sure.

T: OK, let's summarise the two experiments. In the first experiment, the more you tried *not* to think about the rabbit the more it came to your mind. Agreed?

G: Yes.

T: OK, that seems to have some similarities with how you try to cope with the image of yourself alone in the psychiatric ward.

You try to push it out of your mind and it keeps coming back. Is that correct?

G: Yes.

T: Right. In the second experiment, while you were deliberately holding the thought in your mind, it seemed to fade.

G: Yes, that's true.

T: Does this seem to be a way of exerting control over your thoughts?

G: I guess so.

T: OK, so what would happen if, instead of trying to push the image of yourself alone in the psychiatric ward out of your mind, you tried to hold it there?

G: I guess it might fade. But I find it upsetting to have those images – I would feel worse.

T: In what way would you feel worse?

G: Well, if I focus on the image, my anxiety will increase and it will just become totally out of control.

T: There is another hypothesis. If we agree that trying to push the image out of your mind keeps it coming back into your mind and that the image and what it means to you trigger the anxiety, then is it reasonable to hypothesise that as the image fades the anxiety will fade as well?

G: I'm not sure.

T: How about if we conduct an experiment now, by recalling one of the images and trying to hold it in your mind and see what happens?

G: Well, it sounds difficult but I guess I'm in the right place should I go completely mad!!

With encouragement, Gill participated in the experiment and made a significant cognitive shift. In evaluating the experiment she observed that, initially, focusing on her thoughts and feelings had seemed like relinquishing control; but in fact, in so doing, rather than her anxiety escalating as predicted, it dissipated. As a result – paradoxically – she felt 'calmer and in control'. She used this strategy outside the session and within three weeks the intrusive imagery had disappeared. At this point, the end of session 12, she reported experiencing anxiety symptoms three or four days a month. Although the initial therapy contract was complete, a number of issues still needed addressing. So a further six therapy sessions were negotiated.

Sessions 13–18

This final stage aimed to examine difficulties in Gill's relationship with David, as well as to begin work on modifying conditional assumptions and core schemata.

In focusing on her relationship with David, she returned to the episode two years previously when he had initiated a relationship with another woman. Up until this time, she said, she had been very dependent on him. The theme that emerged with his infidelity revolved around abandonment, and Gill said, 'If David had gone, there would have been nothing left in my life and I'd have been alone.' She cited this period as the onset of her anxiety problem, during which she had concluded that she was the only person she could rely on. However, as the anxiety worsened she lost her sense of self-reliance, which accentuated her sense of aloneness. She described her feared consequences of 'going mad' as her own abandonment of herself. This information was added to the formulation.

When Gill and the therapist focused on difficulties in her relationship with David, the following problems emerged:

1   Gill was taking responsibility for keeping the peace in the relationship and sorting out his problems in the business.
2   She was having difficulty expressing her opinions to David.
3   He was having difficulty expressing his wants, needs and feelings.

Thus, the couple tended to use avoidance as a coping strategy for dealing with emotional issues. These issues were explored through Socratic questioning:

Therapist: Gill, two themes seem apparent here: you take
    responsibility for keeping the peace in your relationship with

David, and you have difficulty expressing your thoughts and feelings to him. Have I understood that correctly?

Gill: Yes, it's a real problem for me.

T: When you talk about expressing your thoughts and feelings, what specifically do you find difficult?

G: What do you mean?

T: For example, do you find it difficult to tell him you love him or is it more a case of having difficulty refusing requests or showing anger?

G: I have no problem telling him I love him – I do it all the time. No, it's more saying 'no' or saying if I'm annoyed.

T: What do you think would happen if, for example, you let David see you were angry?

G: Well, when I do lose my temper he doesn't speak to me for a couple of hours.

T: How does it make you feel when that happens?

G: Guilty. I want to make peace.

T: What is it that makes you feel guilty in that situation?

G: I always think I've done something wrong. It's my fault. I need to put things right.

T: What do you need to put right?

G: Things between us. Make peace, be friends.

T: So you have the thought that when you argue and David stops speaking, you're not friends?

G: Yes.

T: So, who has stopped being friends with whom? David with you or you with David?

G: David with me, I guess.

T: Now, when you think about that – you argue and David stops being friends with you – what is upsetting about that?

G: I'm not sure.

T: Try to focus on it now. You feel guilty – any other feelings?

G: I guess I feel anxious as well.

T: Right, so you feel guilty and anxious when you think about the fact that David is not speaking to you. Does this say something about you specifically?

G: Well, you stop speaking to people you don't like, don't you?

T: So – have I understood correctly? – you think David doesn't like you when he stops speaking?

G: Yes.

T: Suppose it were true, David didn't like you – what would be the consequences?

G: He would leave me.

T: And if he left, what would be the consequences?

G: It all comes back to the same thing: I'd be alone and abandoned.

T: Right. So it seems that in these conflict situations you seem pretty convinced that David doesn't like you.

G: I don't know why David stays with me.

T: What do you mean?

G: Well, I don't see what he likes about me. That's why I try so hard to be a perfect wife and mother and keep things running smoothly for him – perhaps then, he'll stay [she starts to cry].

T: You seem really sad and upset. I know it may seem hard to focus on things, but what is going through your mind right now?

G: [crying] I don't know why he stays with me. I'm so pathetic. Except, he probably feels sorry for me because I'm so dependent and insecure. He tells me he loves me, but how could you love someone so weak? Look at me, crying like this.

From this exercise further information was gathered regarding Gill's core schemata: a primary one, 'I'm emotionally weak and vulnerable'; and a secondary one, 'I'm unlovable'. This also allowed for a collaborative formulation of her conditional assumptions:

- 'I must keep the peace at all times, or I will be abandoned.'
- 'I must keep control of every aspect of my life [myself, work, relationships], or I will lose everything [family, home, sanity].'
- 'I must be self-reliant because others will let me down and I'll get hurt.'

Through a process of negotiation it was decided that David's attendance at a session would be beneficial. He participated actively, and a further maintaining factor to Gill's current problem was identified. This related to the way in which she interacted with David. She continually made negative predictions about how he would respond to things she did and said. This would be accompanied by daily seeking reassurance that he loved her and that their relationship was happy. This pattern had existed throughout their married life, and he found it exasperating. He acknowledged that he had difficulty communicating his thoughts and feelings and that he was prone to moodiness.

The therapist, Gill and David together negotiated a behavioural test: David was not to give reassurance when Gill requested it. Initially this increased her anxiety, but she quickly implemented strategies from earlier in therapy and identified and challenged her negative thoughts. The couple also discussed the lack of communication in their relationship, and began to consider marriage guidance.

Over the next month Gill continued to report improvement, and collated further data for the formulation. She observed that from her mother's emotional unavailability and the unpredictability in her home environment, due to tension and arguments when her uncles drank, she had learned:

1   to be self-reliant at all times;
2   to try to keep the peace and take responsibility for other people's concerns and distress;
3   that men leave – her father left when she was a baby, and her mother was very bitter;
4   that, not having been allowed, as a child, to discuss her father, the implicit message was: 'Avoid discussing upsetting subjects' – and this had been carried on into her relationship with David.

The final stage of therapy was to begin work on modifying conditional assumptions and core schemata: significant work had already focused on the issue of control, and therapist and patient now together developed an action plan to undermine this further (see p. 204 for an example).

A plan was also devised to work on the belief: 'I must keep the peace at all times, or I will be abandoned.' This involved Gill identifying issues that she was reluctant to discuss with David. Next, she was to identify her negative predictive cognitions about discussing these issues, and from this develop a behavioural test to ascertain their validity. She was also to keep an ongoing log of the outcome data from these behavioural tests. In conjunction with this aspect of treatment she was asked to read *Love Is Never Enough* (Beck, 1988), a book which examines relationship difficulties from a cognitive perspective.

By session 18 Gill reported experiencing anxiety symptoms approximately once every six weeks. She was, though, able to deal with these reasonably well. She had also virtually eliminatd her reassurance-seeking behaviour and no longer experienced intrusive imagery. At her own request, she terminated therapy. She wanted to consolidate her gains and continue to work on her relationship with David. She did, however, express interest in some joint sessions with her husband at a future date. She found the recommended literature very valuable, and thought that couples therapy based on Beck's work would prove beneficial. She had begun to implement some of this herself, and she felt her relationship with David was becoming more open.

FINAL FORMULATION

The final formulation, developed by Gill and the therapist, is presented in Figure 4.7. Most of the information, which represents her understanding of the problem on completion of therapy, was generated by Gill.

OUTCOME

At the end of treatment, the psychometric measures that had been taken at assessment were taken again, and demonstrated

Figure 4.7 Final formulation

Predisposing factors forming psychological vulnerability

Early experiences

- Absent father who left when Gill was 6 weeks old
- Unavailable mother, who was bitter about her circumstances and complained about having to bring up a child alone
  Message: 'People are unreliable'
- Unpredictability, arguments/tension due to uncles' behaviour when drunk – Gill tried to keep the peace/exert control
- Not allowed to discuss her father
  Message: 'I don't talk about upsetting things'
  Always felt vulnerable, insecure; sought reassurance

Formation of basic assumptions and core schemata

'I must keep the peace, or I will be abandoned'
'I must keep control over every aspect of my life, or I'll lose everything'
'I must be self-reliant, because others will let me down and I'll get hurt'
'I'm emotionally weak and vulnerable'
'I'm unlovable'
'Others are unreliable'
'The world is unpredictable'

Precipitating factors to the problem

Critical incident

David initiated extramarital relationship
Financial difficulties in business due to customers not paying bills

Basic assumptions and core schemata activated

Negative automatic thoughts

Maintaining factors to the problem

Anxiety symptoms

behavioural
subtle avoidance
reassurance-seeking

motivational
loss of pleasure

affective
fear

physiological
arousal

cognitive
cognitive avoidance

the following changes: BDI: 6; DAS: 72; HS: 2; BAI: 6; HRSD-17: 0. The changes in scores over the course of treatment are shown in Figure 4.8.

Figure 4.8   Histogram of scores on pre- and post-treatment questionnaires

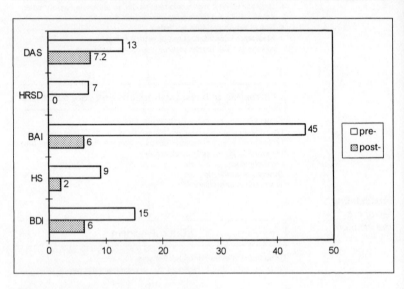

DAS score reduced by a factor of 10

DAS	Dysfunctional Attitude Scale
HRSD	Hamilton Rating Scale for Depression
BAI	Beck Anxiety Inventory
HS	Hopelessness Scale
BDI	Beck Depression Inventory

RELAPSE-PREVENTION

The final two therapy sessions were devoted to identifying and implementing relapse-prevention strategies. One of the central goals of cognitive therapy is to enable the patient to use self-help strategies and to implement these to maintain treatment gains.

With this in mind, a review of treatment was undertaken which examined the following points:

1   What made Gill vulnerable to the problem in the first place?
2   What life stressors triggered the current problem?
3   What factors maintained the problem?
4   What strategies have been learned in therapy to deal with the problem?
5   What future high-risk situations may leave Gill vulnerable to a return of the problem?
6   What plans can be devised to deal with these high-risk situations?

Gill and the therapist used these questions as a guide for drawing up a blueprint for relapse-prevention (for an example of such a blueprint see Table 7.8, p. 210). Gill participated actively in this exercise, and identified a number of areas which might present a risk of her anxiety returning. These can be summarised as follows:

• financial stressors in the business;
• taking responsibility for David's and Ellen's problems;
• tension in her relationship with David.

Plans were devised to anticipate how Gill might handle these potential stressors, to build in strategies that would demonstrate her own coping resources, and to undermine the perceived threat inherent in the situation. A further aspect of relapse-prevention involved continuing to modify conditional assumptions and core schemata. Thus, flashcards were introduced, aimed at further understanding the origins of the underlying beliefs and at devising a concrete and specific action plan – this included short-term and long-term goals with the aim of modifying the cognitive, emotional and behavioural manifestations of the beliefs (for an example of this, see Table 7.6, p. 204).

Gill had already started work on modifying conditional assumptions, and had begun to make some inroads. This aspect of therapy is often difficult for the client. By definition, conditional assumptions involve value judgements and often need to be viewed in terms of how helpful or unhelpful they are to the client, as opposed to relying solely on evidential challenges to weaken their grip. An example of this can be seen in Table 4.2.

Table 4.2 Helpful and unhelpful aspects of holding the belief, 'I must be self-reliant because others will let me down and I'll get hurt'

Helpful	Unhelpful
1 It offers some protection in that if I don't rely on others, they can't let me down and I won't feel hurt or disappointed 2 I have real-life experience of being let down badly (mother, David), so this is self-preservation	1 It stops me getting close to people and enjoying the benefits of sharing things with others 2 It is unrealistic because there is an expectation within it that people should be 100% reliable all of the time, which is impossible; as a result, I set others up to 'fail' by my standards, so they can't win, even in everyday situations, and I get upset 3 It is impossible to be 100% self-reliant, and in trying to live by this rule I am depriving myself of learning from my experiences with others and finding out if some people can be trusted some of the time

In addition, behavioural testing is a core feature of modifying cognitive vulnerability, given that conditional assumptions represent the individual's set of rules which govern his or her action in and interaction with his or her environment. Gill had some difficulty devising behavioural tests, so examples related to specific beliefs were developed within the sessions and incorporated into the action plan.

DISCUSSION

Gill had eighteen sessions of cognitive therapy, from which she derived considerable benefit. When she was asked what aspect of treatment she had found most helpful, she highlighted the formulation, working on intrusive imagery, and modifying underlying beliefs. In addition, the opportunity to involve David in therapy sessions had enabled the couple to address a long-standing maladaptive pattern of interaction between them. This had opened up new avenues of communication, as well as highlighting areas for future work.

David was somewhat reticent about participating formally in sessions, but one of Gill's short-term goals was to discuss with him the communication difficulties in their relationship and try to come to some agreement regarding a future course of action. Therapy ended with an agreement that if the couple decided to use therapy as a way of improving their level of communication, then it would be available to them through the Cognitive Therapy Centre. It was anticipated that this would not involve more than six to eight sessions, but a break of at least six months from the end of individual therapy was deemed appropriate. This would give Gill time to consolidate her gains from treatment, as well as allow the couple to establish what aspects of their relationship required modification. A time lapse would also be important in terms of reorientating the session work away from an individual- to a couple-focused intervention.

5

A Case of Panic Disorder

Stephen – '. . . when you have eliminated the impossible, whatever
remains, *however improbable*, must be the truth' (Sherlock Holmes)
Sir Arthur Conan Doyle

A number of experimental studies testify to the fact that extreme fear dramatically increases physiological arousal, as well
as cognitive and behavioural dysfunction. Much of the work has
employed rather artificial fear-induction scenarios. Marshall's
observations of veteran combat soldiers has ecological validity
and is therefore of more clinical interest (Marshall, 1978). He
found that during battle soldiers' performance was dramatically
impaired on a number of behavioural measures. Indeed, on
average per engagement, only 30 per cent of the field soldiers
managed to fire at the enemy: many froze; some hid or ran;
others became disorientated; some failed to load their guns
correctly, and so on.

It is worth noting that many of these behaviours have their
parallels in clinical panic. Despite Marshall's findings, the soldiers had tended not to view their difficulties as strange nor as a
sign of some sort of disorder, because they could attribute their
reactions to the very real stimuli of the battle. In many respects
these causal attributions are the key feature distinguishing
'normal' from 'abnormal' fear (that is, panic attacks). Hence we
can loosely define a panic attack as an extreme and unexpected
fear reaction produced in response to either a seemingly innocuous, or an undefined, stimulus.

In the general population, panic attacks seem to be fairly common. A study by Norton *et al*. (1985) found that 34 per cent of young adults had experienced a panic attack within the previous year. It seems, therefore, that the occurrence of panics is a problem when they are recurrent and unexpected; and in such cases the condition may be termed panic disorder. Prevalence data from the USA's National Institute of Mental Health's epidemiological catchment area survey (Robins and Regier, 1991) suggest a six-month rate of 0.8 per cent for panic and 3.8 per cent for agoraphobia – a commonly associated condition. Other studies have found higher rates: for example, Reich (1986) found a six-month prevalence rate for panic of 3 per cent, and for agoraphobia 6 per cent. The rates appear to be higher for women than for men – 60 per cent higher for panic, and 30 per cent for agoraphobia. It is worth noting that it is generally believed (Roth and Fonagy, 1995) that, even amongst those who are identified as having such disorders, somewhere in excess of 50 per cent go untreated, due to issues of accessibility of treatment and cost-effectiveness.

DEFINITION OF PANIC DISORDER

Since *DSM*-III-R (American Psychiatric Association, 1987), panic disorder is no longer a separate diagnostic category but must now be defined with or without agoraphobia. Therapists need to be careful when distinguishing between panic with and without agoraphobia, as their patients' avoidance behaviours can often be quite subtle. A summary of the diagnostic criteria is provided in Table 5.1, overleaf.

THE COGNITIVE MODEL

The cognitive model of panic disorder (Beck *et al*., 1985; Clark, 1986; Salkovskis, 1988) is based on the premise that sufferers have a heightened tendency to react to fear elicited by ordinary bodily sensations. This sensitivity is thought to be a consequence of interoceptive conditioning and catastrophic

Table 5.1 Diagnostic criteria for panic disorder with agoraphobia (summarised from *DSM*-IV)

Panic disorder
- Presence of panic attacks – discrete period of intense discomfort, in which 4 or more of the following 13 symptoms have developed abruptly and reached a peak within 10 minutes: palpitations, sweating, trembling or shaking, chest pain or discomfort, breathing difficulties, nausea, feelings of unreality, feelings of choking, dizziness, fear of losing control, fear of dying, numbness or tingling sensations, chills or hot flushes.

- Nature of panic attack – (1) recurrent and unexpected; (2) succeeded by one or more of the following: fear of additional attacks, worries about consequences of the attacks (e.g., having a heart attack, 'going crazy'), significant change in behaviour resulting from the attacks (e.g., avoidance)

- Exclusion – attacks are due neither to a general medical condition nor to any ingested substance (e.g., drugs, coffee); attacks cannot be accounted for better by other anxiety-related disorders, such as social phobia, obsessional–compulsive disorder, post-traumatic stress disorder, separation anxiety disorder

Agoraphobia
- Fear of situations in which escape is difficult or help is not available in the event of panic; through fear, the person either restricts travel or needs companion when away from home – or endures agoraphobic situations despite intense anxiety

- Exclusion – anxiety or phobic avoidance is not better accounted for by another anxiety disorder

---

misinterpretation of bodily sensations. Since fear is usually accompanied by autonomic arousal, an individual who is fearful of bodily sensations will be susceptible to feed-forward escalation of symptoms. Clark (1989) considers that the triggers in panic can be wide-ranging, both internal and environmental. He also suggests that there are two forms of panic: (1) anxious attacks – those which are preceded by anxiety-provoking events, or some form of fearful anticipation, and (2) 'out of the blue' attacks – those with no obvious precursor. A vicious cycle is hypothesised, the probably trigger being some slight change in bodily sensation, which is then perceived as threatening; this results in a state of apprehension, which leads to the person focusing on bodily sensations; these sensations are processed catastrophically (catastrophic body interpretations – CBIs), and the individual feels unable to cope. An adapted form of Clark's (1986) model is summarised in Figure 5.1.

Figure 5.1 Panic cycle

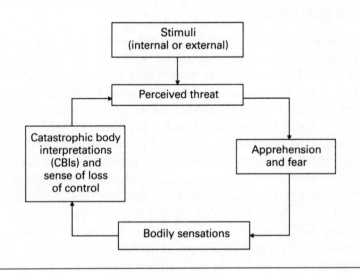

Perceived fear of the panic attack makes the patient both hypervigilant and internally focused. The hypervigilance and internal focusing result in greater sensitivity to changes in physiology, and thus increase the probability of the onset of an attack. Clark and Ehlers (1993) and McNally (1991) have recently reviewed the empirical evidence in support of this cognitive hypothesis. The conclusion is that there is, indeed, evidence that patients with panic disorder tend to misinterpret bodily sensations more than other anxious and non-anxious individuals (Clark *et al.*, 1988; Foa, 1988; Chambless *et al.*, 1984). The model has led to the development of treatment approaches aimed at identifying and changing the patient's misinterpretations of bodily sensations: Barlow and Craske's (1989) panic control treatment, and Salkovskis and Clark's (1991) cognitive therapy treatment for panic. Aspects of these approaches are illustrated in this chapter.

STEPHEN

THE REFERRAL

Stephen was referred by his general practitioner. He was described as having 'chronic panic with agoraphobia', both of which had been resistant to previous psychological interventions (eclectic and group anxiety-management therapy). His problems had recently become worse; he now required his wife to travel with him whenever he left the house. A self-employed salesman and ex-professional rugby player, he had two children, both still living at home. His mother had died ten years earlier, and his father had recently been diagnosed as having dementia. He was not currently taking medication, and had stopped drinking coffee and alcohol a short time before.

The GP requested an assessment to see if Stephen was suitable for cognitive therapy. It appeared that he had been a regular visitor to her surgery, and was continually requesting reassurance regarding pains in his chest and heart. In recent months he had had numerous tests, which concluded that he was a healthy individual.

THE ASSESSMENT

The main part of the assessment took place during the first three sessions. In this phase, a diagnostic interview was conducted; a detailed history was taken; Stephen was socialised to the model; and he was taught how to complete the monitoring and diary sheets correctly.

Symptom profile

Stephen met the criteria for *DSM*-IV (American Psychiatric Association, 1994) panic disorder with agoraphobia. He had experienced a number of recent and unexpected panic attacks, which had occurred within a four-week period of one another. He lived in constant fear of having further attacks, and was experiencing a number of physical symptoms – shortness of breath, depersonalisation, dizziness, palpitations, sweating, and pains in his arms and chest. Before attending the Cognitive Therapy Centre he had received a full physical check-up and there was no evidence of any organic factors being responsible for his problems. Stephen also met the agoraphobic criteria (*DSM*-IV). He had a fear of being in places or situations from which escape was difficult. As a result of his fear, he restricted his travel and, as already mentioned, always needed his wife with him when away from home. There was no evidence of his problem being a social phobia, as the panic attacks were not triggered by social attention; neither was his symptom profile consistent with any of the other anxiety disorders.

Baseline measures (mood measures) were taken after his initial screening session (these are presented with the outcome data on pp. 142–3). As can be seen from these data, Stephen was not suffering from depression, which was a good prognostic indicator for improvement.

History of the disorder

Stephen's first panic attack occurred when he was sixteen, following a particularly acrimonious row with his father. After experiencing a series of further panics around the age of seventeen, he was put on diazepam. He remained on a daily dose of diazepam until his early thirties. After a difficult withdrawal from the medication, he coped with his anxiety by reverting to alcohol misuse. The anxiety, and the heavy drinking, eventually resulted in his having to curtail his career as a professional rugby player. His agoraphobia became more acute, and it was about this time that he started insisting on his wife travelling with him. In addition to the anxiety, he considered himself to be 'a bit of a hypochondriac' – he felt that this had been the case since his early twenties. He considered that the preoccupation with his health might also have had something to do with his being a keen sportsman, since 'good health is an important predictor of good performance'.

Stephen claimed that he has been aware of a background of constant tension in his life since his teens. But there were specific occasions when the panic symptoms had been worse. He had a particularly bad spate of attacks following (1) a bad leg injury which threatened his rugby career, (2) the death of his mother, (3) withdrawal from diazepam, and (4) difficulties in his current job, coinciding with his father's diagnosis of dementia. These latter difficulties were the reason for his seeking help at present.

He had attended a short course of psychotherapy twelve years earlier, and a group for anxiety-management nine years earlier. It appeared that he had obtained temporary benefits from both of these treatments, but relapse had occurred one month and three months after therapy, respectively.

Personal background

Stephen's current problems appeared to have had their origins in his difficult childhood. He was the oldest of three children living with his parents in the northwest of England. He reported that there was a lot of tension at home because of parental conflict. His father was an oil-rig worker who spent long periods away from the family. Stephen described him as an aggressive individual, who paid little attention to his children: 'He ignored us most of the time, which was good because he terrified us all of the time.' He described his mother as a weak, dependent person: she was in constant need of support from other people, particularly men. This neediness often led to her becoming involved in short, furtive relationships. Stephen was greatly affected by the home situation. Nevertheless, despite his fear and confusion, from his early teens onwards he felt responsible for supporting and protecting his mother and siblings.

Clearly, this was a great burden on him, which became evident around the age of sixteen. It was at this time that he experienced his first full-blown panic attack, while travelling on a ferry following a row with his father. After another particularly bad row, in which Stephen had tried to intervene to protect his mother, he was thrown out of the house. From that time on, he returned home only when his father was on the rigs.

Presentation

Stephen was a tall, well presented man in his early forties. He spoke confidently, and seemed fairly comfortable in the therapeutic situation. He had read a number of self-help books just before attending the session, and so was familiar with many of the terms associated with anxiety. He appeared motivated and enthusiastic at the prospect of carrying out homework tasks. This dynamism was maintained throughout the therapeutic relationship, and he worked hard to overcome his problems.

During his initial interview, he described his problems as:

- 'a constant sense of tension, made worse by minor stresses, such as telephone calls, chores, etc.';
- 'frequent mini-panics and occasional major ones';
- 'an inability to leave the house without my wife, and a need to know where she is at all times'.

Summary of the assessment

The assessment established that Stephen was suffering from panic disorder, a chronic difficulty that he had suffered from with varying degrees of severity since his mid-teens. The problem appeared to become worse during times of acute life stress. After one particularly difficult time following the end of his career as a rugby player, he developed additional agoraphobic symptoms. Recent work difficulties and his father's diagnosis were the proximal precursors of his current problems.

In the past his panic had been partially controlled by anxiolytics. Ater a difficult withdrawal period, he reverted to alcohol as a coping mechanism, which brought with it its own additional problems. Previous therapy had provided temporary relief only, and his symptoms had returned shortly after terminating the treatment. Stephen was referred by a rather exasperated GP who was somewhat tired of her patient's catastrophising and constant need for reassurance.

At the initial assessment session, it was confirmed that he was suffering from panic with agoraphobia. He presented as a confident, well motivated man, but admitted that his wife was sitting in the waiting-room: '. . . if she hadn't come, I wouldn't have been able to get here.' Because of his positive attitude and his keen acceptance of the model (see next section, Suitability for Short-term Cognitive Therapy), and the encouraging outcome studies of cognitive therapy with panic disorders (Clark *et al.*, 1994), a good outcome was predicted.

SUITABILITY FOR SHORT-TERM COGNITIVE THERAPY

Stephen was rated highly suited to cognitive therapy (see Table 5.2). There was clear evidence of his taking personal responsibility for change, and his enthusiasm to engage in the homework tasks indicated a good degree of alliance potential both in and outside the sessions. It appeared that he was able to focus well on relevant issues, and discriminate well between the distal and proximal causes of his difficulties. Obviously, their chronicity was an issue of concern, and understandably the fact that he had not benefited greatly from previous psychotherapeutic treatments made him a little cautious about the prospect of a long-term recovery. The only other slight concern was the large number of safety behaviours in which he engaged, which included continually checking his pulse, avoiding situations, and using objects or people as props. These were behaviours that he wrongly perceived as helping him to prevent the onset of a panic attack.

Table 5.2   Suitability for Short-term Cognitive Therapy Rating (Safran and Segal, 1990)

Suitability ratings (poor 0–5 good)

1	Accessibility of automatic thoughts	3.5
2	Awareness and differentiation of emotions	3.5
3	Acceptance of personal responsibility for change	4.0
4	Compatibility with cognitive rationale	4.0
5	Alliance potential (in session)	4.0
6	Alliance potential (out of session)	4.0
7	Chronicity of problems	2.0
8	Security operations	3.0
9	Focality	4.0
10	Patient optimism/pessimism regarding therapy	3.5

Total score 35.5

INITIAL FORMULATION

The case formulation is presented in diagrammatic form in Figure 5.2 (overleaf), which attempts to summarise the important issues succinctly, using the specific example of Stephen's going to the bank to ask for a loan.

It was hypothesised that his childhood and consequent life events had led to the formation of various dysfunctional unconditional and conditional beliefs, which were catastrophic and hypochondriacal in nature. At times of increased stress a characteristic vicious cycle became activated, involving perception of threat, hypersensitivity to bodily sensations, CBIs and safety behaviours.

TREATMENT

The plan

Treatment is presented in distinct therapeutic phases; but, in reality, therapy was a continuous process. The general principles of treatment were:

1   identifying Stephen's catastrophic interpretations of bodily sensations (CBIs);

Figure 5.2 Initial formulation

Distal circumstances
- Poor, inconsistent, chaotic and violent parenting
- Poor parental support
- Childhood anxiety
- Premature notions of responsibility
- Growing preoccupation with health

Proximal circumstances
- Use of diazepam
- Withdrawal of diazepam
- Use of alcohol
- Loss of career
- Current work problems
- Mother's death and father's dementia

Basic beliefs

Unconditional: 'I'm vulnerable – my heart is defective'
Conditional: 'If I panic, I'll lose control completely – if I get too frightened, my heart will stop'

Precipitating event
Visit to bank manager to ask for loan

Perception of threat
Fear

Safety behaviours
- Taking wife along
- Holding on tightly to briefcase
- Sitting near to door
- Continuously checking pulse at wrist
- Avoiding eye contact with bank manager

Bodily sensations
- choking
- palpitations
- nausea
- sweating

Catastrophic thoughts
'My hand is shaking – she'll see there's something wrong with me'
'My heart is racing – I'm going to break down in her office'
'If she refuses my application I might panic – my heart might stop. If I die, how will my wife and kids cope?'

2   Helping him to generate alternative, non-catastrophic interpretations of his bodily sensations;
3   testing out the validity of his catastrophic and non-catastrophic interpretations by discussion and behavioural experiments.

The main focus of this work was aimed at the panic rather than at the agoraphobic symptoms. It was felt that the cognitive and behavioural tasks employed in treating the panic would produce the necessary shift with respect to the agoraphobic symptoms (Michelson and Marchione, 1989). In addition, because the agoraphobia was seen as secondary to the panic, the latter was seen as the main focus of therapy. It is worth noting that the work outline below is not meant to be an exhaustive review of the techniques used with people with panic disorder; but, rather, it represents the flexible application of a range of these methods within a 'real-life' setting.

Treatment took place over a period of three months with a total of nine sessions; the first four were weekly and the remainder were spaced over two weeks or more.

PROGRESS OF THERAPY

Treatment progressed rapidly, owing to Stephen's high level of motivation and his general suitability to the cognitive therapy model. The different features of the treatment are explained in more detail below.

1   Identifying catastrophic interpretations

Throughout the treatment Stephen was encouraged to keep a log of his progress. This initially involved writing down (a) his personal beliefs about his condition, and (b) any metaphors or folk psychology he used to explain it. He wrote the following:

- 'Because the heart is a muscle, pains in my chest suggest it's getting tired and cramped.'

- 'tension in my arm or chest is the first sign of heart disease.'
- 'One day, perhaps while asleep, I will just stop breathing and die. I'm afraid if I take a breath that's too long, the whole system will collapse.'

Obviously, such fears needed to be dealt with. Stephen's third hypothesis, 'his respiratory fear', was addressed with a mixture of education and behavioural-paradox work. Firstly, the therapist took time to discuss with him the biological nature of respiration – the fact that his breathing was a reflex reaction that would not suddenly stop when he was not paying attention to it. Secondly, he was asked to test out his belief behaviourally: he was encouraged to try to stop his breathing by holding his breath. By failing to do this, he learned (a) some new information about his respiratory system, and, perhaps more importantly, (b) the concept of experimenting with his untested predictions.

An important part of the treatment involved keeping panic diaries, in which he was required to:

- identify the situation in which the panic occurred;
- identify the associated bodily sensations;
- record any catastrophic bodily interpretations;
- produce alternative/rational responses;
- rate his conviction;
- identify 'safety behaviours'.

As part of his diary-keeping and thought-monitoring procedures, Stephen was asked to identify any of the cognitive distortions ('twisted thinking') that he commonly engaged in. Through examining his diaries, he realised that he frequently used the following distortions and biases:

selective abstraction – he tended to focus on the threatening elements of the situation while ignoring the context.

'Although my heart seems OK today, I've just noticed this strange pain in my arm.'

catastrophising – he tended to dwell on the most extreme negative consequences in situations, and exaggerated the probability of their occurrence.

'The pain in my chest is cancer – I'm certain of it.'

magnification/minimisation – he emphasised the potential dangers, and minimised or ignored the non-threatening signs.

'Although I've not died so far, I've been stressed for so long my heart is bound to have been affected.'

As one might imagine, these distortions tended to amplify his anxiety.

Another method of identifying Stephen's catastrophic interpretations was through Socratic questioning. Questions such as 'What is the worst thing that could happen?' enabled him to describe his specific fears in detail. By elucidating these fears, he was also able to think through some potential coping strategies.

2 Generating alternative, non-catastrophic interpretations

This aspect of treatment involved, firstly, providing a cognitive explication of his symptoms and behaviours through psycho-education; and, secondly, helping him to generate more functional interpretations.

(a) *Education*

One of the most powerful tools in the fight against panic is to inform the patient about the panic cycle – also known as the fight/flight response. In Stephen's case, he was aware of the fight/flight response from his previous therapy. He had found it very instructive, particularly the information on (1) the physical effects of panic; (2) the impact of adrenaline surges; (3) the problem of excessive oxygen intake due to overbreathing; and (4) hyperventilation in general, and the fact that it *does not* cause panic despite the manifest symptoms being so similar. He had attended a stress-management course nine years previously, and still practised the breathing and relaxation exercises (see Bernstein and Borkovec, 1976), which took the edge off his symptoms.

Stephen felt that the other useful tool from his previous therapy, particularly for the minor panics, was the mnemonic, WASP – 'Wait, Absorb, and Slowly Proceed'. He felt that this helped during an attack because it emphasised his need first to 'check' the panic and not try to escape, then to try to distract himself by defocusing from the self, and when the attack was passing to reorientate himself and slowly go on.

In addition to the theoretical information regarding fear, the therapist was able to use information from the diaries to construct an idiosyncratic explication which increased the validity of the approach for him. The following questions were helpful in guiding Stephen to understand his cycle of panic:

- 'As you experienced these bodily sensations [dizziness, palpitations], what was going through your head?'
- 'When you were thinking about having a heart attack, how did you feel?'
- 'As you felt this fear, did you do anything to help yourself to control the panic?'

This form of questioning was used to analyse a number of his panic attack scenarios; he found it helpful in that it increased his understanding of his problem and led to decatastrophising the interpretations attached to bodily feelings.

(b) *Thought-challenging*
Through the correct use of his diaries, Stephen became accustomed to identifying his automatic thoughts, linking them with his bodily sensations and then successfully challenging them. Unlike many other panic patients, he did not experience dysfunctional imagery. If this had been the case, some form of imagery-modification technique would have been employed (Clark, 1989, pp. 68–9).

He did, however, display a feature common to panic sufferers, in his need to seek constant reassurance: 'Are you sure my heart is OK?' This situation was discussed early on in therapy, and it was conceded that even if the whole session was spent reassuring him about the strength of his heart it was not going to change his belief. So he was encouraged to try to stop seeking reassurance from the therapist, his GP and others, and see whether this increased his anxiety and his panic attacks (on pp. 102–3 there is a more detailed discussion of the issue).

This latter feature serves to illustrate that the beliefs of people with panic are difficult to shift. They are not readily changed by simple disputation alone, and are resistant even when there appear to be lots of disconfirming evidence available. Nonetheless it is important, through Socratic questioning and other self-exploratory techniques, that the therapist help the patient to discover for himself that his CBIs stem from erroneous beliefs. An excellent example of effective questioning techniques is provided in Clark (1989, pp. 76–8). Here the patient is helped to challenge his erroneous belief that he will 'faint and collapse in a panic attack'. This example also illustrates that a patient's dysfunctional beliefs are far stronger during the panic experience than outside of it (as was the case with Stephen). For instance, outside of the attack situation, Stephen's belief rating concerning a heart attack was 40–50 per cent, but during an attack it was 100 per cent. In consequence, it was considered important to try to introduce some flexibility into his beliefs and get him to challenge his assumptions while actually experiencing the attack. This was done, as illustrated in the next section, through behavioural experimentation.

3   Testing out the validity of catastrophic and non-catastrophic interpretations by discussion and behavioural experiments

Socratic questioning and rational responses do not appear to have the same impact in anxiety as in other disorders. Indeed, it is quite common for a person to understand intellectually that there is no danger, but still feel afraid. So behavioural tests are a vital component of change. But before using behavioural tasks with Stephen it was important to examine the behaviours that he was inadvertently using to maintain his problems.

(a) *Analysis of safety behaviours*

As part of one of his homework assignments, Stephen was asked to monitor his behaviour in different settings and identify his safety behaviours. They included continually checking for changes in his pulse; holding himself tense; breathing deeply; avoiding stressful situations; using objects or people as props. He was then asked to (i) specify exactly how each assisted him in preventing a panic attack, (ii) determine the reality of this perception, and (iii) specify any other effect the safety behaviour might have on him (Table 5.3). He soon came to realise that many of these behaviours actively exacerbated his panic and further increased the focus of attention on his own bodily sensations.

(b) *Hypothesis-testing through behavioural experimentation*

Before engaging in any particular behavioural task, it was important to get Stephen to make a prediction about the difficulty and significance of successfully carrying it out. Firstly, this helped in setting up a desensitisation hierarchy, with the most difficult tasks at the top and the easier ones at the bottom. Secondly, it prevented him rationalising away any successes. Indeed, it reduced the likelihood of his denying the therapeutic impact of any successful performance. The following exchange illustrates his problem with rationalisation:

Therapist: How long is it since you've climbed two flights of stairs?

Stephen: About six or seven months – last time I had an attack.

T: Now that you've done it, has it changed the way you think about your heart?

S: Well, not really! You see, these stairs aren't as steep as normal ones, and in addition you were here to help me . . . I know you wouldn't make me do anything too difficult. Now, if I was by myself, I might over-exert myself.

Table 5.3 Perceived function, actual function, and other potential effects of safety behaviours

Type of safety behaviour	Perceived function	Reality of this perception	Other potential effects
1 Taking my wife with me	• To calm me down	She tends to make me more tense	Increases the likelihood of my having a full-blown panic attack
	• If I am driving and I faint or have a heart attack, she could control the car	In reality she would not be able to take the car over	I might kill both of us Her presence makes me feel 'I'm weak', 'I'm a failure'
2 Gripping on to objects (e.g., to a cup) when feeling an attack coming on	• To calm me down	Makes my whole body tense	Increases my tension, and makes me think about my body even more
	• To stop others noticing that I am shaking	I start noticing pulse in my hand and arm	As above, and I look so tense people will probably notice there is something wrong – so I might call more attention to myself

Once the predictions were establishing, the behavioural testing began. The following three methods of testing were employed.

1 *Reproducing panic sensations within therapy* To show that the causal stimuli were innocuous, it was important to get Stephen to demonstrate the sorts of things that brought on the symptoms. Initially he was extremely reluctant to attempt to reproduce a panic, because of his fear of losing control. He also

claimed he was not sure how to bring on an attack. But this was immediately remedied when he was asked to show how he breathed during an attack – on attempting to do so, he was surprised to find that he felt an attack starting. It was informative for him to notice, after further investigation, that many of his safety behaviours (such as checking his pulse) had a tendency to bring on attacks.

Specific panic induction techniques were also used to demonstrate the sorts of stimuli, and the resulting catastrophising, that were responsible for his attacks. Two examples were the stand/sit technique and word-priming. The stand/sit technique required Stephen to stand and sit repeatedly for a period of forty-five seconds. This simple but rather energetic task produced a number of sensations that he associated with heart problems – blurred vision, tension across his chest, increased heart and pulse rates. The word-priming technique involved him reading the following word list slowly, from left to right:

Word combinations

chest pain . . . heart attack
dizziness . . . collapse
breathlessness . . . choke
palpitation . . . die

The purpose was to initiate panic symptoms in order to illustrate the powerful effect that thoughts could have on his body and feelings. Choosing word combinations consistent with his own particular fears was important, so as to increase their power and relevance for him – for instance, he associated chest pains with heart attacks. With Stephen, though, the technique was only slightly effective.

2 *Testing out the consequences within therapy* The fear of testing out the consequences of a panic attack was one of the major maintaining factors of Stephen's panic. For example, he would not use stairs because he feared that his defective heart

might give way and then he would collapse: 'Even if I don't die, I'll cause such a fuss [crowds, ambulances, etc.] that I'll lose all confidence about going out again.' Therefore, it was important for Stephen to use stairs repeatedly. With the experience he had gained from his previous cognitive therapy exercises, he was now in a position to explain the mechanics, the process, of his panic. He rapidly acknowledged that his difficulties stemmed from his catastrophic interpretations of the physiological changes that were taking place naturally as he climbed the stairs. He felt that the sensations might be even more acute for him at present, because of his lack of fitness (he had stopped doing regular exercise because of his fear of its consequences).

3   *Dropping safety behaviours*   As outlined earlier, safety behaviours, which up until this point Stephen had perceived as his salvation, only exacerbated the problem. So it was most important to help him to drop them. Using the example provided in the formulation (see Figure 5.2), he was asked to role-play the bank manager scenario. The therapist encouraged him to repeat all of the behaviours he had used in the original setting (breathing, manner of sitting, speaking, and so on). One of his interesting discoveries was that his posture (rigid and tense), and his tendency to grip objects tightly (to prevent people seeing him shaking), made him more sensitive to his bodily sensations. Thus by altering his posture and reducing the strength of his grip, he became less sensitised to his bodily sensations and, in turn, more relaxed.

In addition, Stephen was encouraged to enter new situations and to try to drop his previously identified safety behaviours. This work involved using a combination of cognitive and behavioural approaches. In one of the examples given in Table 5.3 (his need to travel with his wife) the cognitive component involved breaking down the function of his safety behaviours as shown in the table, while the behavioural component involved collaboratively setting up a step-by-step hierarchy of tasks aimed at helping him to travel by himself. Stephen was asked to keep a record of his anxiety levels during such tasks. After an initial increase, as he became more comfortable with abandoning his behavioural crutches, his ratings dropped.

FINAL FORMULATION

Panic disorder is distinct from the other emotional disorders in the simplicity of the cognitive formulation, which is constructed as early as the first session of therapy. Details are added as therapy progresses, pertaining to the individual's idiosyncratic automatic thoughts and safety behaviours, and with less emphasis on developmental factors.

Stephen's therapy enabled him to understand the subtleties of his escape behaviours and gain access to automatic thoughts. Little work was done on the developmental factors beyond psycho-education relating to the formulation. The issues of responsibility and control had clearly arisen from his parenting – his need to protect his mother and the unpredictability as far as his father's violent behaviour was concerned. Triggering the relevant circumstances made sense in terms of Stephen's perceived fear of actual loss of control. He was able to understand how his parents' 'failures' had laid a vulnerable foundation to his personality functioning, encouraging a propensity to panic; and, in turn, how his avoidance strategies had allowed his proclivity to develop into panic disorder. The final formulation was therefore a fleshed out version of the initial one shown in Figure 5.2.

OUTCOME

1 *Statistical outcome data*
A battery of psychometric questionnaires was given to Stephen throughout the treatment phases, in order to examine his progress. The anxiety measures used were:

- Beck Anxiety Inventory (BAI) (Beck and Steer, 1990); people with anxiety disorder have a mean score of 23.49, and a standard deviation of 12.39.

- State–Trait Anxiety Inventory – state version (STAI-S) (Speilberger *et al.*, 1970); see p. 64 for norms.

The depression measures used were:

- Beck Depression Inventory (BDI) (Beck *et al.*, 1961).
- Hamilton Rating Scale for Depression (HRSD) (Hamilton, 1960); see p. 64 for norms.

Table 5.4 demonstrates that Stephen's main problem was one of anxiety rather than depression. Indeed, he scored within the 'normal' range on depression measures. Thus, the improvement over therapy is reflected in the anxiety scores. It is noteworthy that most of the improvement took place in the first half of treatment, which is consistent with the recent empirical findings of Clark *et al.* (1994).

Table 5.4   Stephen's pre-, mid- and post-treatment psychometric measures

Session		Anxiety		Depression	
		BAI	STAI-S	BDI	HRSD
1	pre-	42	57	12	8
5	mid-	18	40	11	7
9	post-	12	38	11	8

Figure 5.3 (overleaf) presents histograms of the data from Table 5.4.

2 Clinical outcome

Stephen was seen over nine sessions. He was fairly quick to accept the cognitive model, as it appeared to fit his experience of the problem. An inspection of his diaries seemed to suggest that his beliefs changed considerably after receiving the formulation, yet those changes seemed to consistently lag behind his behavioural experimentation. This suggests that the testing out of

Figure 5.3   Stephen's anxiety and depression measures

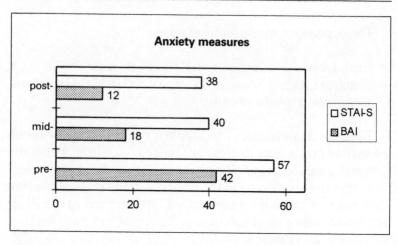

STAI-S   State-Trait Anxiety Inventory – State Version
BAI   Beck Anxiety Inventory

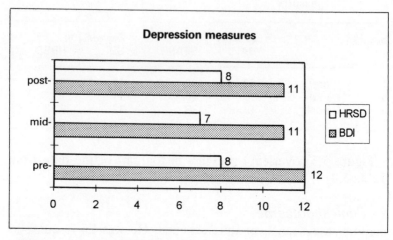

HRSD   Hamilton Rating Scale for Depression
BDI   Beck Depression Inventory

his catastrophic interpretations was a crucial factor in the process of change.

By the end of treatment he was able to travel freely by himself, and he experienced no panic attacks during the months following the final therapy session. The six- and twelve-month follow-ups revealed that he was still symptom-free, although during a number of stressful life events, such as his father's recent death, he experienced a series of minor panics.

RELAPSE-PREVENTION

In the penultimate session, therapy began to focus on relapse-prevention: the therapist set a homework assignment which involved a series of questions (see Figure 5.4, overleaf), which were then discussed at the final session. Special emphasis was placed on preventing the re-establishment of safety and avoidance behaviours.

As Stephen got up to leave after the final session, the therapist was somewhat reassured regarding his prognosis by his parting observation:

Stephen: I realised the other day that this sort of work involves you being a bit like a detective – a sort of Sherlock Holmes. You go on the facts, rather than your perceptions or assumptions.
Therapist: Elementary, my dear Stephen, elementary.

DISCUSSION

Stephen had undergone nine sessions of cognitive therapy over a period of three months. Progress was maintained at the six-month and twelve-month follow-ups. Evidently he responded well to cognitive therapy as predicted in Safran and Segal's (1990) suitability scale. His acceptance of the model and keen motivation greatly assisted his swift progress. His ability to collaborate and work hard both in and out of the sessions was also an important contributing factor.

Figure 5.4 Relapse and maintenance questions

Assess gains made
- What behaviour/feeling/attitude changes have occurred?
- What are the objective differences between now and before?
- Have I achieved the goals specified in the problem list?

Identify important lessons learned in CT
About myself:
- What have I learned about myself from the formulation?
- What are the typical sorts of cognitive biases I engage in?

About the disorder:
- What is the model of the disorder?
- How is it maintained?
- What role do my avoidance and safety behaviours play in maintaining it?

Identify high-risk situations
- List the situations that are still difficult, frightening or depressing
- Take at least two of the situations and plan how to deal with them, using the insight and skills obtained through CT

Identify early signs of relapse
- List the signs of early relapse – e.g., beginning to take wife with me when she is not really needed; making excuses and avoiding situations

Determine what to do if relapse occurs
Minor relapse:
- What have I learned from this relapse?
- What do I need to do to stop it happening in the future?

Major relapse:
- What would constitute a major relapse?
- What is my emergency plan?
- Have I got the addresses of people (friends, GP, CT centre) that I might need to contact?

This marked degree of progress must not be wholly attributed to his general suitability to short-term cognitive therapy, however, because research (Clark *et al.*, 1994) has indicated that 90 per cent of patients treated with cognitive therapy become free of panic within 12 sessions, and on average this is achieved after only 5.5 treatment sessions. On the strength of these results, Clark and his colleagues are currently attempting to produce an empirically valid but briefer cognitive therapy treatment package for panic.

Despite the overall success of the treatment, Stephen reported the occasional recurrence of symptoms after particularly difficult life events. For example, as mentioned earlier, he experienced a series of panic attacks following the death of his father in the eighth month after therapy. However, within a matter of days he was able to halt his catastrophising by using the therapeutic and relapse-prevention work. Since then he has experienced only minor difficulties, and says that it is difficult to imagine how he used to be.

Of note in this case is the amount of change, including evidence of maintenance, in the face of post-therapeutic stressors, without direct work on underlying schemata. Why is this so, given that the theory of cognitive therapy would predict that, without such work, long-lasting results are unlikely? What happened with Stephen – and this is characteristic of so many patients with panic disorders – is that the behavioural experimentation seems to have contradicted powerfully the assumption of personal vulnerability underlying the problem.

The short-term focused approach outlined in this study has appeared to be sufficient for long-lasting change – this is an important point to make. Cognitive therapy is a highly efficient form of psychotherapy which delves into developmentally focused work only if the clinical evidence shows it to be necessary, the major indicator being lack of symptomatic change. Stephen was changing rapidly without recourse to early issues beyond those mentioned in the formulation section (pp. 131–2; 142). Had this not been the case, then schema-focused work would have been indicated, as indeed it would have been if he had relapsed after therapy. Normally, it becomes evident early on whether or not symptom-focused therapy is going to suffice, as the patient presents in such a fashion as to indicate a mixed diagnosis and/or personality problems.

6

A Case of Obsessional–compulsive Disorder

John – 'You are the sum of your achievements'

The fourth and most recent edition of the *Diagnostic and Statistical Manual of Mental Disorders* (American Psychiatric Association, 1994) categorises obsessional–compulsive disorder as one of the anxiety disorders. Recent community studies have estimated a lifetime prevalence of 2.5 per cent and a one-year prevalence of 1.5 to 2.1 per cent. The disorder is equally common amongst men and women. It usually begins in adolescence or early adulthood, but it may begin in childhood. Modal age at onset is earlier in men than in women and, for the most part, it is gradual. The majority of individuals follow a chronic waxing and waning course, with exacerbation of symptoms that may be related to stress. About 5 per cent of people follow an episodic course, with minimal or no symptoms between episodes.

DEFINITION OF OBSESSIONAL–COMPULSIVE DISORDER

Obsessional–compulsive disorder is characterised by the occurrence of intrusive and upsetting thoughts which the patient usually reports as senseless, and which are accompanied by the urge to 'put right' or neutralise. Neutralising behaviour can take the form either of overt actions such as washing or checking, or of cognitive behaviours such as thinking a 'good thought' whenever an obsessional intrusion occurs. Neutralising behaviour, either cognitive or overt, usually happens repetitively and is often identified as the patient's main reason for seeking treatment.

It is important to understand that the obsessions are not simply excessive worries about real-life problems. This distinguishes the disorder from general anxiety disorder. Rather, they are egodystonic – that is, experienced as alien, not within one's control and not the kind of thought one would expect to have or want. Such thoughts are, therefore, also distinguished from depressive ones, which involve mood-congruent and egosyntonic ruminations – for example, of being worthless. Obsessions are, though, recognised as entirely the product of one's own mind. Commonly they take the form of believing that one has been contaminated, or of having repeated doubts about one's actions, or needing to have things in a particular order, or having aggressive or horrific impulses.

Compulsions contain the vital element that the individual feels driven to perform a particular act in order to relieve the distress caused by the unwanted thoughts. The stereotypical acts can sometimes be highly elaborate, without the individual being able to indicate why she is doing them. They are clearly excessive in nature and are commonly unconnected in any realistic way with what they are designed to neutralise or prevent.

DSM-IV defines obsessions as 'recurrent and persistent thoughts, impulses or images that are experienced as intrusive and inappropriate and that cause marked anxiety or distress.' And compulsions are defined as 'repetitive behaviours (e.g. handwashing, ordering, checking) or mental acts (e.g. praying, counting, repeating words silently)' the goal of which is to prevent or reduce anxiety or distress, not to provide pleasure or gratification. In most cases the person feels driven to perform the compulsion to reduce the distress that accompanies the obsession or to prevent some dreaded event or situation.

A diagnosis of obsessive–compulsive disorder is made in the presence of the factors outlined in Table 6.1, in addition to the presence of either obsessions or compulsions.

Table 6.1   Diagnostic criteria for obsessional–compulsive disorder (summarised from *DSM*-IV)

---

1   Obsessions and/or compulsions are present
2   It is recognised that the obsessions and compulsions are excessive or unreasonable (this does not apply to children)
3   The obsessions and compulsions cause marked distress, or are time-consuming (take up more than one hour a day), or significantly interfere with the individual's normal routine, job or social life
4   If another Axis I disorder is present, the content of the obsessions or compulsions is not restricted to it – e.g., guilty ruminations in the case of depression, or preoccupation with food in the case of an eating disorder.
5   The disturbance is not due to the direct physiological effects of drugs or a physical medical condition.

THE COGNITIVE MODEL

Cognitive–behavioural formulations

Until the 1980s behavioural therapy was the treatment of choice for obsessional–compulsive disorders. But reports of outcome studies have revealed important shortcomings in this approach, leading to the claim that true success rates are less than 50 per cent, even in highly selected populations; non-compliance with and non-acceptance of treatment have been critical factors (Salkovskis, 1989).

Cognitive frameworks have attempted to overcome some of the problems with behavioural procedures. The simplest example is essentially an extension of behavioural principles: that obsessional fear is maintained through the prevention of reappraisal of the feared stimulus. However, this fails to account fully for the phenomenology of obsessional–compulsive disorder (Beech and Liddel, 1974; Rachman, DeSilva and

Roper, 1976; Roper and Rachman, 1975; Roper, Rachman and Hodgson, 1973). As discussed in Chapter 2, Salkovskis' extended cognitive formulation (1985) is empirically encouraging (Emmelkamp, 1987; James and Blackburn, 1995). It starts from the premise that intrusive thoughts are a normal phenomenon (Rachman and DeSilva, 1978; Salkovskis and Harrison, 1984) and do not automatically have affective connotations, but acquire emotional properties as a result of appraisal. Intrusive thoughts are deemed to be adaptive and functional in the sense that they are integral aspects of creative problem-solving, persisting only to the extent to which they have implications for intentional behaviour or deliberate thought (Salkovskis, 1985, 1988). This is advantageous for selecting the most relevant and important cognitive data.

The characteristic pattern of thoughts and neutralising behaviours in an obsessional–compulsive disorder results from the interaction of pertinent types of intrusive thoughts with certain underlying beliefs. These beliefs are of the type which overemphasise responsibility for possible adverse consequences of one's harmful thoughts and actions. If the intrusive thoughts run counter to an individual's beliefs, then these beliefs will lead him to resist the occurrence of the thoughts because of the anxiety they produce and, when this does not succeed, to neutralise them. The significant underlying beliefs appear to be those concerning responsibility and blame (Salkovskis and Warwick, 1988), which result in appraising the intrusions in terms of responsibility for future harm. The consequent attempts at neutralising such thoughts then prevent the reappraisal of true risks and have the effect of amplifying pre-existing beliefs about responsibility. It is proposed that the sufferer's individual developmental history may include experiences of actual and/or perceived problems caused by not taking sufficient care, and/or specific teaching from key adult figures in strict codes of conduct and in responsibility. Passing on responsibility to others through reassurance-seeking, and getting others to carry out checking tasks, are common clinical manifestations of such schemata.

Treatment focuses on the main cognitive–behavioural factors

in the model: reducing avoidance behaviour and increasing exposure to problem situations and thoughts; modifying attitudes concerning responsibility; modifying appraisal of intrusive thoughts; preventing the neutralising that follows the appraisal of responsibility; and increasing exposure to responsibility, both directly and by stopping reassurance-seeking.

The constructivist formulation

The constructivist's starting-point is different from Salkovskis'. Whereas Salkovskis lays emphasis on early messages of responsibility, Guidano and Liotti (1983) attribute the genesis of the disorder to a specific type of pathological attachment that is characterised by ambivalence and that has supplied the child with two distinct and opposite interpretations of self: that one is equally lovable and unlovable, worthy and unworthy. The disorder is explained in terms of the need for a unitary non-contradictory image of self. This is psychologically encapsulated by an endless search for certainty and order, and entails constructing rigid attitudes around precise rules and perfectionistic behavioural strategies. The obsessional–compulsive paradox is neatly elucidated: highly valued certainty leads to systematic doubt about everything.

The model describes the psycho-social context in which the ambivalent attachment occurs: a highly verbal but emotionally lacking parenting which demands from the child absolute love and affection and adult maturity and responsibility, with emotional control being obtained through moral values and ethical principles. Incompatible emotions are 'forbidden', leading the individual to exclude and control mixed feelings. This requires him to engage in cognitive and behavioural strategies that make sense in terms of the concrete stage of childhood during which they are developed as strategies for emotional 'control'. It follows that precipitating events will be those that herald the surfacing of mixed emotions. These include (1) adolescence, when there is a drive towards detachment from the family and towards an independent relationship with reality, but when the 'distorted' self-image makes such separation problematic; (2) the making and breaking of affectional bonds at any time during the lifespan, when integrating new experiences into a functionally rigid view of self will be necessarily difficult; (3) life events which nullify the individual's search for certainty, such as interpersonal problems in significant relationships, separation, loss or illness of significant others, disappointments or failure at work.

The main focus of treatment in this model is to alter the perfectionist attitude and the need for certainty. The first step is to exploit this attitude, recommending that the patient should not commit himself to too much and that he accept from the start that therapy itself will give only partial relief. This approach offers a number of advantages to obsessional patients: the therapist is being honest and, since obsessional individuals attach great importance to ethical behaviour, this will foster a good therapeutic relationship; the idea is being suggested that something can be done without implying that it needs to be complete and perfect, thus laying the foundation for working at beliefs regarding perfectionism and certainty; the patient is not led to believe that he is going to be forced to dismiss his rituals, and so anticipatory anxiety and problems with compliance are reduced; and by recognising the protective value of the fears and rituals, the therapist can prepare the way for an exploration of the connection between his symptomatology and tacit self-knowledge.

Treatment then proceeds along behavioural therapy lines, using direct and concrete techniques intermingled with psycho-education of the nature and origin of fears and rituals with respect to notions of the self and of the world, and specifically recognising and explaining the very basic experiences of early learning and early attachment. Techniques of distancing and decentring are employed, as well as of identifying and clearly verbalising central irrational beliefs or assumptions. Practice in translating emotional into verbal experiences is an integral part, as are techniques for maintaining the restructuring schematic process.

JOHN

THE REFERRAL

John was referred to the centre by his GP. He was thirty years old, with a sixteen-year history of obsessional–compulsive disorder. He had already had twelve sessions of behavioural therapy, which had created intolerable levels of anxiety and had not had lasting effects beyond the end of treatment. This was six months before the referral to cognitive therapy. Clomipramine had had some effect, but he found the side effects too uncomfortable to continue. He was finding it increasingly difficult to sustain his role as a lecturer at the university. He had read about cognitive therapy and had expressed interest in trying it out.

THE ASSESSMENT

Symptom profile

John presented with two kinds of obsession: firstly, ideas of having been contaminated by parasites through touching children or objects that had come to be associated with the obsession; secondly, repeated doubts of not having locked up his flat, or of not having switched off electrical appliances. He reported both overt and covert neutralising behaviours. Overt ones included cleaning and checking rituals. These entailed washing his hands up to fifteen times in succession, until his skin was red-raw; or showering for an hour while following a stereotypical washing routine; or checking switches and door locks – at worst, up to two hours at a time. Covert strategies included counting in multiples of five and prime numbers. These numbers had a 'magical' quality which could cancel out the sense of non-completion or uncertainty that accompanied his obsessions.

In terms of appraising his symptoms, John was aware that he believed that if he did not carry out the rituals 'properly', then something bad would happen. He was not sure what form the portent took, but sensed danger – a fire, people coming to some kind of harm and so on. And there was a pattern to the symptoms. They were worse after returning from football practice and before going to work in the mornings, and particularly bad when leaving his house to visit his parents in Scotland. John was prepared to consider that proximal precipitating factors could be related to stress, but was not aware of the cognitive impact of such stress.

History of the disorder

The obsessional–compulsive disorder appeared to have been precipitated by a discrete event – when he contracted threadworms at the age of fourteen. He was very ashamed about this and remembered being quite devastated. It occurred around the same time that his sister left home for university, and when work became an altogether more serious matter at school. He was finding it difficult to live up to others' expectations of him academically, receiving fairly average grades in tests. He focused specifically on the infestation as the precipitating factor, and was initially 'closed' to the relevance of these other contextual factors.

The symptoms were at their worst when he was eighteen, during his A-level year and the lead-up to leaving home and going to university. Ever since, they had waxed and waned. The two years preceding cognitive therapy had been a particularly protracted and distressing episode, coinciding with taking up his post as lecturer at the university, where he had been unhappy – again believing that he was not living up to others' expectations of him.

Personal background

John was the second of three children, born to intellectual parents. His mother was a teacher and his father a solicitor. He had a sister three years older, to whom he had been very close in childhood. His brother was two years younger and was very disruptive, causing family rows by refusing to conform. John was his brother's opposite. He never spoke his mind and would always try to keep the peace. His mother had had health problems for as long as he could remember. She was menopausal during his adolescence, and was phobic about cancer. She was very difficult to live with because of her bad temper and critical stance. Her own mother had died of cancer and this had been a major event in the family. John was able to express in an intellectual way a profound regret about his relationship with his mother, particularly in terms of its lack of emotional warmth. His father was emotionally uninvolved and distant, being interested only in academic achievement. There was a sense in which John never felt that he lived up to his expectations.

He was aware of a strong need to escape his family situation, which he achieved at eighteen when he left for university. He had since returned home as little as possible, and was aware that when he did his symptoms were particularly problematic.

Presentation

John presented as an emotionally controlled person and would consider how he responded to questions very carefully. He was hard-working and achievement-motivated, and invested strongly in being liked. This extended to his behaviour in therapy, when he would noticeably try to please his therapist and avoid confrontation. On one occasion he positively construed the therapist keeping him waiting for thirty minutes in terms of an excellent opportunity to 'gather his thoughts'. His cognitive avoidance was apparent in his tendency to forget to chronicle specific cognitions – or, indeed, to forget to bring his diary to therapy. His emotional avoidance was apparent in his marked inability to experience or label emotional states in the here and now or, indeed, from the past. His intellect and verbal ability were of a quite different order. He was able to describe his symptomatic disorder in an 'advanced' way, and enjoyed the concrete psycho-educational aspect of therapy.

Typical automatic thoughts included:

- 'I feel out of my depth.'
- 'Everyone expects more of me than I can give.'
- 'I want to do well, but I have always been a 55 per cent person.'
- 'People expect me to be confident and capable.'
- 'I worry about not being confident and capable.'
- 'I feel that I ought to be going "hell for leather", but for what?'
- 'I feel I am just trundling along.'

Summary of the assessment

John was suffering from an obsessional–compulsive disorder. There was no evidence of any other Axis I diagnosis. He had clear-cut obsessions and compulsions and fulfilled all the additional criteria outlined in Table 6.1. Distal precipitating factors involved an actual experience of contamination at the age of fourteen, of which he had felt totally ashamed and out of control; and feelings that mirrored those he was generally feeling about himself, in terms of not living up to others' expectations as far as his achievements and responsibilities were concerned. Feelings were disallowed by his parents, and so John managed them by developing an obsessional–compulsive mechanism of avoidance. Proximal precipitating and maintaining factors were the achievement expectations in his new job at the university, which was threatening to expose him as a failure. The lack of emotional expression in his psychological functioning was testimony to how well the obsessional–compulsive mechanism was allowing him to avoid feeling states. This was causing him difficulties in establishing and maintaining meaningful emotional relationships with the opposite sex.

SUITABILITY FOR SHORT-TERM COGNITIVE THERAPY

The information collated during assessment gave a good idea of John's suitability for cognitive therapy. The Safran and Segal Suitability for Short-term Cognitive Therapy Rating Scale

(1990) was applied (scores out of 5 are given in parentheses after each item below).

In terms of his suitability, the picture appeared to be a mixed one. On the positive side, John could easily access and articulate automatic thoughts, including – of particular importance – those relating centrally to his conception of self (5); he perceived an appropriate level of personal responsibility for change (5); he viewed the cognitive model as compatible with his problems, and understood and accepted the value of the 'active' aspects of treatment, such as homework (4); he engaged quickly with the therapist and achieved 'empathic resonance' (4); he could work in a focused way, identifying problem areas and comfortably working within the structure of the session (4); he responded well to the inductive guided-discovery questioning format, and was comfortable in the collaborative empirical stance; and he displayed a reasonable amount of hope that therapy would be of value (3).

However, on the negative side John necessarily had difficulty in experiencing and differentiating emotional states (1); he was encountering big problems with establishing stable and trusting relationships outside of therapy, with marked evidence of conflict avoidance and of ambivalence (1); his problems were of sixteen years' duration and therefore chronic (1); and his cognitive and emotional avoidant mechanisms were very apparent (2).

His suitability score was 30, which indicated that he was moderately suitable for short-term cognitive therapy. The emotional issues were the main area of concern in terms of prognosis, and would, it was felt, most probably require further treatment at a later stage. The fact that the disorder extended back to adolescence and not into childhood was a positive indicator for short-term therapeutic results. It was unlikely that there would be an abundance of the early maladaptive phenomenology normally associated with the personality-disordered patient, and his behaviour in therapy was consistent with this opinion.

INITIAL FORMULATION

Pertinent obsessional–compulsive developmental factors appeared to be present: namely, that John had received intellectualised parenting which lacked emotional demonstration and supplied him with powerful messages of personal responsibility and high codes of conduct. There appeared also to be an ambivalent element, leading to the equal and contradictory messages to do with personal worth of the type outlined in the section on the cognitive model (p. 150). The content of his thoughts alludes to the presence of dysfunctional schemata in relation to his self-worth; he was overly dependent on others' opinions of him, and he demonstrated this attitude through seeking achievement and being personable. Precipitating circumstances appeared to involve the issue of the potential loss of other people's positive opinion, through personal error, failure or unacceptability. The two types of intrusions – of repeated doubts and of contamination – were being appraised in terms of the harm that they would do to this external source of value. Neutralising behaviours made sense in dealing with the intrusions and the associated distress caused by the automatic thoughts (see Figure 6.1, overleaf).

TREATMENT

The plan

The overall goal of treatment was to remove John's need to engage in the ritualistic behaviour, by helping him to reappraise the intrusive phenomenology so that it would no longer have affective connotations. Systematic unravelling of the obsessional–compulsive syndrome in a manner that impacted at both the symptomatic and the underlying assumptive levels was required. In order to make symptomatic impact, the ritualistic behaviour needed to be reduced so as to provide the 'space' for reappraisal work. Assumptive change needed to involve understanding the developmental aspects in terms of their

Figure 6.1 Initial formulation

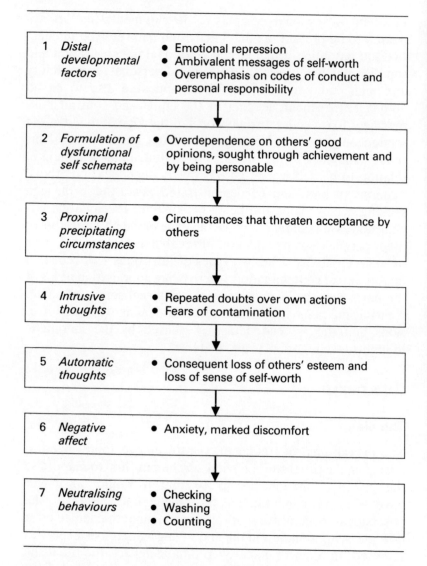

1	*Distal developmental factors*	• Emotional repression • Ambivalent messages of self-worth • Overemphasis on codes of conduct and personal responsibility
2	*Formulation of dysfunctional self schemata*	• Overdependence on others' good opinions, sought through achievement and by being personable
3	*Proximal precipitating circumstances*	• Circumstances that threaten acceptance by others
4	*Intrusive thoughts*	• Repeated doubts over own actions • Fears of contamination
5	*Automatic thoughts*	• Consequent loss of others' esteem and loss of sense of self-worth
6	*Negative affect*	• Anxiety, marked discomfort
7	*Neutralising behaviours*	• Checking • Washing • Counting

psychological viability, and to provide John with new experiences so that reconstruction could occur.

Treatment was planned in three stages, which the initial,

middle and final stages in Figure 6.2 roughly represent.

Figure 6.2   The three stages of treatment

Initial stage (sessions 1–3)

1   Establish rapport: listen carefully, instil hope
2   Establish goals
3   Establish a psychological understanding; psycho-educate; measure; monitor
4   Establish a common language for the purposes of data 'shorthand' and data 'reduction'
5   Arrive at an initial formulation

Middle stage (sessions 4–8)

6   Establish the links between the symptoms and emotional avoidance in the 'here and now'; link present events with other present events (lateral linkaging); discover general rules from specific circumstances
7   Uncover the developmental context of emotional avoidance
8   Make links between past and present issues (vertical linkaging)
9   Flesh out the formulation collaboratively
10 Test out the formulation with homework assignments, using the therapeutic relationship where appropriate
11 Begin to identify schemata

Final stage (sessions 9–12)

12 Act against 'old' assumptions with homework assignments
13 Utilise the therapeutic relationship in understanding assumptions, and when it is necessary to confront emotional avoidance
14 Reconstruct early assumptions
15 Establish goals for the future
16 Discuss methods of relapse-prevention
17 Summarise therapy and identify any problems of understanding

---

Each stage encapsulates a number of 'items' in the therapy, which were neither mutually exclusive phenomena nor carried out in a certain order. They give some idea of the amount of work involved in the twelve-session package described in this chapter; the skill of the therapist lay in linking the items together, flexibly and effortlessly, and in inductively inviting the patient to share in this psychological process so that later he could begin to make the links for himself. The guiding principles outlined in Chapter 1 were central to the change process, making treatment a psychotherapy art form rather than a collection of techniques.

The next section describes what happened in each phase of therapy.

PROGRESS OF THERAPY

Sessions 1–3

The first task was to allow John space to describe the problem fully to the therapist, and for the therapist to empathetically feed back an understanding of the complex and distressing nature of the problem while reducing the amount of information that needed to be handled. This was done for a number of reasons: (1) patients with obsessional–compulsive disorder happily continue to describe *ad infinitum* the minutiae of their condition, leaving little time for anything else in the session. They do this, firstly, because they are seeking reassurance about the status of their symptoms by making sure that nothing is left out and that there can be no doubt that the therapist has understood; and, secondly, because they are subtly passing on responsibility to the therapist; (2) obsessional–compulsive symptoms are experienced as a chaotic and complicated mass of thoughts, reducing the patient to a state of helplessness. By reducing the data to simpler categories the patient is provided with an early sense of control and a method of communicating in short-hand so that therapy time is used optimally.

It was important at this point for the therapist to instil a sense of hope, by emphasising the commonality of the categories in which the symptoms fell without inadvertently reinforcing John's need for reassurance or coming across as discounting the idiosyncrasy of his experience. This illustrates the complexity of establishing rapport, or 'empathic resonance'. It involves listening to details attentively enough to instil in the patient a sense of being understood, while avoiding being 'sucked in' and ovewhelmed by them; instilling realistic hope, but not reassurance; providing a model that is common across individuals, but one that offers enough scope for valuing the individuality of the patient.

After collaboratively agreeing on symptom categories, John began to monitor his symptoms using the diary outlined in Figure 6.3.

Figure 6.3   Symptom diary

Day	Time/ duration	Type of intrusion (C or D)	Intensity of intrusion (1–10)	Level of conviction (1–10)	Type of ritual (W, Ch or N)	Tenacity of ritual (1–10)	Trigger/ context WK PP

C   contamination
D   doubts
W   washing
Ch   checking
N   counting
WK   something particularly stressful at work
PP   physical contact with others

He was explicitly told just to monitor the intrusive thoughts and the compulsive behaviours and not to attempt to make any changes at this stage. This was so as to reduce the threat of the procedure and also to communicate on the part of the therapist an understanding of the functional significance of the symptoms and, additionally, to allow the therapist to collect some pre-intervention baseline information. What happened was that John, like so many sufferers from this condition, reported fairly immediate change in his symptoms. This was for two reasons. Firstly, the monitoring task had given him a sense of 'control' by simplifying the diffuse and profuse phenomenology into discrete categories. Secondly, by virtue of the 'distancing' effect that this type of recording has on symptoms, the immediate distress of the intrusions was reduced, resulting in a negative feedback effect on the symptom cycle.

As the diary (Figure 6.3) shows, John's obsessions were of two types: contamination (C) and doubts (D); and his rituals were of three types: washing (W), checking (Ch) and counting (N). Obsessions were rated according to intensity and conviction, the latter often being the first dimension to change, with intensity lagging behind. Rituals were recorded not just in terms of their occurrence but also according to the tenacity or strength with which they were carried out – another indicator of change to watch out for. The triggers or context, commonly the least obvious aspect to the patient, included going to work on days when there was something he found particularly stressful (WK), and returning from places where he had been in close physical contact with others (PP), such as football practice, crowded shops.

John's symptomatic pattern began to emerge very quickly. Like most obsessional patients, he had no difficulty in filling in such a complex diary as it satisfied his need for perfectionism and certainty. The pattern was:

$$PP \rightarrow C \rightarrow W$$
$$WK \rightarrow D \rightarrow Ch$$

This was a revelation to him, because he had not hitherto realised to what extent his symptoms were related to stress. Having established this very simple psychological link and a common language, the therapist then proceeded to explain the cognitive model of obsessional–compulsive disorder, deliberately using John's idiosyncratic symptoms to arrive at a personalised explication.

John and his therapist were then able to ascertain more about stress factors in his life. It appeared that there were several issues in his relationships at work and in his private life. At work he was very unhappy. He felt undervalued by his boss and pressurised into producing research of which he did not feel capable. With girlfriends, he had never been able to experience deep emotion, liking the courtship but finding it difficult to sustain any further relationship. More recently it was becoming a bigger issue, as he was of the age when his peers were marrying and having children.

This was a significant turning-point in the therapy. John and his therapist had established that the obsessional–compulsive symptomatology was just the tip of the iceberg. He could now understand that his therapy goal was not merely to deal with the symptomatology, as he had initially thought, but also to sort out his relationship and work problems. At this stage he was toying with the hypothesis that the latter might even be integral to the symptomatology.

So by the end of session 3, John and his therapist had achieved the first five points outlined in Figure 6.2.

Sessions 4–8

Therapy proceeded to consolidate the material that had begun to emerge in relation to stress at work. John acknowledged that his relationship with his boss was very strained – it was one in which he was trying to appear capable and confident, but in which he also needed to feel liked. It became apparent that, although there were certain issues specific to this particular relationship, they amounted to general rules that he applied to most of his relationships. This is an example of what is termed 'lateral linkaging' – that is, when the patient becomes aware of how a specific event in the here and now is related to other ongoing events, and so exemplifies general rules rather than being merely a specific incident. The rule that John was able to uncover about himself was: 'In order to be liked, I have to be capable and confident.' He began to realise how much he invested in being the nice guy and in pleasing others at the expense of his own feelings and needs. A downward arrow exercise, analysing the contamination intrusions, revealed the following supporting data:

John: I might be contaminated.
Therapist: And if you were, then what?
J: I could contaminate others.
T: What would this mean to you?
J: It would be embarrassing and they would be angry with me.
T: And so, if they were angry with you?
J: They wouldn't like me any more.
T: And what would be the significance of this?
J: That I wouldn't like myself.

By means of inductive questioning, he was able to make a link with the way it was with his mother, whom he would always 'keep sweet'. She was a worrier and needed protecting, and was prone to outbursts of violent temper. This is an example of 'vertical linkaging' – that is, making a cognitive connection between events or circumstances in the past and events or circumstances in the present. John was assisted in making these links through guided-discovery techniques, always ending the linkage with a present situation and relating it to the problems for which he had come for therapy. This linkaging technique was central in fleshing out the initial formulation. The formulation was always the key point of each session, and homework assignments naturally followed from the formulation work.

The assignment that followed at this point was to focus on the energy John was expending in keeping relationships sweet. The results were conclusively supportive, and this had a marked impact on his understanding of himself. He began to spontaneously link aspects of his relationship with his boss to his relationship with his father, particularly in relation to his father's critical stance. With him, John had never felt that he came up to the mark. He felt average and boring, and conformed with his parents in an attempt to keep the peace. At this point he began to report the emotional concomitants to his intrusions. He described a portentous feeling of being smothered and overwhelmed, and of wanting to escape. Until then he had not been able to construe an emotional aspect to his symptomatology. He began to remember pertinent pressurising events from adolescence – for instance, being emotionally blackmailed into singing in the church choir and into playing the organ. This was highly significant, given that at the beginning of therapy he had been unable to do so. Now he was remembering both at a cognitive and, albeit to a lesser extent, at an emotional level. This was evidence that therapy was having an impact on his schematic organisation in terms of the reduction in his cognitive and emotional avoidance strategies.

John completed this stage of therapy by working his memories into the framework of the schema: 'In order to be loved, I have to achieve and keep people sweet.' He had learned that he viewed achievement, being acceptable and being loved synonymously, and that they were all integral to his view of himself.

Sessions 9–12

The next important link involved helping John to understand the part his symptomatology was playing in avoiding the anxiety caused by holding such an externalised and precarious self schema.

He was able to help himself here. He had come up with an important observation: that his symptoms were at their worst whenever he visited his parents. Now that he was becoming clearer about the genesis of his self schema, he could accept that returning to the original psychological circumstances would necessarily be problematic but also an extremely valuable learning experience. An assignment was agreed upon whereby he was to return home, observe the psychological interactions in his family and focus particularly on the way this made him feel. Using the formulation, John and his therapist came up with a number of hypotheses:

1   that his family shy away from emotional expression;

2 that to go against family opinions is anxiety-provoking;
3 that the patterns of his symptoms wax and wane according to these emotional issues.

John's task was to seek information for and against these hypotheses. The visit turned out to be psychologically successful, and allowed further therapeutic progress. He had gathered a plethora of supporting data and had also been able to act against his assumption that he must always keep his parents sweet. In fact, he had found himself disagreeing with his father over a matter relating to his young nephew joining the church choir. His father disapproved of the boy's resistance, and John was able to take his side. His father came out with a telling statement which, for John, summed up his whole psychological disturbance – 'You are the sum of your achievements.'

John confronted his father about this, and no devastating consequences followed. This was a vital relearning experience, because it had chipped away at his dysfunctional self schema, allowing him the opportunity to consider an alternative viewpoint. He reported important changes in his symptoms. When he had been playing with his sister's children, he had become aware of the portentous feeling described earlier as well as intrusions of contamination. He found that he could insert alternative cognitions into the situation, such as 'These are just intrusive thoughts and I should not attach any significance to them.' The result was that he could control the urge to perform his rituals and did not need to avoid playing with the children as he had always done in the past. He had learned experientially a major psychological lesson, aided by the explicit formulation constructed in his therapy.

Therapy proceeded to help John make more vertical linkages, and psycho-education now focused on schema mechanisms. More significant data emerged concerning the time when the symptoms had emerged, when he was fourteen: his first significant relationship with a girlfriend came to an end. His exploration of how he felt about this event led him to consider that there was a pattern to his choice of women – they were women who, by virtue of their stage in life and their career ambitions, were safe as far as long-term commitment was concerned. Here he made a connection with his need to avoid rejection. Assignments turned to acting against his assumptions about women: he began to assert his needs with his current girlfriend, despite her resultant anger and, in challenging her, recognised a similarity between his mother's personality and his choice of girlfriends. Schematic mechanisms of maintenance and avoidance had prevented him from moving from the position where his perception of his self-worth was dependent on approval. After all, if he risked getting intimately close only to be rejected, this would confirm his feared belief that he was, indeed, worthless. By not taking the risk, the belief could never be disconfirmed.

Therapy articulated this dilemma, and assignments were constructed to help him take increasing risks with people. They involved setting up situations both in and out of work where he would explicitly not go along with others' expressed opinions. The results proved positive. He asserted himself with his boss over the matter of some menial and unrewarding tasks, and the result was a fairer distribution of work across the department. In his relationship with his girlfriend he began to engage in more personally rewarding activities and pursuits, and one consequence of this was that he observed fewer 'put-down' comments from her.

John began to consider the broader issue of his career. He was able to understand that his needs were never going to be met in his current job, and so he began to consider alternative options. By the end of therapy he had applied for a job abroad. He was also considering non-university jobs. He knew in his own mind that he did not want to be an academic and that his strengths were in training and supervision of staff – an area he was going to pursue after therapy. He found his decision to change career 'strangely liberating'. What was most important to him was that he was pursuing it for himself. He had stopped feeling inadequate or a failure at work, and he reported a major reduction in his symptomatology. He no longer felt the need to stay at work 'out of hours', and had begun to express his opinions to good effect in meetings.

In all, treatment lasted for twelve hourly sessions spaced at two- or three-week intervals. The spacing was important, given the wealth of work required outside the sessions. John's concluding remarks about his therapy were very telling in relation to schematic change: 'The world is a lot less frightening and a lot more exciting. I'm doing things I could not have imagined. I thought it was my symptoms that were preventing me from doing them, but I now see that it was me.'

FINAL FORMULATION

The final formulation (see Figure 6.4) contained more detail, but essentially was not very different from the initial one. The hypotheses regarding the developmental context proved to be correct, and therapy had uncovered a lot more details of it. The dysfunctional schemata were more specific in the formulation. Two parallel dimensions to the schemata were made explicit: firstly, 'responsibility' and 'capability'; and secondly, 'acceptability' and 'likeability'. Both were psychologically precarious and produced symptomatology that made sense in terms of averting the consequent anxiety. The two dimensions were themselves causing tension in the sense that it was hard to sustain being both good and liked. Characteristically of obsessional–compulsive disorders, the intrusions themselves were not directly linked in a realistic way to the activating circumstances. Nevertheless, they had become the focus of attention and interacted with the dysfunctional schemata in such a way as to produce negative affective connotation and the need to ritualise as a way of reducing the distress.

Note that the formulation contained elements of both Salkovskis' model and the constructivists' outlined on pp. 150–3: Salkovskis (1985) concentrates on the issue of 'responsibility', whereas the issue of 'likeability' is more compatible with Guidano and Liotti's (1983) explication in terms of attachment.

Figure 6.4 Final formulation

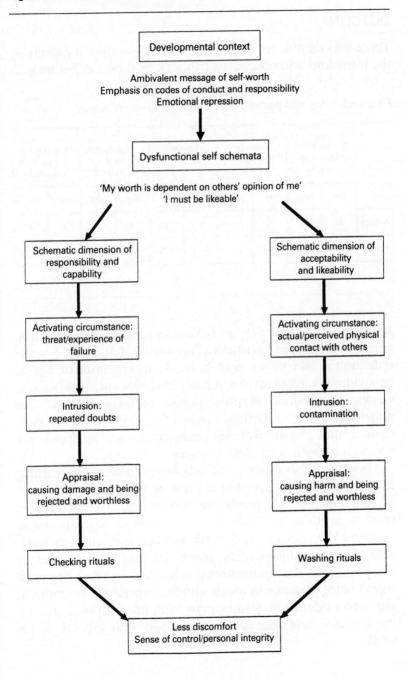

OUTCOME

There was an observable reduction in all monitored aspects of the intrusions and obsessions (rituals), as shown in Figure 6.5.

Figure 6.5   Pre- and post-treatment symptomatology scores

	Duration (mins) of intrusion per episode		Intensity of intrusion (1–10)		Level of conviction		Tenacity of ritual (1–10)		Duration (mins) of ritual per episode	
	pre-	post-	pre-	post-	pre-	post-	pre-	post-	pre-	post-
Average	57	16	7	3	8	2	8	1	37	8
Range	29–132	2–30	4–9	1–5	7–10	1–5	6–9	1–3	15–140	0–16

John reported that, despite having intrusions, he could stop himself engaging in his rituals. This was, he felt, related to the reduction in his conviction of them. He also reported being less behaviourally avoidant in a number of significant areas, such as voicing his opinion in professional meetings and with his girlfriend, going on certain pieces of equipment in the gymnasium, and playing with his young nieces and nephews. He was well pleased with these changes.

There was also evidence of schematic change. By learning that he had heavily invested in pleasing others at the expense of fulfilling his own needs, he had begun to challenge the need to continue to do so. He had begun to separate out in his mind the issues of self-worth and achievement – at least, achievement in his parents' terms. He had pieced together the genesis of the dysfunctional schemata and had begun to report being far more in touch with the experience of emotion. He cited evidence of getting angry with his girlfriend, of feeling anxious, and indeed of satisfaction with aspects of his work.

RELAPSE-PREVENTION

Several elements of the therapy were important here:

1   summarising the material learned in therapy, by collaboratively preparing written synopses and diagrammatic illustrations of key points, so as to provide him with ready access to information if and when he should require it in the future;

2   the final formulation and handouts on the cognitive model, in particular on schematic organisation and processes, so as to provide him with the necessary self-help material for the future;

3   developing contingency plans for further symptomatic flashpoints, or for dealing with potentially triggering circumstances (given the ongoing changes that he was introducing into his life, setbacks were likely);

4   listing strategies that he found useful in therapy, so that he would have ready access to information on how to deal with future difficulties, practically and pragmatically;

5   working at developing his confidence in coping independently, by means of the therapist gradually handing over more and more of the responsibility for the work in each session, becoming less and less directive, and leaving increasingly longer intervals between sessions, so as to phase out help gradually;

6   planning follow-up sessions some time after treatment had ended, to maintain motivation for continued change.

DISCUSSION

The first point to make about this case is how much change was possible in only twelve sessions. And change was not just at a symptomatic level, as would be the case with purely behavioural intervention, but also at a schematic level. It is this that makes for a more optimistic prognosis. John was able to take on board fairly swiftly the cognitive model of his disorder, and was comfortable with the collaborative inductive style of therapy. The therapist was able to exploit cognitively his well developed intellectual capacity and, through skilful and intuitive questioning and synthesising, as described on p. 17, was able to help him to uncover and deal with the emotional problems underlying his symptoms.

Notice how little direct and explicit work was done on the actual symptomatology – in contrast with behavioural therapy. Instead, the main focus was on developing the formulation and on constructing assignments to test it out. Symptomatic change occurred as a secondary aspect to this process which, through the gradual reconstruction of personal experiences, decreased the need for avoiding anxiety and thus the need for engaging in symptoms. Indeed, by not directly tackling the symptoms, the therapist circumvented the level of resistance to change often observed in behavioural therapy. Respecting the emotional function of the symptoms was a key factor in changing them.

Crucial to change were a number of factors: the exploration and learning about early developmental issues; the linking of past issues to present problems; delving into the past only when there was an explicit rationale for doing so, based on the formulation.

From the evidence of schematic change, John's prognosis is fairly good. He made more headway with the problem area of work, and less with his intimate relationships – which may need more extended schema-focused therapy at a later date. It is, however, important to allow a period of time out of therapy before making this decision, so as to see (1) how much new psychological strategy he can maintain from his short-term therapy, and (2) whether or not he is able to continue to make headway without more formal cognitive therapy, depending on how much schematic reconstruction based on new life experience occurs.

The case has tried to illustrate how a rationalist and a constructivist viewpoint can be integrated to form a package of cognitive therapy that is bigger than the sum of its parts. It has not been possible in the space available to go into detail about the specific use of the therapeutic relationship. But it should be noted that, as well as using it as a vehicle for testing out hypotheses, interpersonal issues between therapist and patient were explicitly discussed in relation to the formulation. In John's case, his need to placate people and to avoid bad emotion naturally extended into his relationship with his therapist. Acting against these assumptions with his therapist was a safe and revealing way of changing.

7

A Case of Bulimia Nervosa

Sophie – Breaking Walls and Building Bridges

In a review of the epidemiology of bulimia nervosa, Fairburn and Beglin (1990) suggest a prevalence rate of between 1 and 3 per cent among adolescent and young women. However, the authors observe that the studies reviewed employed a range of methodologies in order to detect cases, and this may have led to an underestimation of the prevalence of eating disorders. In addition, Herzog *et al.* (1991) suggest that if individuals with a subclinical diagnosis are included in the statistics, the prevalence rises to between 5 and 15 per cent. Few data are available concerning the prevalence of eating disorders among men. The fourth edition of the *Diagnostic and Statistical Manual* (*DSM-IV*) of the American Psychiatric Association (1994) estimates the prevalence of bulimia nervosa among men at one-tenth of that in women.

DEFINITION OF BULIMIA NERVOSA

The diagnostic criteria for bulimia nervosa, as defined in *DSM-IV*, are summarised in Table 7.1. Reviewing the eating disorder literature, Garner and Garfinkel (1985) concur with this definition and, in addition, observe that this presentation typically occurs in conjunction with depressive and anxiety symptoms and impaired social function.

Table 7.1 Diagnostic criteria for bulimia nervosa (summarised from *DSM*-IV)

---

1 Recurrent episodes of binge eating, characterised by:

- eating, in a discrete period of time (any 2 hours), an amount of food that is larger than most people would eat during a similar period and under similar circumstances
- a sense of lack of control over eating during the episode

2 Recurrent inappropriate compensatory behaviour in order to prevent weight gain, such as self-induced vomiting, misuse of laxatives, diuretics, enemas, fasting or excessive exercise

3 Binge eating and inappropriate compensatory behaviours both occurring, on average, at least twice a week for 3 months

4 Self-evaluation unduly influenced by body shape and weight

Fairburn emphasises the apparent lack of restraint which characterises bulimia nervosa, and suggests a number of factors to account for this phenomenon. Firstly, he suggests that individuals who present with the disorder often have a family history of obesity. As a clinician, he operates from the premise that body weight is genetically determined and that individuals with bulimia nervosa tend to be constitutionally overweight. Consequently, in their attempts to diet they are pitting themselves against biology. Secondly, Fairburn highlights a family history of substance-abuse among sufferers, particularly the use of alcohol to deal with distressing emotions. In addition, sufferers often possess personality traits of extraversion and lack of control, with an underlying chronic low self-esteem. A tendency towards perfectionism in combination with difficult life circumstances often functions as a precursor to the emergence of the disorder. Finally, Fairburn places much emphasis on the role of sociocultural factors in the genesis and maintenance of bulimia nervosa. He views the disorder as originating from failed attempts to diet driven by cultural standards which equate happiness, success and desirability with the attainment of a svelte physique.

THE COGNITIVE MODEL

Fairburn and Cooper (1989a) have developed a cognitive–behavioural model that aims to account for the maintenance factors in bulimia nervosa (Figure 7.1). This offers a means of conceptualising the disorder in cognitive and behavioural terms, and forms the basis of a treatment rationale. They emphasise the following aspects as part of that rationale.

1   Dieting is a common behaviour in Western society, and one that most women engage in to a greater or lesser extent. Dieting predisposes an individual to binge eating through a combination of psychological and physiological mechanisms. Reasons for dieting are complex, but many women develop a preoccupation with their shape and weight. For some this can become excessive, and as a result they adopt strict and inflexible dietary rules to which they rigidly adhere. Any deviation from the rules, however small, is viewed by the bulimic person as evidence of lack of control and of failure. This is usually followed by temporary abandonment of the rules, the behavioural consequence of which is bingeing. Equally, if a person is underweight as a result of dieting and/or restrained eating, physiological mechanisms within the body will be automatically triggered. These stimulate the organism to engage in the activity of eating, which is essential to survival. In consequence, these physiological mechanisms will increase the likelihood of over-eating if the person concerned is eating less than is necessary. Binge eating, in someone concerned with weight and shape, reinforces the act of dieting. This, in turn, leads to further bingeing and so a vicious cycle is established.

2   Once the vicious cycle is established, the individual seeks other methods of controlling her weight and shape. Self-induced vomiting, the use of diuretics and laxatives and excessive exercising all reinforce binge eating. Reinforcement occurs because

the person mistakenly believes that these strategies are effective in reducing calorie-absorption. This removes the perceived negative consequences of overeating – namely, weight gain, and the restraint is reduced. Thus a second vicious cycle is established between binge eating and purging behaviours.

3   Individuals who are excessively concerned about their weight and shape tend to judge their self-worth according to these criteria. So the archetypal super-model body shape gains highest currency. Such a value system increases the likelihood of engaging in dieting behaviour. A third vicious cycle is thus established between dieting and concern about shape and weight.

Figure 7.1   Cognitive–behavioural model of the maintenance of bulimia nervosa

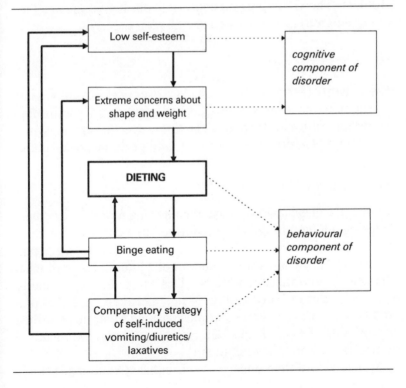

4   Individuals who are extremely concerned about their shape and weight frequently describe underlying thoughts and feelings of failure, ineffectiveness and worthlessness – generally described as low self-esteem. Excessive concern about shape and weight, dieting, binge eating and purging behaviours reinforce low self-esteem, and so a fourth vicious cycle is established.

SOPHIE

THE REFERRAL

Sophie was referred by her general practitioner at her own request to the Cognitive Therapy Centre. The referral letter was short, diagnosing the problem and indicating that Sophie had specifically requested that her parents not be informed of her problem. The GP expressed concern about her young age (she was seventeen) and requested she be seen urgently.

THE ASSESSMENT

Assessment of her problems took place over three sessions, using psychometric measures, interview and baseline self-monitoring to gather information regarding three specific areas: symptomatology, history of the disorder, and personal background.

Symptom profile

Sophie, a college student, described her main problem as daily bingeing and vomiting. This conformed to a consistent pattern of restrained eating between the hours of 11 am and 5 pm, during which she ate a small amount of a limited range of what she called 'non-forbidden foods'. This was followed by one to three episodes of binge eating, usually between the hours of 5 and 10 pm, during which she would consume what she described as 'forbidden foods' (Table 7.2). Episodes of binge eating lasted between five and thirty minutes.

Sophie would then engage in self-induced vomiting, usually

five to ten minutes after the binge. Vomiting was induced with relative ease, using the index finger, and always happened at home in the bathroom. The frequency of such vomiting was between one and three episodes a day, one of which would always be before going to bed. At assessment, Sophie was unable to identify triggers to bingeing episodes, and viewed self-induced vomiting as a way of eliminating calories. She described an erratic eating pattern governed by self-imposed rules regarding the acceptability of eating certain foods (Table 7.2). She also preferred to eat alone, but did not hoard food. She was a vegetarian, partly on account of her beliefs regarding animal rights and partly as a means of controlling her calorie intake.

Table 7.2   Hierarchy of foods

Non-forbidden foods

low-fat yoghurt	baked beans	cauliflower
apples	cucumber	broccoli
oranges	black coffee	grapefruit
pears	black tea	onion
tomatoes	courgettes	dry toast
lettuce	pepper	

Slightly forbidden foods

rice	sweetcorn	banana
wholemeal bread	orange juice	cottage cheese
pasta	milk	kidney beans
soup	Marmite	coleslaw

Moderately forbidden foods

cheese	reduced-fat spread
veggie burger	ice-cream
eggs	reduced-fat
baked/boiled	mayonnaise
potatoes	

Forbidden foods

cakes	chocolate	sweets
biscuits	chips	roast potatoes
pastry	curry	fried foods
butter/margarine	sugar	crisps

Sophie had a body mass index (BMI) of 15, which is within the underweight range (Fairburn and Cooper, 1989b). She weighed herself once a week.

She did not use laxatives or diuretics as a means of weight control and did not exercise regularly. She would, however, on occasions when she perceived she had overindulged, carry out an exercise programme in her bedroom. This would happen approximately once every three to four weeks for five to ten minutes, and consisted of sit-ups. The purpose of this activity was to burn calories and to flatten her stomach.

When the therapist discussed body image with Sophie, it became clear that she did not have a current perception of herself as fat. But she was preoccupied with the importance of having a flat stomach, and expressed an exaggerated fear of weight gain in this area of her body. She also perceived herself as less desirable than other women in her peer group and tended to compare herself unfavourably with them, in terms of both physical appearance and personality. Beliefs elicited focused on judging self-worth and success in terms of physical appearance, as well equating the attainment of happiness and fulfilment with the possession of physical perfection.

Sophie described her mood as fluctuating daily. She reported that it could drop quite rapidly at various points throughout the day. She was unable to identify triggers to this pattern. When she felt low, she became irritable and socially withdrawn. She made no links between periods of low mood and the pattern of binge eating and purging that she described. She reported her concentration and memory as normal, as was her sleep pattern. When questioned, she did not describe any suicidal ideation. Her alcohol intake, at a level of 5–10 units a week, was within recommended limits. She did not use recreational drugs. Her problem did not cause menstrual irregularities. When differential diagnosis was considered, Sophie's description of her difficulties did not meet diagnostic criteria for major depression, nor was there any indication of an Axis II disorder.

Baseline psychometric measures scored were as follows:

- Beck Depression Inventory: 25
- Hopelessness Scale: 3
- Dysfunctional Attitudes Scale: 150
- Hamilton Rating Scale for Depression: 5
  (For guidance on the norms for the above measures, see p. 64.)
- Eating Attitudes Test (EAT): 42
  Garner and Garfinkel (1979) indicate in their validation study of the EAT a cut-off score of 30, where patients with anorexia and normal controls overlap. Higher scores indicate increasing severity of the disorder. The maximum score is 117.
- Bulimia Inventory Test Edinburgh (BITE): symptom scale: 22; severity scale: 11
  Henderson and Freeman (1987) define two scales on the BITE. On the symptom scale scores of 20 or more indicate highly disordered eating patterns and the presence of binge eating (maximum score 30). On the severity scale scores of 5 or more are considered clinically significant, and scores in excess of 10 indicate extreme severity (maximum score 18).

History of the disorder

Sophie recalled first experiencing discontent regarding her physical appearance at the age of ten. At this time she was overweight and was being teased about it by her family and peers at school. She found this very upsetting, and recalled becoming socially withdrawn.

A year later, her mother took her to the family doctor and requested her daughter be put on a diet. The doctor considered this inappropriate, advising that the weight would probably drop of its own accord as she moved through adolescence. Sophie felt humiliated by this experience, regarding her mother as insensitive and unsupportive. When she embarked on secondary education, the teasing about her weight escalated to verbal taunts (particularly from boys) such as 'Blubber guts' and 'Fatso'. She described herself as an 'outcast', and felt helpless to defend herself. She confided in no one about how distressed she felt.

At thirteen Sophie began to restrain her eating. This, in turn, precipitated bingeing. After reading a magazine article on the topic of bulimia nervosa, she learned the tactic of self-induced vomiting as a means of weight control, and over the next year her weight reduced significantly. Her weight loss and resultant model-like figure were praised by family and friends, who told her how attractive she now looked. She recalled feeling extremely angry that, because of weight loss, she was suddenly perceived as acceptable. Consequently, she felt very ambivalent regarding her new-found popularity, particularly towards the boys who had taunted her.

Sophie had never confided in anyone about her problem, and at assessment expressed uncertainty regarding her mother's knowledge of her difficulties. Since onset, the bulimia had been reasonably stable, although there had been a worsening in terms of the frequency of bingeing and self-induced vomiting since taking her GCSEs at sixteen. She could not articulate any reason for this, but as a result had sought treatment. She had done so without the knowledge of her parents, and asked the therapist not to involve them in the treatment.

The maintaining factors of Sophie's problems appeared to be the self-defeating cycle of bingeing and self-induced vomiting, stringent self-imposed rules regarding food consumption, and low self-esteem.

Personal background

Sophie was born and brought up in a Derbyshire village. She was the eldest of three, having a brother of fourteen and a sister of eleven. She described her childhood as 'unhappy', and cited her relationship with her father, whom she described as 'strict' and 'controlling', as the main reason for this. From an early age she recalled her father determining what activities the family engaged in, and setting rigid rules regarding behaviour, manners and social pursuits. Sophie regarded her father as emotionally 'cold' and 'undemonstrative'. He was also prone to temper outbursts, which would result in his not speaking for several days. On occasion he hit her for 'misbehaving', and often told her she 'deserved it'. At the time of assessment she had not spoken to her father for a year, since he had slapped her face and called her 'a slag' when he discovered she had a boyfriend.

Sophie cited an equally emotionally cold relationship with her mother, whom she described as 'selfish' and 'unsupportive'. Her parents had a particularly difficult marriage, characterised by frequent explosive arguments. Her mother used Sophie as a confidante regarding the marriage – a pressure that she found difficult to bear. She described herself as having little respect for her mother for not standing up to her father's behaviour. She also expressed anger at her mother's seeming inability to support her children, and recalled often feeling she was an inconvenience to her.

Her relationship with her siblings was fraught, and they had frequently argued. She now had little contact with her brother and sister. Sophie's self-perception was as an introverted and nervous person. Junior school had been particularly difficult because of what she termed a personality clash with a male teacher: she described having 'temper tantrums', for which she was punished both at school and at home. She always had one or two friends at school, but described difficulties in 'getting close to people'. She socialised weekly, visiting the cinema, pubs and nightclubs.

Sophie said that she had some difficulty relating to men. She entered her first relationship at the age of sixteen, and it lasted three months. This was also her first sexual experience – she had intercourse on one occasion, after which the boy concerned ended the relationship. In retrospect she saw that she had not wanted this aspect of the relationship to develop, but had felt peer pressure to conform. She considered herself 'cheapened' by the experience, especially when she discovered the relationship had been the result of a bet among a group of boys. Understandably, she became hostile towards other men who attempted to initiate any form of relationship with her. She had four female friends with whom she regularly socialised. She was studying for A levels at a local sixth-form college, but found it quite stressful in terms of the workload and a perceived pressure to plan her future career, about which she was very uncertain. Three evenings a week she worked as bartender in a local pub.

Presentation

After three assessment sessions, the impression gained of Sophie was of an introverted young woman who was very unsure of herself. She experienced difficulty in discussing her problems, and could not readily access a vocabulary to articulate and label her thoughts and feelings. She appeared nervous when speaking, as well as having difficulty at times maintaining eye contact. The overall impression was of someone holding back from engaging in the therapy sessions. However, if the focus of discussion moved away from herself, she did become more animated, particularly when describing the creative writing she produced at the college.

Summary of the assessment

Sophie presented with a moderate form of bulimia nervosa. Central to her difficulties appeared to be a low self-esteem, particularly in terms of how she perceived herself in an interpersonal context and her ability to relate to others. Hypothesised core self schemata revolved around themes of worthlessness and inferiority. This self-view appeared to have been well established in early childhood as a consequence of the controlling and demeaning behaviour of her father and the emotional distance of her mother. This was exacerbated by teasing and bullying about her shape and weight, and so by the time she was ten lovability and acceptability had become equated with being thin – an erroneous way of thinking inculcated by family and peers and never challenged by adults, including teachers, or friends. This was reinforced when, at the age of thirteen, Sophie began to induce vomiting and lost weight, obtaining a model-like figure over the next two years. However, the resultant praise and attention from those around her, rather than raising her self-esteem, created ambivalence. Part of her, at least, rejected the implicit assumption shared by people in her environment that weight loss somehow made her a different, more acceptable, person. It is hypothesised that this is the rescue factor that led her not only to seek treatment, but also to benefit from it.

SUITABILITY FOR SHORT-TERM COGNITIVE THERAPY

Suitability for treatment was formally measured using the Safran and Segal (1990) Suitability for Short-term Cognitive Therapy Rating Scale (aspects of the cognitive therapy process are rated on a scale of 0–5). High ratings indicate a good prognosis and low ratings indicate a poor one. The total maximum score possible is 50.

1 *Accessibility of automatic thoughts* At assessment Sophie was unable to identify specific automatic thoughts, but could discuss general themes that caused her distress (1).

2 *Awareness and differentiation of emotions* She was unable to articulate or label emotions and, on questioning, used words such as 'uncomfortable' and 'confused' to describe how she felt. She did, however, report fluctuations in her mood (2).

3 *Acceptance of personal responsibility for change* That she had sought help on her own initiative, without parental support, gave some indication that she accepted responsibility for change. This was confirmed during assessment when she said that she viewed her binge eating and self-induced vomiting as a problem, and commented: 'I know I'm the only person who can change things, but I need help to do that' (5).

4 *Compatibility with cognitive rationale* When the therapist shared the cognitive rationale with Sophie, she stated that she could understand it in principle but had some reservations about how it applied to the problem she described (3).

5) *Alliance potential (in-session evidence)* Throughout the assessment she was hesitant, and at times had difficulty maintaining eye contact. But as sessions progressed she did engage to some extent in the therapy process, and appeared a little more at ease (2.5).

6 *Alliance potential (out-of-session evidence)* From Sophie's description of her relationship with her parents and siblings, it was clear that she had little experience of forming any trusting bonds with other people. However, she did have a number of female friends with whom she had established and sustained friendships over a number of years (3).

7 *Chronicity of problems* She described a four-year history of bulimia nervosa, with a significant worsening of the problem in the year before seeking treatment (3).

8 *Security operations* While she experienced difficulty in discussing her problems and displayed some avoidance of anxiety-provoking topics, as the assessment sessions proceeded she did gradually begin to engage more. There did not appear to be any major security operations that contra-indicated short-term therapy, although some reservations were noted (3).

9 *Focality* She was readily able to focus on a specific topic, and after initial hesitancy would attempt to discuss it in some depth (3.5).

10 *Patient optimism/pessimism regarding therapy* Sophie did not express overt pessimism regarding the usefulness of therapy and, while not spontaneously optimistic, she did give some indication that it might be beneficial to her (3).

The overall score of 29 highlighted some reservations regarding prognosis. However, it was to her credit that, at the age of seventeen, Sophie was able to acknowledge that she had a problem. Anecdotal evidence from researchers such as Fairburn (1992), which is borne out by the author's own clinical experience, suggests that many women view bingeing and self-induced vomiting as an acceptable form of weight control. It was also noteworthy that Sophie had sought help on her own initiative. However, it was reasonable to hypothesise that, given her experience in relationships to date, confiding and asking for help with the expectation of receiving support were going to be something of an anathema to her. In contrast, her symptomatology was not extreme, and the actual pattern of the bulimia was relatively stable.

INITIAL FORMULATION

As we have already seen, a fundamental aspect of cognitive therapy is the development of a formulation of the problems described by the client. The spirit of cognitive therapy insists that this be collaborative, and guided by the client as much as possible. Thus limits are placed on the therapist's hypothesis regarding the pyschological mechanisms that drive the disorder. Given that Sophie experienced difficulty articulating and labelling her thoughts and feelings, the initial formulation, which followed Beck's (1976) model for the development and maintenance of emotional disorders, was limited. This initial formulation is described in Figure 7.2, overleaf.

TREATMENT

The plan

The proposed treatment plan followed the Fairburn and Cooper model, which proposes three distinct phases; these are not described in detail here (see Fairburn and Cooper, 1989a).

Phase 1 This phase lasts four weeks, with twice-weekly appointments. The rationale for session frequency is that of facilitating engagement in the process and tasks of therapy, as well as seeking to establish rapid behavioural change which aims to disrupt the vicious cycle of bingeing and vomiting. Disrupting this cycle involves a number of steps:

- self-monitoring (an example of food and drink consumption is shown in Table 7.3, p. 191);

Figure 7.2   Initial formulation

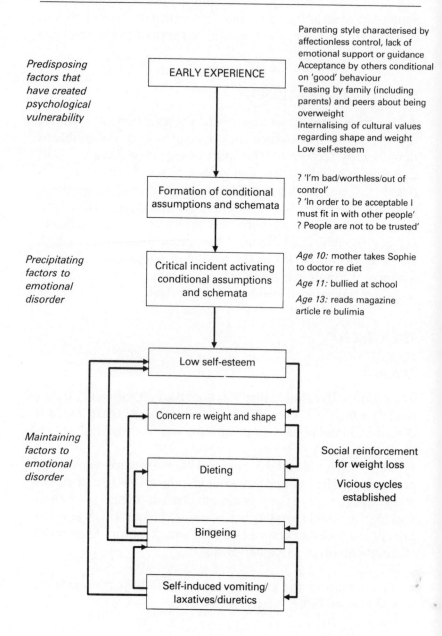

Predisposing factors that have created psychological vulnerability

EARLY EXPERIENCE

Parenting style characterised by affectionless control, lack of emotional support or guidance
Acceptance by others conditional on 'good' behaviour
Teasing by family (including parents) and peers about being overweight
Internalising of cultural values regarding shape and weight
Low self-esteem

Formation of conditional assumptions and schemata

? 'I'm bad/worthless/out of control'
? 'In order to be acceptable I must fit in with other people'
? People are not to be trusted'

Precipitating factors to emotional disorder

Critical incident activating conditional assumptions and schemata

Age 10: mother takes Sophie to doctor re diet
Age 11: bullied at school
Age 13: reads magazine article re bulimia

Low self-esteem

Concern re weight and shape

Maintaining factors to emotional disorder

Dieting

Social reinforcement for weight loss

Vicious cycles established

Bingeing

Self-induced vomiting/ laxatives/diuretics

Table 7.3 Self-monitoring

Time	Quantity	Food/drink	Binge?	Vomit	Laxative?	Reasons/thoughts
10.30 am	1	low-fat yoghurt cup of black coffee				hungry
12.30 am	1	salad sandwich banana				still hungry, a bit greedy
5 pm	1	veggie burger				hungry
6 pm	3	slices of bread				tired, confused
6.20 pm	1 1	veggie burger bag of crisps	yes	yes		What a pig!
8.30 pm	7	chips (taken from brother's plate)	yes	yes		bored, trying to do homework and couldn't
10 pm	1 3 2	bowl of ice-cream biscuits slices of bread	yes	yes		pathetic, I've blown it again, I'm useless
11 pm	1	Eccles cake		yes		

- weekly weighing;
- selling the model to the patient;
- education;
- implementing a regular eating pattern;
- stimulus-control strategies;
- alternative behaviour;
- the therapist giving information regarding self-induced vomiting.

Phase 2 This phase of treatment lasts eight weeks, with appointments scheduled at weekly intervals; it is cognitively orientated, and client and therapist focus on the following:

- the elimination of dieting behaviour;
- the relationship between thoughts, feelings and behaviour in the context of the disorder – this involves the identification and modification of automatic thoughts, conditional assumptions and core schemata;
- developing problem-solving skills;
- body image disturbance.

Phase 3 This phase lasts eight weeks, with sessions spaced at fortnightly intervals; it represents the relapse-prevention aspect of treatment. Usually clients still experience symptomatology – this improves after discharge.

PROGRESS OF THERAPY

Phase 1

One of the first steps in treatment was to develop collaboratively a prioritised problem list, as well as to establish treatment goals. Sophie's prioritised problem and target statements, written using her own terms of reference, are summarised in Table 7.4.

Further aims of this phase were to:

- establish a sound therapeutic relationship;

Table 7.4   Prioritising problems and establishing targets

Problems	Targets
1 Bingeing and vomiting daily	To be able to reduce bingeing and vomiting behaviour by 90%
2 Lack of confidence in social situations, leading to avoidance behaviour	To be able to enter social situations and feel less self-conscious
3 Lack of support at home, leading to feelings of not coping with stressful situations – for example, examinations	To be able to develop a range of coping strategies that rely on a support network that extends outside the home, for dealing with stressful situations

- sell the cognitive–behavioural model of bulimia nervosa to the patient, including discussing the psychological and physiological processes which maintain the problem;
- educate Sophie regarding the adverse consequences of bingeing and vomiting behaviour as well as of the use of laxatives and diuretics;
- introduce a regular eating pattern;
- disrupt the vicious cycle of bingeing and self-induced vomiting;
- identify the connection between thoughts, feelings and behaviour within the context of the disorder.

Initially, Sophie experienced difficulty in engaging in treatment. She cancelled two of her first four sessions, and did not complete the negotiated homework assignments for the first two weeks. She also had a tendency to arrive between ten and twenty minutes late for appointments. This pattern of behaviour was congruent with the initial hypothesis made at assessment. Given her home environment, building trust and developing a confiding relationship were going to be difficult for her. Equally, the chaotic nature of a disorder like bulimia often interferes with the treatment process itself, in that dichotomous reasoning and behaviour often predominate. For instance, a perception of not having completed one aspect of homework, such as keeping a food diary, quickly accesses global judgements of failure. The behavioural correlate of this is giving up not only on the activity itself but on therapy as well.

At session 3 this hypothesis was shared with Sophie. Guided discovery was used to explore difficulties that she might have been experiencing with therapy, as follows:

Therapist: Sophie, do you have any specific item for your agenda today?

Sophie: No, not really.

T: OK. If it's all right with you, I'd like to spend the initial part of the session today talking about our meetings together.

S: OK.

T: We've had three sessions together so far. How are you finding treatment?

S: [silent, looking at the floor] A bit difficult.

T: Yes, I wondered if you were finding things a bit hard going. Is that why you cancelled our last two appointments?

S: Sort of. [silence]

T: Sometimes people find treatment difficult for one reason or another, and this can put them off attending the sessions. You said earlier you were finding our sessions a bit difficult. Do you feel able to discuss the difficulties with me?

S: [silent, tearful] I don't know.

T: Sophie, you seem really sad right now. What's going through your mind?

S: [silent] I don't know. I feel confused.

T: From what you've told me so far in our sessions together, this 'feeling confused' is quite a common experience for you.

S: Yes.

T: This feeling also seems to cause you problems when you are getting to know people.

S: I guess so.

T: Last time we met, Sophie, you talked about feeling as if there were walls between you and other people. I wonder, do you feel as if there is a barrier between you and me?

S: Yes. I feel I can't communicate properly when I'm here and I

can't get across my feelings. I just feel distant and find it hard
to talk.

T: Are you able to say what it is that makes it hard to talk?

S: I'm not sure.

T: Before you come to the sessions, how do you feel?

S: A bit worried.

T: A bit worried. What is it you worry about?

S: I worry about what to say and how I come across.

T: When you say you worry about how you come across, what is
your view of how you come across?

S: Introverted and not very talkative.

T: So, what you're saying is that one of the reasons why you
cancelled the sessions was worrying thoughts that you were
coming across as introverted and not very talkative?

S: Yes.

T: OK. You identified these feelings as something you wanted to
try to change in treatment. Yet it also sounds as if the feelings
may stop you coming to sessions. That sounds like another one
of those self-defeating vicious cycles we talked about.

S: Yes, it does a bit.

T: Right. When you think back to the last time we examined
self-defeating vicious cycles, what conclusions did we come to
about what kept them going?

S: I'm not sure.

T: How about looking in your therapy folder for the piece of
paper with it written on?

S: [several minutes later] Here it is.

T: What does it say?

S: The cycle is kept going by self-criticism and negative expectation of doing everything perfectly. [Sophie shows the piece of
paper]

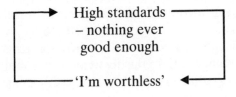

T: Do you think this is what might be going on here?

S: What do you mean?

T: Are you in this situation criticising yourself and discounting your achievements?

S: What achievements?

T: Well, you've been talking twenty minutes now and we've found out a fair bit of information about your problem.

S: I suppose we have. [smiling] I never thought of it like that.

From this, a strategy was devised to try to facilitate optimum engagement in therapy. Firstly, a practical problem was addressed: activity-scheduling was used in order to set aside specific time for therapy work at home. This was set at half an hour a day between 5 and 6 pm. Secondly, at the end of each session Sophie and the therapist summarised what aspects of herself and her problem had been shared that day, as well as identifying her thoughts and feelings relating to the work of the session. The rationale for this was to begin to focus on the interpersonal aspect of her problem and to try to build some positive self-esteem in this context.

Sophie responded well to the educational aspects of treatment as well as to the cognitive–behavioural model of the disorder. However, as is often the case, she found the prospect of instituting an eating pattern based on food-consumption every three to four hours somewhat daunting. As a first step, she was asked to categorise foods as illustrated in Table 7.2, p. 181.

Initially, the regular eating pattern focused on foods from the first two categories that Sophie could eat without experiencing high levels of distress. However, this highlighted once more the dichotomous reasoning inherent in the disorder, and trying to eat more regularly led to an increase in bingeing and self-induced vomiting. This was tackled by focusing on bingeing behaviour, by using the 'I think I am going to binge' form (Table 7.5). This has four main purposes: firstly, to identify triggers to bingeing; secondly, to examine the role of thoughts and feelings in relation to binge eating; thirdly to identify a range of alternative behaviours that are incompatible with binge eating (for

Table 7.5   The 'I think I am going to binge' form

Use this form next time you know you are going to binge. Use it as a way of getting yourself to sit down and think hard about the reason why you want to binge. You may find that once you can identify the reason another, better, solution becomes apparent.

Note   You will be able to use this form only early in the cycle of events. It is not usually possible to sit down and think sensibly when you are very distressed, just before a binge.

Date   12/8/1993   *Time*   6 pm

Place   home

How strong is the urge to binge (1–10)?   6

How to you feel?
   Upset, fed up.

Why do you want to binge? Is there something upsetting you?
   I'm trying to do some project work for college. Don't know how to start. I've been trying for ages now. I just can't get my head round it.

What did you decide to do instead of binge?
   Take the dog for a walk. Ring Alison and ask if she can help me with the work and try to solve the problem together.

How did you feel once you realised you were not going to binge?
   Relieved. Pleased. It passed quite quickly once I tried to sort out the problem.

What do you think you have learned from this experience?
   There are reasons why I binge. Trying to sort out the reasons helps. If I can find the problem and try to solve it I don't get so upset, and I don't feel upset very long. I can sometimes control my binge eating – but will I next time?!

---

example – take the dog for a walk, ring my friends, tidy my bedroom, have a bath); and finally, to evaluate the outcome of resisting the urge to binge. During phase 1 the following triggers to binge eating were identified:

- 'if I have something I don't want to do or I'm not sure how to do – for instance, going to work, college projects';
- 'if I have nothing constructive to do';

- 'if I'm hungry';
- 'if I think I've not got on with people or I think I've been "quiet" in social situations';
- 'when I have thoughts about being directionless and not knowing where my future career lies';
- 'when I'm watching television and eating at the same time';
- 'when I feel angry or upset or down';
- 'when I'm tired';
- 'when the house is empty';
- 'when I perceive rejection by others'.

Sophie found this aspect of treatment something of a revelation. She used the form consistently and discovered that bingeing 'temporarily blocks things out'. Exploration during treatment sessions identified that the 'things' she was seeking to block were painful emotions. Further discussion of family interactions revealed patterns of emotional avoidance in both her parents, not only in terms of avoiding conflict (her mother), but also avoiding showing love, affection and care (both parents). This was related to the current problems she was experiencing in an interpersonal context, which were characterised by difficulty in identifying her feelings on some occasions or, more often, difficulty in showing her feelings for fear of rejection. In response to this, self-monitoring to identify connections between thoughts, feelings and behaviour was introduced.

As a means of undermining some of the triggers to bingeing, the therapist introduced prospective-activity scheduling. The aim was to structure the day in advance, planning activities after meals and at times when there was an increased likelihood that Sophie would start binge eating.

By the end of phase 1, she had made these gains:

1 She had developed a sound, confiding relationship with the therapist.
2 She had identified a number of recurrent triggers to binge eating and had successfully implemented a range of strategies to

tackle them, to the extent that there had been a 50 per cent reduction in the frequency of binge eating and in self-induced vomiting. These strategies included:

- structuring her day;
- identifying thoughts and feelings associated with her problem.

Phase 2

The main emphasis of this phase was on identifying the links between thoughts, feelings and behaviour. Having established these links in the maintenance of the disorder, attention turned to challenging unhelpful thinking patterns surrounding food, shape and weight, and Sophie's negative self-perceptions during interactions with her peers. There was also an increased focus on formulation, in terms of identifying the underlying conditional assumptions and core schemata. Once these were identified, work was directed at modifying them.

At the beginning of this phase Sophie reported feeling low in mood, and was very tearful during one particular session. This in itself was a positive step, as it indicated that she felt able to trust the therapeutic relationship sufficiently to show her real feelings. She had not done any homework and described herself as a 'complete failure' at everything, including treatment.

First, a treatment review was carried out, examining gains to date and the area of improvement, as an evidential challenge to her thoughts about failure. Dichotomous reasoning and behaviour were identified, and a daily list of achievements was introduced. The aim of this was to begin building positive self-esteem, by asking Sophie to pay attention to what she had achieved rather than to what she had *not* done. She had experienced considerable distress at work in the previous week, and this was investigated as follows. A comparison of her current job in a bar (which she found difficult) was made with her previous job in a clothes shop (about which she had felt very confident). The following points emerged:

Clothes shop

1 on the shop floor, able to move around
2 colleagues all the same age
3 customers the same age or younger, and looking at clothes, not her
4 customers anonymous

Bar

1 trapped behind a bar
2 being observed by others, particularly men
3 customers mainly older men
4 customers regulars, pressure to make some form of relationship
5 felt on show, self-conscious, 'people judging my appearance/performance'
6 self-perception as shy, but needed to be outgoing

The overriding issue that emerged from this exercise was the importance of control within the context of Sophie's problem. Thus a further important trigger to binge eating was a perception of being out of control. Equally important was the observation that she felt more out of control when interacting with men, particularly when they were older than herself. She was able to relate this directly to her interactions with her father, and identified always feeling worthless and inferior in relation to him.

Despite an increase in the level of distress she was experiencing, Sophie did not report an increase of binge eating and vomiting. Indeed, for the first time since the problem had begun, at session 12 Sophie reported three days when she was not engaged in binge eating and self-induced vomiting.

By this stage in the treatment she was more able to identify and label emotions and associated thoughts. The next step was to introduce methods of challenging thoughts, which followed the format outlined by Beck (1976). She quickly utilised this aspect of therapy, particularly in establishing behavioural experiments to test the validity of her automatic thoughts. Two such important experiments were devised by Sophie, on her own initiative. Firstly, she confided her bulimia to a close friend. Rather than the predicted revulsion and rejection, her friend responded with care and comfort, as well as offering practical support.

This prompted Sophie to confide in her mother that she was visiting a 'counsellor', although she did not discuss the details of her problem. Her mother responded with sympathy and articulated her own discomfort with family relationships, putting it down to the difficulties her husband had in communicating his feelings appropriately. Her mother then attempted to instigate a number of family discussions regarding emotional issues, which led to increased family tensions. In relation to this, Sophie identified the following thoughts and feelings:

Emotions

Guilt 70%	'It's my fault. I caused a problem between my parents.'
Anger 100%	'My father is insensitive and cold. He is so unreasonable. It's not fair.'
Sadness 90%	'My family is so unhappy – no wonder I am the way I am.'

These thoughts and feelings were discussed in therapy and appropriate challenges developed.

Over the period of the next two sessions Sophie encountered a number of difficult situations:

- negotiating her hours with her boss;
- avoiding social situations with a friend;
- not attending college because of feeling 'distant' and 'not fitting in'.

Once more she became very tearful in the sessions and, through guided discovery, the following were hypothesised:

- conditional assumption: 'Unless I keep control of myself and my emotions, people will discover I'm worthless and reject me.'
- Schema: 'I'm inferior.'

By session 15, Sophie's binge eating and self-induced vomiting had been reduced by 70 per cent. She also regularly experienced several days when she would not engage in this behaviour at all. In examining the triggers to the remaining episodes of bingeing and vomiting, three issues emerged:

1 'If I don't binge and vomit I feel "out of control".'
2 'If I stopped bingeing I would lose one way of dealing with strong emotions.'
3 'If I stopped bingeing and vomiting I might gain weight and be more unhappy with my appearance.' In parentheses she wrote: '(However, I know I could lose weight and still be unhappy.)'

These issues were tackled by challenging the inconsistencies within the statements, drawing on alternative strategies for dealing with emotions, and beginning to address issues surrounding weight and shape – including beginning to eat 'forbidden foods'. It was also noted that direct work at the level of conditional assumptions and core schemata was necessary, and the sessions began to focus on early experiences that might have accounted for the formation of the specific beliefs she held. Once more she was able to use therapy in a constructive way.

She learned that not speaking to her father was her only way of exerting 'control', and that this was something she transferred to interactions with other men. Equally she observed that, given her relationship with her father, it was understandable that she experienced difficulty in trusting men. From this she devised the behavioural test of initiating conversation, when she found herself in a social context, rather than holding back and waiting for someone to speak to her. This had a dramatic effect on her sense of control, as well as giving her a sense of having something in common with other people.

By the end of phase 2 of therapy, Sophie had:

1 instituted a regular eating pattern, including some forbidden foods;

2   reduced the incidence of binge eating and self-induced vomiting;
3   identified connections between thoughts, feelings and behaviour in relation to her bulimia;
4   begun to challenge her thoughts and to behave differently in social situations, which had led to an improvement in her mood and a reduction in her anxiety symptoms;
5   developed some understanding of how her problems began and what maintained them.

Phase 3

The main aims here were the consolidation of previous gains, the modification of conditional assumptions and/or core schemata, and relapse-prevention work.

Fennell (1992) estimates that it takes eight months of consistent work to modify one conditional assumption. The work is initiated in the final phase of therapy, and an action plan is devised such that the client can continue to work on this important area after discharge. A flashcard with a specific and concrete action plan was drawn up with Sophie. (An outline of this method is shown in Table 7.6, overleaf.) Throughout the course of therapy emphasis had been placed on building positive self-esteem. This had included strategies such as a daily list of achievements pinned to the bedroom wall, and Sophie giving herself credit for them with rewards. In addition, focus had been aimed at her contribution to tackling her problem within the sessions, as well as using cognitive therapy to challenge self-criticism.

In order to continue work on self-esteem, during the final phase of therapy an exercise was implemented which involved looking specifically at the role of schemata. Sophie was asked to draw up a list of ten self-referent positive attributes not related to physical appearance. The therapist and three of Sophie's friends also drew up a list of what they considered her positive attributes.

Patients' response to this is variable. Those who have a fragile

Table 7.6 Flashcard for challenging conditional assumptions

I hold the belief that
  Unless I keep control of myself and my emotions, people will
  discover I'm worthless and reject me.

It is understandable that I hold this belief because . . .
  1
  2
  3

However, this belief is unrealistic because . . .
  1
  2
  3

This belief is also unhelpful because . . .
  1
  2
  3

A more helpful belief is . . .
  1
  2
  3

*Because I have held this belief for a long time it is going to be difficult
to challenge. The following action plan is aimed at modifying this
belief*
  [specific and concrete strategies]

---

self-esteem may refuse to participate in the exercise, or become
very distressed at the prospect of even considering positive
statements about themselves. Clinically this may be explained in
terms of the strength and rigidity of the schema being challenged, and it can be an indication of the presence of an Axis II
disorder. This usually requires more long-term schema-focused
cognitive therapy.

Sophie responded with some reticence to the exercise, but
managed to produce a list and asked her friends to do the same.
The lists were then collated and Sophie was asked for her
immediate thoughts and feelings regarding attributes identified.
She expressed some surprise and pleasure regarding other

people's observations, and quickly identified discrepancies between her perception of herself and other people's.

Secondly, she was asked to categorise the attributes as follows:

1 those she could accept as true;
2 those that seemed plausible but not wholly acceptable;
3 those she found herself unable to accept.

These are illustrated in Table 7.7.

Table 7.7   Sophie's list of positive attributes

---

1 *Positive attributes about myself that I can accept*

self-reliant	considerate
responsible	polite
reliable	helpful

2 *Positive attributes about myself that are plausible*

hard-working	generous
tenacious	good at taking initiative
creative	mature

3 *Positive attributes about myself, observed by others, that I cannot accept*

supportive	intelligent
good fun	interesting
kind	sensitive
caring	warm

Several behavioural tests were devised to examine these. Firstly, she was asked to collect daily examples of the attributes in category 1. The aim was to shift her focus from negative self-criticism towards building a positive self-view. This had a profound effect for Sophie, simply because it shifted the focus from negative to positive events and attributes. Secondly, she and her three friends were asked to keep a daily log of the attributes in category 2. Enlisting the help of friends was vital because it offered an alternative perspective which maintained dissonance between self-evaluation and evaluation by others. Again, this reaped positive benefits for Sophie, in terms both of beginning to change how she viewed herself and of starting to form confiding relationships with others.

Finally, attention was turned to the attributes in category 3. Clinical experience suggests that attributes the client cannot accept are often related to the core schemata, and this appeared to be so for Sophie. Thus attention was turned to the formulation and to the role of underlying beliefs in maintaining low self-esteem. The first step in challenging these was for Sophie to write down her thoughts and feelings about each attribute. This typically involved identifying thinking errors such as emotional reasoning, plus challenging thoughts such as: 'Elaine only said I was caring because she felt sorry for me.' Secondly, Sophie was to ask her friends to keep a daily diary of these attributes – she would show them how to do it – over several months. Finally, she was asked to engage in a behaviour congruent with the attributes, and to monitor her thoughts and feelings as well as the response of others. Role-play was used in the session to practise this strategy, and reverse role-play was used to challenge negative automatic thoughts. Obviously this element of treatment, which required repetition over several months, was implemented as a long-term strategy for undermining the cognitive vulnerability factors in low self-esteem.

An important outcome from the self-esteem work was Sophie's realisation that her friends shared many of her worries and concerns about how they viewed themselves. This opened the way for the use of bibliotherapy to explore some of these issues. Books recommended included *The Beauty Myth* (Wolf, 1990), *Tomorrow I'll Be Slim* (Gilbert, 1989), *Never Give Up* (Fleming, 1992), *Womansize* (Chernin, 1983) and *Sugar and Spice* (Lees, 1993). Also, Sophie began to question the validity of her self-view and acknowledge that, whatever she might think, others did not view her in the same way.

Upon completion of phase 3 of therapy, Sophie had:

1 reduced the incidence of binge eating and self-induced vomiting by 95 per cent;

2   actively engaged in challenging distressing thoughts and feelings;
3   participated more actively in social activities and subjectively reported a reduction in interpersonal sensitivity with friends and work colleagues.

In addition:

4   Although communication at home remained difficult, she was better able to build alternative supportive and confiding relationships with her friends.

FINAL FORMULATION

The final formulation was developed with Sophie, and is presented in Figure 7.3, overleaf.

OUTCOME

At the end of therapy, the measures that had been taken at assessment were taken again, demonstrating the following changes:

- Beck Depression Inventory: 3
- Hopelessness Scale: 0
- Hamilton Rating Scale for Depression: 0
- Dysfunctional Assumptions Schedule: 75
- Eating Attitudes Test: 12
- BITE: symptom scale: 6; severity scale: 3

Figure 7.4 (p. 209) illustrates the reduction in binge eating and self-induced vomiting across treatment.

RELAPSE-PREVENTION

Relapse-prevention forms an integral aspect of cognitive therapy. It is particularly important in the treatment of bulimia

Figure 7.3 Final formulation

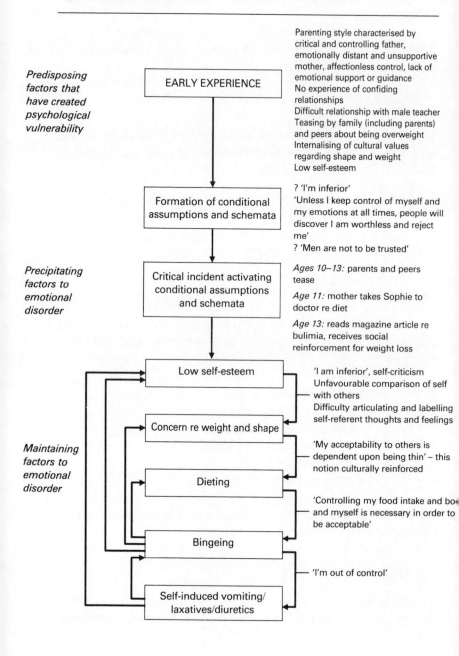

Predisposing factors that have created psychological vulnerability

EARLY EXPERIENCE

Parenting style characterised by critical and controlling father, emotionally distant and unsupportive mother, affectionless control, lack of emotional support or guidance
No experience of confiding relationships
Difficult relationship with male teacher
Teasing by family (including parents) and peers about being overweight
Internalising of cultural values regarding shape and weight
Low self-esteem

Formation of conditional assumptions and schemata

? 'I'm inferior'
'Unless I keep control of myself and my emotions at all times, people will discover I am worthless and reject me'
? 'Men are not to be trusted'

Precipitating factors to emotional disorder

Critical incident activating conditional assumptions and schemata

Ages 10–13: parents and peers tease

Age 11: mother takes Sophie to doctor re diet

Age 13: reads magazine article re bulimia, receives social reinforcement for weight loss

Low self-esteem

'I am inferior', self-criticism
Unfavourable comparison of self with others
Difficulty articulating and labelling self-referent thoughts and feelings

Concern re weight and shape

'My acceptability to others is dependent upon being thin' – this notion culturally reinforced

Maintaining factors to emotional disorder

Dieting

'Controlling my food intake and bo[d] and myself is necessary in order to be acceptable'

Bingeing

'I'm out of control'

Self-induced vomiting/ laxatives/diuretics

Figure 7.4 Frequency of binge eating and self-induced vomiting across treatment

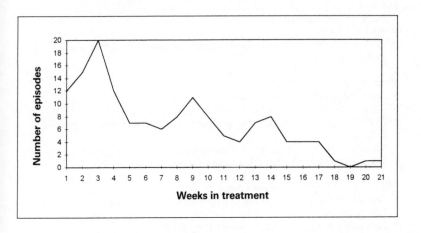

nervosa because, should it persist in the long term, the disorder presents the individual with a number of physical health risks, including problems such as infertility and osteoporosis. By challenging her identified conditional assumptions, Sophie had already begun some of this work and had thus begun work on building positive self-esteem. These strategies were aimed at undermining her psychological vulnerability to relapse.

Working collaboratively, Sophie and the therapist drew up a summary of treatment and a blueprint for relapse-prevention (illustrated in Table 7.8, overleaf).

DISCUSSION

Sophie had twenty sessions of treatment over five months. Despite initial reservations regarding her suitability for a short-term cognitive–behavioural approach, she engaged in therapy and derived considerable benefits. Not only did she succeed in virtually eliminating her binge eating and vomiting behaviour, but she participated actively, and engaged in the process of

Table 7.8 Blueprint for relapse-prevention

What made me vulnerable to developing the problem in the first place?
- Lack of confidence
- Self-criticism
- Difficulty identifying my feelings (these were related to early childhood experience)

What have I learned in treatment?
- I can now identify triggers to binge eating
- I can now eat regularly (3 meals and 3 snacks a day)
- My first thoughts about myself are not necessarily true; I am self-critical
- My view of myself is not the same as other people's view of me
- People do like me and think that I have positive attributes

What areas leave me vulnerable?
- Not planning my day or structuring my time, which may lead to binge eating
- Not addressing problems when they arise
- Being hard on myself and discounting my achievements
- Conflicts at home
- Meeting new people
- Relationships with men

What strategies can undermine these vulnerabilities?
- Persisting in implementing conditional-assumption action plan
- Continuing to work on 'positive attributes'
- Monitoring and challenging my thoughts – particularly in a crisis
- Being aware of situations that may trigger my conditional assumptions and core schemata
- Continuing with my regular eating plan
- Planning my day in advance, giving it structure and purpose
- Trying actively to develop confiding relationships but remembering that this takes time and investment; using friends to build a mutual support network
- Monitoring successes and rewarding myself for persisting in tackling problems; watching out for dichotomous thinking and behaviour

Dealing with a setback
- Don't give up
- Use treatment folder to get back on track
- Ask friends for help
- Write problems down – try to solve them
- Ring therapist for advice
- Start all this sooner rather than later

What are my personal strengths?
- I'm hard-working and persistent in tackling a problem
- I'm mature and responsible in seeking help and using it constructively
- I have lots of initiative and creativity
- I'm self-reliant
- I'm friendly, warm(ish!) and sensitive, with things to offer others

---

learning to identify her thoughts and feelings and of testing their validity in real-life situations. So by the end of treatment she was beginning to develop a new perspective in terms of how she defined herself and her relationships with other people.

Her age had the potential for creating blocks to treatment, in that many of her constructs regarding herself, the world and her relationships with others were still developing. At times this made formulation difficult, because stepping back and seeking direction from a half-drawn map often led into uncharted waters. However, this may have been what enabled her to utilise treatment; and it is to be hoped that therapy has at least equipped her with the skills to build a more positive self-view and a compass to determine her own route in life.

An aspect of treatment that she found puzzling was the use of bibliotherapy to try to examine social constructs of female body image and behaviour. Image was very important to Sophie, and this was heavily reinforced by her peer group. Equally, she viewed the recommended literature as endorsing a feminist viewpoint – which was not only beyond the realms of her experience within her peer group, but was also a construct with which she could not identify.

After discharge, Sophie went to work abroad, and follow-up arrangements were not implemented. Two years later she wrote thanking the therapist for the help she had received. She had continued to improve, having one brief setback for a month, three months after discharge, which she dealt with effectively. She said she felt more at ease with herself and more able to be herself with other people. She ended her letter with the following Shakespeare sonnet (in Harrison, 1950) which, she said, encapsulated how she felt about people's tendency to make false comparisons based on external appearances:

> My Mistress' eyes are nothing like the sun;
> Coral is far more red than her lips' red;
> If snow be white, why then her breasts are dun;
> If hairs be wires, black wires grow on her head.
> I have seen roses damask'd, red and white,
> But no such roses see I in her cheeks;
> And in some perfumes is there more delight
> Than in the breath that from my mistress reeks.
> I love to hear her speak, yet well I know
> That music hath a far more pleasing sound;
> I grant I never saw a goddess go –
> My mistress when she walks treads on the ground.
>   And yet, by heaven, I think my love as rare
>   As any she belied with false compare.

8

A Case of Long-term Problems

Luke – 'I am a lone lorn creetur . . . and everythink goes contrairy with me'

Charles Dickens, *David Copperfield*

Among patients with long-term problems, those with residual psychotic symptoms and those with personality disorders pose the greatest challenge in therapy. In this case study, a patient presenting with an Axis I disorder (major depression) and an avoidant personality disorder (APD) is described. As mentioned in Chapter 2, the elaboration of clear and specific criteria in *DSM*-III-R and *DSM*-IV has facilitated research and the development of treatment approaches in this area.

Personality disorders are highly prevalent in the clinic. Turkat and Maisto (1985) found that 50 per cent of psychiatric patients present with personality disorders. Shea *et al.* (1990), in the NIMH outcome study comparing cognitive therapy, interpersonal psychotherapy and imipramine with clinical management and placebo in the treatment of major depression (Elkin *et al.*, 1989), reported that 74 per cent of the 178 patients satisfied criteria for at least one symptom of personality disorder according to *DSM*-III-R. Fifty-seven per cent had more than one symptom, and 53 per cent had symptoms belonging to more than one cluster of personality disorders:

Cluster I, described as 'odd–eccentric', includes paranoid, schizoid and shizotypical personality disorders; Cluster II, described as 'dramatic-erratic', includes antisocial, borderline, histrionic and narcissistic; Cluster III, described as 'anxious-fearful' includes avoidant, dependent and obsessive–compulsive personality disorders.

At the end of treatment, patients with personality disorders showed lower levels of functioning in their social and leisure activities than other patients, but their responses to the different treatments (cognitive therapy, interpersonal therapy or medication) did not differ significantly. On the other hand, Rush and Shaw (1983) commented that patients with personality disorders do not respond well to cognitive therapy, and Mays and Franks (1975) have suggested that one of the main causes of poor response to psychotherapy is the very presence of personality disorders. Tyrer *et al.* (1993) also reported in their outcome study of patients with generalised anxiety disorders, panic disorder or dysthymia that, overall, personality disorders had a negative impact.

In a review of epidemiological surveys, Weissman (1993) found that 10–13 per cent of personality disorders were diagnosed in community samples or in samples of relatives of patients with psychiatric problems. Although she estimated the lifetime prevalence of personality disorders to be low, ranging from 0.4 to 5.6 per cent, their chronic nature and associated psychopathology and social dysfunction lead to their high prevalence in the clinic. Co-morbidity typically includes depression (as mentioned above), generalised anxiety, simple phobias, agoraphobia, social phobia, alcohol abuse, obsessive–compulsive disorder and dysthymia (see Swartz *et al.* (1990) for co-morbidity with borderline personality disorder).

DEFINITION OF PERSONALITY DISORDERS

DSM-IV defines personality disorders according to clusters of traits or characteristics which are distinguished from personality traits because they have become 'inflexible, maladaptive, and persisting and cause significant functional impairment or subjective distress' (American Psychiatric Association, *DSM-IV*, 1994, p. 633). As many of the features described in the personality disorders are also present in Axis I disorders, diagnosis must be made cautiously during an acute Axis I disorder, and only if the dysfunctional personality features appeared before early adulthood and characterise the individual's long-term functioning.

Table 8.1 summarises *DSM*-IV criteria for personality disorders.

Table 8.1   General diagnostic criteria for personality disorders

---

1   An enduring pattern of inner experience and behaviour, which deviates markedly from cultural norms in two or more of the following areas:
    * *cognition* (perception and interpretation of self, others and events)
    * *emotional response* (range, intensity, lability and appropriateness)
    * *interpersonal functioning*
    * *impulse control*

2   *The enduring pattern is*
    inflexible and pervasive across a broad range of personal and social situations;
    stable and of long duration, with onset dating back to adolescence and early adulthood;
    not due to or a consequence of another mental disorder;
    not due to the physiological effects of a substance or a general medical condition.

The definition of personality disorders is not without its controversies. It is clinically based and largely ignores basic personality research in psychology. The overlap between the personality disorders puts in question their specificity and their heuristic value. Rutter (1987) concluded that he saw 'little justification for the retention of trait-defined personality disorders' (p. 453) and that, instead, personality disorders would be better 'characterised by a persistent, pervasive abnormality in social relationships and social functioning generally' (p. 454).

THE COGNITIVE MODEL

Beck *et al.* (1990) present a model of the personality disorders which is primarily inspired by clinical practice. In view of the characteristic long-standing problems found in these disorders, the authors share with psychoanalysts the belief that 'core' problems must be identified and modified. Although originally inspired by ideas from the 'ego analysts' such as Adler, Horney, Sullivan and Frankl, Beck and his colleagues propose that the core cognitive structures are not unconscious and unavailable to the patient, and that the products of these structures are largely within the realm of awareness (Ingram and Hollon, 1986). The role of the cognitive therapist is to train the patient to become more conscious of the general themes of these cognitive products, and of their associated feelings and behaviours, and thus become able to identify and modify core structures.

Beck's theory is anchored in a genetic and evolutionary view of personality. It is assumed that personality patterns reflect strategies that have been selected through evolution to facilitate survival and reproduction. Variations of these primitive strategies can be observed in an exaggerated form in syndromes such as general anxiety or depressive disorders, but also in personality disorders. The way in which information is evaluated, through information-processing and affective processes, triggers these evolutionarily based strategies, which may be adaptive or maladaptive. A situation is evaluated through the core, relatively stable, structures termed schemata. This model is represented in Figure 8.1.

The conceptualisation of personality traits as basic strategies which reflect underlying schemata, instead of being motivational drives, is central to Beck's cognitive theory of personality disorders and forms the basis of his treatment methods. The dysfunctional schemata and their associated strategies render

Figure 8.1 Personality disorder as inherited and learned survival
strategies

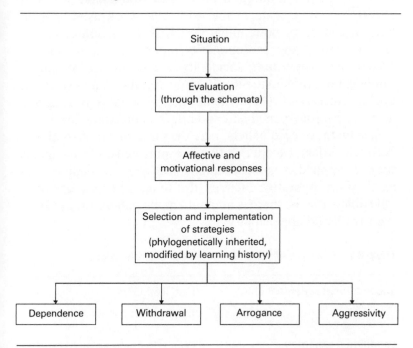

the patient vulnerable to a whole range of stimuli, because those
schemata and strategies are overgeneralised and rigid. Thus, the
dependent individual is vulnerable to loss of affection and
support from others; the narcissistic individual is vulnerable to
situations which appear to decrease his self-importance; the
avoidant individual is traumatised in any social or professional
situation where self-assertion or decisiveness is needed.

In ethological terms, the behavioural, cognitive and affective
strategies in personality disorders can be seen as the survival of
naturally selected automatic processes which might have been
adaptive in more primitive times, but which are no longer so.
They give rise to behaviours which are harmful to the individual
and/or to society. For example, highly predatory behaviour may
have been helpful for survival in the early development of man,

but in our social milieu it may be overly aggressive and 'antisocial'. Similarly, exhibitionistic display would have served to
attract help or a mate in the wild, but, when used as a behavioural strategy now, might be labelled 'histrionic' or 'hys-
terical'. Thus, any evolutionarily based behaviour, such as
predation, competition, sociability and avoidance of danger,
can become problematic if it is *excessive, inflexible and uncontrolled*. Beck *et al.* (1990) define the personality disorders in
terms of overdeveloped and underdeveloped strategies.

Schemata, or core beliefs, play the same role in Axis II as in
Axis I disorders, except that they are more generalised – that is,
they are applied to more situations; they are more stable – that
is, they are operative most of the time; and they are more
inflexible – that is, there is no doubt in the patient's mind about
their truth and applicability.

Table 8.2 Example of schemata in personality disorder

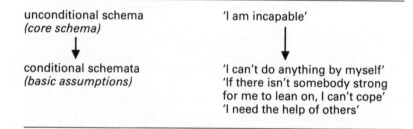

An example is given in Table 8.2. These rigid, pervasive and
negative schemata deal with information in three ways:

1 by screening out information which disconfirms the schemata;
2 by processing information which confirms the schemata;
3 by distorting positive or neutral stimuli into negative information which confirms the schemata.

Typical self-perceptions, evaluations of others and schemata
accompany each of the personality disorders. These cognitive

profiles are often shared across the disorders, the difference occurring in the characteristic behavioural strategies and the internal and external control systems. Control systems, according to Beck *et al.* (1990), are reflected in the typical self instructions found in the different disorders: for example, 'Don't trust anybody', in the paranoid patient; 'Keep at a safe distance', in the schizoid patient; 'Do everything they want', in the dependent patient; 'Draw attention to yourself', in the narcissistic patient; and 'Don't stick your neck out', in the avoidant patient.

Young (1990) and Young and Klosko (1993) propose a schema-focused approach for the early maladaptive schemata (EMS) encountered in personality disorders. Young makes two useful contributions to the theory and treatment of these disorders. Firstly, he delineates the processes which ensure the enduring quality of early maladaptive schemata:

schema-maintenance processes   The cognitive distortions, maladaptive behaviours and environmental influences which block adaptive change in the schema.

schema-avoidance   Conscious and automatic processes, which are developed to avoid the intense pain associated with the triggering of the schema. These include cognitive, affective and behavioural avoidance strategies.

schema-compensation   The development of strategies which camouflage the schema – for instance, extremely autonomous attitudes and behaviours in the dependent individual, or narcissistic behaviours in the person with a worthlessness schema.

Secondly, Young (1990) has developed very clearly defined therapeutic methods in which he emphasises the use of the therapeutic relationship and of affective methods in the treatment of personality disorders. These have been stressed less by other cognitive therapists.

In the specific area of *borderline personality disorder* Linehan (1993a, 1993b) has developed a package called dialectical behaviour therapy (DBT), which is based on a bio-social theory of the borderline personality. She stresses the social system in which the patient exists, which is often harmful. Therefore the borderline patient must learn social and self-control skills to influence that environment. Secondly, the dichotomous thinking style of the borderline patient and his or her extreme behaviours and emotions are seen as dialectical failures. The patient is stuck in opposing forces (thesis and antithesis) and unable to move to synthesis. Therapy is aimed at facilitating synthesis. Thirdly, the DBT therapist is conscious of the changing nature of reality. The therapist, the patient and the environment change over time, and the therapist should aim at becoming more comfortable with the concept of temporal change.

Finally, the main deficit in borderline personality disorder is seen as the emotional disregulation which derives from emotional vulnerability and maladaptive emotional regulation strategies. These deficits are seen as partly biologically determined and partly as resulting from an invalidating and negative environment in childhood.

DBT involves a broad array of cognitive and behavioural methods, in individual and group format, aimed at helping the patient develop psychological skills. Layden et al. (1993) also describe cognitive–behavioural methods specifically for the borderline patient. Although their treatment methods do not differ from those of Beck et al. (1990) and Young (1990), more theoretical emphasis is put on Ericksonian and Piagetian stages of development. They propose that the unsuccessful resolution of each developmental period leads to specific early maladaptive schemata in the borderline patient.

LUKE

THE REFERRAL

Luke was referred by a local community mental health team (CMHT). He was described as a 25-year-old unemployed male with chronic social and relationship difficulties. The referral outlined a difficult childhood, and four suicide attempts. Before the CMHT's assessment, he had spent two years in private counselling with little progress. He was formally diagnosed as having depression, and was currently on antidepressant medication.

THE ASSESSMENT

Symptom profile

Luke met several of the criteria for avoidant personality disorder (see *DSM*-IV, American Psychiatric Association, 1994, pp. 664–5). For example, apart from his father, there had been only one person with whom he had ever felt comfortable and whom he classed as a 'friend'. He was extremely anxious and avoidant in most social situations, and even had difficulties walking down the street during the day for fear of being seen as 'different'. Observations of him in company revealed him to be awkward, shy and apprehensive. With strangers his speech was slow and his eye contact poor. Luke found one-to-one situations easier than groups, but even then he required time before he established a relaxed body posture. However, despite his relationship difficulties, he had a great desire to be accepted by others and to form friendships.

He met the criteria for clinical depression (see p. 59), and scored high on the Hopelessness Scale – the scores are summarised on p. 245. He also displayed social phobia, agoraphobia and mild panic symptoms. But unlike these anxiety disorders, which are underpinned by worry, Luke's problems appeared to stem from a fear of intimacy as opposed to a fear of personal disaster. Most of these problems seemed to have persisted with varying degrees of severity at least since early adolescence, if not before.

At the initial screening interview, he summed up his problems as:

- 'a tendency to avoid relationships because I'm afraid of them – I'm afraid that others will not like me';

- 'difficulties going out by myself, particularly during the day, because people think I look odd';
- 'occasional drinking binges and frequent use of sleeping tablets';
- 'general boredom'.

History of the disorder

The anxiety and avoidance appeared to be lifelong. He remembered feeling an outsider in the school playground at the age of five or six. At primary school he recalled wandering around the school perimeter by himself, unsure whether he'd be accepted by the other children. Schooling remained difficult, and the first of four separate suicide attempts occurred at the age of twelve following a return to school after the holidays. His reasons for the attempt were given as:

- 'I didn't like the kids.'
- 'There was no privacy.'
- 'I wasn't doing the subjects I wanted to do.'
- 'I felt I'd rather be dead than go through another four years.'

He had a long history of contact with the psychological services, stemming back to the age of twelve, after his first overdose. He had made subsequent overdose attempts at the ages of seventeen, twenty and twenty-one. He claimed that these 'real' attempts followed periods of extreme loneliness and hopelessness: 'Although I feel lonely most of the time, sometimes it strikes me that it's never going to change.'

Before being referred to the Centre, he had received two years of private treatment. This appeared to have been a mixture of Gestalt and psychodynamic therapy, which had been more supportive than therapeutic. Throughout the eighteen months of cognitive therapy he took antidepressant medication, prescribed by a consultant psychiatrist.

Personal background

He was an only child, although there had been an older brother who had died in infancy five years before Luke was born. His parents were in their mid-forties when he was born. He appears to have gone through the normal childhood milestones (walking, talking, and so on) at the appropriate ages. The first time he remembered feeling different from others was around the age of four or five. He recalled feeling awkward and shy with other children, and made very few friends during his early school years. He claimed that there had been only one 'real' friend in his life. He had met this person (Susan) four years previously, but unfortunately she had subsequently moved abroad. Susan still kept in contact with Luke by correspondence, but her current boyfriend was unhappy with this arrangement.

Luke's mother was a social worker and his father had owned and run a grocery shop. His father died when he was eight years of age, and this had upset him at the time: 'Dad, apart from Susan, was the only one who came near to understanding me.' There was little evidence of maternal bonding: 'My mother never showed me much attention – she was more interested in her job'; 'I hated her for sending me to boarding school; she just wanted me out of the way.' There was a clear feeling on his part that his mother had never liked him, and he felt that she had both abandoned and rejected him.

Luke said that his schooling was 'unhappy, lonely and isolating'. He described himself as a very shy boy, who found speaking out difficult. For a period of his early childhood he stuttered badly, which made him more self-conscious. His quiet demeanour seemed to attract taunts and bullying from other children; this resulted in some early school avoidance. From the age of ten he went to a private boarding school in Kent, and spent a large percentage of his free time either in his room or on solitary walks. Despite being intelligent, he took a perverse pride in being unteachable. He was determined that he was not going to pass any exams – 'I don't want the teachers to bask in reflected glory.' He left school at sixteen without any formal qualifications, and went on a number of government training courses. Once again he found it very difficult to mix with the other course members, although on one of these courses he met Susan.

At assessment, he was unemployed and living by himself. He led a very unstructured life, using drink and sleeping tablets as ways of coping. He succinctly described his present lifestyle thus:

> I hate being by myself, but can't get on with other people – they scare me! I'm different to them, and they always spot it quickly . . . Each day sort of merges into another . . . most of the time it's OK, I can cope. I get up late, watch a couple of videos, play on my computer, have something to eat at 3 pm, and then read my sci-fi books until children's programmes start on the TV. I watch TV for the rest of the night, take a few sleeping tablets and go to bed – it's a routine! I don't go out much except when I run out of food. I'll choose a quiet time, when there are no schoolchildren about, and do a big shopping. If I'm lucky, my mother does the shopping for me. Occasionally, I feel really bad – I start to think, 'Is this what my life is always going to be like?' At these times I lock myself into the bathroom and lie on the floor; after a few hours I fall asleep and the worst will have passed.

Presentation

When the therapist collected Luke from the waiting-room at his first interview, she sensed an atmosphere of fear. He was a small, pale, well kempt individual. When she introduced herself his eyes barely lifted in acknowledgement of her presence, and he moved slowly and hesitantly towards her office. Once in the room, he sat down heavily and it was as if he had enveloped himself in an invisible protective cloak. The therapist knew that this was going to be a tough one! Fortunately, as time progressed the barrier began to lift, although for the first three sessions he continued to present as a rather shy, awkward man. By the fourth, however, he was clearly beginning to enjoy the therapeutic relationship. He now settled quickly – and this later transpired to be a regular pattern for him in therapy, probably because the therapeutic situation was one of the few opportunities in which he was able to talk without fear of rejection.

Summary of the assessment

Luke was a 'normal'-looking young man with chronic social and relationship difficulties, who met the criteria for avoidant personality disorder (APD). For most of his life he had found mixing with other people extremely difficult, and this often left him feeling lonely, isolated and on occasion hopeless. He had made four serious suicide attempts, and still considered this a viable option if things got too bad. He had a poor relationship with his mother, and felt that she did not like him; he claimed these feelings were reciprocal.

He was currently living alone in a city flat, not daring to go out during the day. He was unemployed and had been so since he'd left boarding school at the age of sixteen. He often got bored with his own company, and this resulted in occasional binge drinking. He also took sleeping tablets, when he was feeling particularly bad. He was on antidepressant medication, and had been for the last five years. He was currently under the care of a local consultant psychiatrist.

From the referral, and from the initial experience of working with him, it was clear that Luke's was going to be a long-term case. Once this had been acknowledged, it was felt imperative to organise some good peer supervision for the therapist during the work to come.

SUITABILITY FOR SHORT-TERM COGNITIVE THERAPY

The suitability scale (Table 8.3, overleaf) suggested that in many respects Luke was not suitable for cognitive therapy. But one must accept that people with personality disorders are invariably difficult to treat, whatever therapeutic rationale is used, and it was encouraging to note that he was positive about the cognitive model, could access some negative automatic thoughts, and showed good collaboration within sessions. There were, however, a number of particularly bad portents for prognosis – in particular, the chronicity of his difficulties and his tendency to avoid issues – both emotionally and behaviourally.

Table 8.3   Suitability for Short-term Cognitive Therapy Rating Scale (Safran and Segal, 1990)

	Suitability ratings (poor 0–5 good)	
1	Accessibility of automatic thoughts	3.0
2	Awareness and differentiation of emotions	2.0
3	Acceptance of personal responsibility for change	2.0
4	Compatibility with cognitive rationale	2.0
5	Alliance potential (in session)	3.0
6	Alliance potential (out of session)	1.0
7	Chronicity of problems	1.0
8	Security operations	1.0
9	Focality	2.0
10	Patient optimism/pessimism regarding therapy	2.5
	Total score	19.5

INITIAL FORMULATION

By the fourth session, the initial formulation had been produced in collaboration with Luke. Much of that session involved constructing the details of the formulation. It was formally written up in a four-page collaborative document, under the headings of Presenting Problem, Background, Formulation and Treatment Plan. It was typed and presented to Luke at the following session, and referred to and revised as treatment progressed. It is important to note that some therapists prefer to share the formulations at a later stage in therapy (see p. 72).

Luke's initial formulation is illustrated by using one of the examples taken from his dysfunctional-thoughts diaries (Figure 8.2). This represents one of the early behavioural tests he was asked to perform – to accept an invitation to a neighbour's

Figure 8.2   Initial formulation

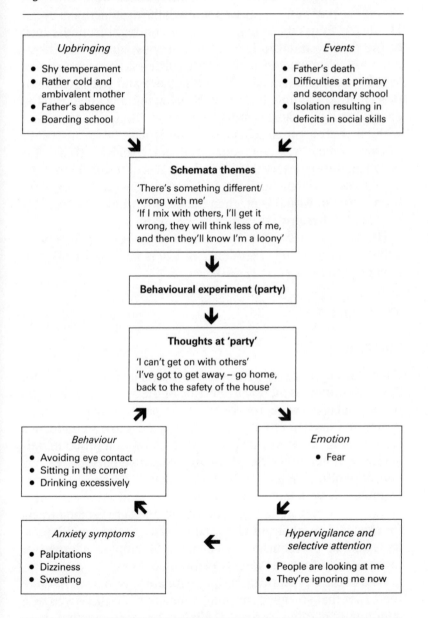

party. As one can see, the schematic themes were activated during the party and expressed through the dysfunctional cycle. He clearly found the situation difficult, and right from the start of the party wanted to leave. But one must admire his determination in staying there, despite his distress. It was interesting to see (under the heading, Hypervigilance and selective attention) that he was able to rationalise what initially appears to be contradictory evidence into a perspective that was consistent with his dysfunctional schemata – that is, that he is 'different'.

This scenario was very typical of other social settings (for instance, during his weekly shopping). It is noteworthy that the only occasions when he didn't feel fearful were those spent with Susan: 'If I'm with Susan, then people will think I'm part of a couple and therefore they'll think I'm normal.'

For a good review of the formulation process of people with avoidant personality disorders, and personality disorders in general, see Beck et al. (1990).

TREATMENT

The Plan

An idealised image of the treatment plan is presented in Figure 8.3. This outline is merely a heuristic of the approach taken. Its basic principles were to (1) build up patient–therapist trust during the assessment stages, and increase Luke's confidence within the first few weeks; (2) provide him with a broad understanding of his difficulties through a cognitive perspective, via educational techniques (this stage included sharing the initial formulation with him and outlining potential treatment procedures); (3) negotiate a plan of action, and agree some targets for change; (4) enhance Luke's self-efficacy, as this was felt to be an essential prerequisite to change; (5) employ a range of techniques to fulfil the targets mentioned above.

One of the key features of the treatment was to instil in Luke the belief that so-called 'normal' behaviour is best viewed as a continuum: in other words, to help him to appreciate that there

Figure 8.3   Treatment plan

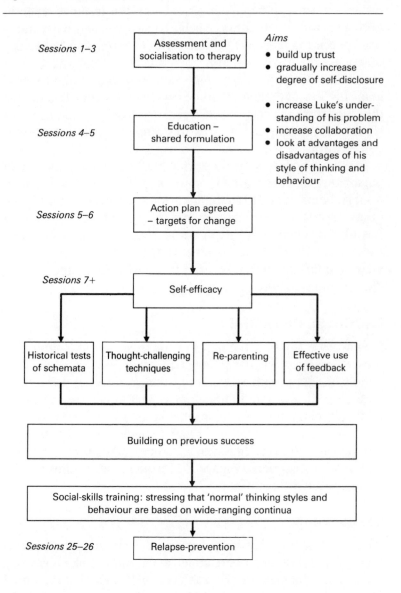

are relatively few absolutes regarding behaviour (that is, 'right' or 'wrong' ways to behave in situations). For instance, even in fairly prescriptive situations, such as being in expensive restaurants, people have many different styles of eating and frequently do not use the correct cutlery. This issue of 'normalising' human variability was particularly important in helping Luke to challenge his 'me' and 'them' attitude (that is, his feeling that he was different from the rest of society). Successfully challenging his rigidity of thinking in this area was a major goal of the therapeutic work.

In schematic terms, the key principles of treating people with personality disorders are (1) to weaken their existing dysfunctional schemata, and (2) to build up more adaptive ones. Unlike other disorders, where it is felt that the patient is aware of what it is like to function 'normally', it is suggested that people like Luke may never have experienced this 'normality'. When viewed in this manner, it is easier to see why the treatment is so much more difficult.

PROGRESS OF THERAPY

It is noteworthy that the methods of treatment are similar to those employed when dealing with other disorders, because people like Luke with avoidant personality disorder suffer from a number of associated difficulties – such as certain aspects of social phobia, panic with agoraphobia, depression and anxiety. The aspects outlined below, which include details of the contents of the various techniques, are some of the more distinctive features of treatment. Figure 8.3 provides an outline of the timing of the interventions.

Sessions 4–6

After the first three sessions of assessment and socialisation into therapy, these sessions were aimed at *educating* Luke regarding the role of schemata in his problems, and at sharing the initial formulation with him. Padesky's (1990) 'schema as self-prejudice' metaphor was used to explain to him how schemata

operate, and with the assistance of Socratic questioning particular biases in information-processing were demonstrated. For
example, Luke was asked to outline a deeply held prejudice of a
friend or relation which he did not hold himself:

Luke: My uncle dislikes women politicians.
Therapist: What would he say if a woman politician made a big
   political gaffe?
L: He'd say something like 'I told you so!'
T: All right, what if she was successful?
L: He'd probably ignore it, or discount it somehow. For
   example, he used to say that Mrs Thatcher was an exception
   to the rule – a sort of 'man's man' with a handbag.

Taken further, this technique helped Luke to appreciate the
various types of distortions used by people to help maintain
their entrenched beliefs. It helped him to appreciate that he
might be adopting similar cognitive biases in his assumption
about being 'different'. The example was further used as a
vehicle by which he could start making suggestions about ways
of trying to change such entrenched views: for instance, by
monitoring distortions, by challenging global statements, by
looking for alternative ways of thinking, and by using facts and
evidence rather than 'emotional' thinking.
   Young (1990) also proposes that educating the patient about
schemata – or, in his language, 'early maladaptive schemas'
(EMS) – is of crucial importance. In order to facilitate this, he
has produced *A Client's Guide to Schema-focused Cognitive
Therapy*. This useful leaflet, which includes a section on 'How
schemas work', was given to Luke and he found it particularly
informative. With the help of the therapist, he recognised that
his cognitive biases, his avoidance of social contacts and his
occasional aggressive and superior attitude were all processes
which maintained the rigidity of his schema of 'being different
from others'.
   Following assessment and introduction to the cognitive
model, Luke started to make some suggestions about specific

treatment targets (that is, an *action plan*). Yet when it came to making a formal action plan he had great difficulties whittling down his problems to manageable goals. As predicted in his Suitability for Cognitive Therapy scores (Table 8.3), he found it difficult to focus on specific issues and break them down into appropriate steps, and was reluctant to take personal responsibility for change.

It started to become apparent at this point, as he was moving into the more active phase of treatment, that he preferred to view the meetings as social support rather than therapeutic sessions. In the past, a lot of the help he had received had been of the former kind, and he had not been expected to work too actively in trying to change. It was clear that the previous passivity would not suit the requirements of cognitive therapy treatment. When this issue was broached directly in session 5, the proceedings became very uncomfortable as he evidently felt threatened. Nonetheless, by the end of that session a formal contract had been achieved, comprising long-term and short-term goals.

Long-term goals Twenty-five sessions of cognitive therapy treatment, by the end of which:

• he would be able to feel comfortable walking in daylight by himself;
• he would be able to speak to other people without feeling fearful;
• he would have reduced his intake of alcohol and sleeping tablets;
• he would go to college and do an introductory GCSE course.

Short-term goals Plans were collaboratively constructed at the end of each treatment session. Here is an example of one of the early homework plans – tasks to be fulfilled before the next fortnightly session:

• take one trip a day out of the house during daylight hours, for a minimum of 15 minutes;

- speak to at least two people during each day – for instance, ask someone the time, ask a shop assistant for help; not bulk-purchase any alcohol;
- clean house and tidy garden, specifically asking to borrow the vacuum cleaner from the neighbour.

In addition to this behavioural work, Luke agreed to keep a record of his progress in a notebook, which would include details of his behavioural and thought-challenging work. This notebook also contained photocopies of his dysfunctional-thoughts diaries and monitoring procedures. Frequent reference to it reminded him of his progress, and of the effective and non-effective aspects of treatment.

Sessions 7–10

Once a good working relationship had been established with Luke, and he had been educated in the cognitive therapeutic style, it was time to move towards tackling some of his initial goals. In order to do this, it was necessary to increase his self-efficacy across a number of situations. So he was asked to select some of his problem situations and to estimate (1) the threat posed by a particular situation, and (2) his own capacity to cope in that situation. Interventions were then planned to give him the opportunity to appraise the problem situations more realistically. For example:

Therapist: When you go into a shop, what are you afraid of?
Luke: If I can't find what I want, I'll have to ask the assistant for help.
T: Now, when you ask for help how do you feel, and what goes through your mind?
L: Threatened, because the assistant might ignore me – sometimes people do ignore me.
T: If you can remember the last time someone ignored you in this sort of situation – what happened?
L: I went to the cheese counter and took a ticket for my turn in the queue. But when it came to my number, someone jumped in front of me.

T: What interpretation did you put on this?
L: They can see that I shouldn't be there. They probably think I'm odd – different from everybody else!

On further examination of this situation, it became clear that Luke was very hesitant in speaking up when his turn came. Indeed, when his number came up he was too anxious to draw attention to himself, and although he spoke to the assistant, his voice was very weak. From his description it was possible to draw up the scenario outlined in Table 8.4, which sets out the perceived threats and provides some potential coping strategies. These practical coping skills allowed him, for the first time, to test out formally his dysfunctional perceptions.

Table 8.4   Problem-solving chart, outlining threats and relevant coping skills

Threats	Coping skills required
1 I will be ignored. People will know I've got it wrong. I will get embarrassed and feel bad 2 The thought that I'm odd and so easily overlooked	• To stand in line and not to one side of the queue • To make eye contact with assistant when my turn comes • To speak clearly – perhaps prepare what I'm going to say while in the queue

As part of this work, some assertiveness skills were introduced and role-played. He found these exercises very difficult, but he conceded the importance of developing such skills.

Sessions 11–20

At this stage the focus turned to challenging Luke's schema, using a variety of methods. His belief that he was 'different' was often recorded at 100 per cent: 'I'm not like other people, and I never have been.' However, the use of a *historical test* – from birth to present day – showed evidence of periods in his life when he felt less 'different'. Therapist and patient constructed a time line to highlight this feature (Figure 8.4, overleaf). The therapist ensured, through guided discovery, that Luke did not at any time give himself a rating of 0 ('I'm totally different'), as this would clearly serve to reinforce this dysfunctional notion. So a technique called the 'continuum method' (discussed in greater detail later) was used, whereby he was asked to think of people from his past, or of whom he was aware, who could be classified as being more different than himself. The people he thought of as more different (or weirder) than himself included Hitler, Jesus Christ, hermits and his mother. Figure 8.4 illustrates the end result of this exercise, which took several sessions.

Following a brief exchange which ended up with the therapist pointing out that there was little evidence that people were looking at him strangely as he walked down the street, Luke remarked: 'It's very clever the way you can trick me into saying that I'm not different, but I know "me" better than you do, and I know what it is really like out there.' The lesson learned from the exchange was that he needed to be more quizzical than direct about his thought/behaviour discrepancies, and hope that he would resolve the inconsistencies in his thinking himself. The revised questioning took the following form – using as an example his reluctance to walk around the town during daylight hours by himself:

Therapist: You said that when you were walking around the park with Susan you didn't feel in any way awkward or different. Is that right?

Luke: Yes, I didn't seem to notice the other people around me.

T: When you were with Susan, did you dress differently, or walk differently – was your appearance different in any way?

L: I don't think so.

T: What was the reason you didn't feel different in this situation?

L: I don't know . . . I suppose it was just that I was more interested in the conversation than what the other people were thinking.

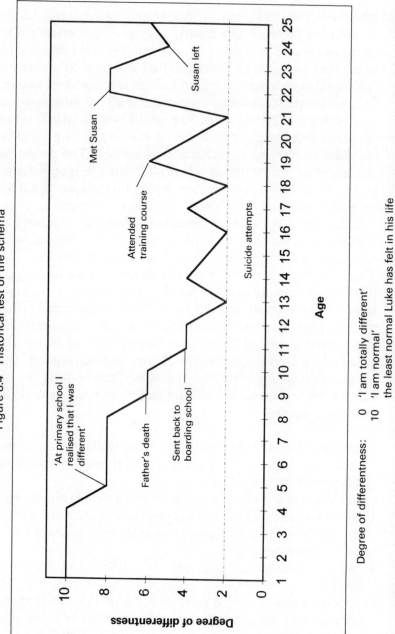

Figure 8.4 Historical test of the schema

Degree of differentness:
0 'I am totally different'
10 'I am normal'
the least normal Luke has felt in his life

T: When you're walking during the day by yourself, do you often worry what other people might be saying about you?

L: Yes, all of the time. I think that they can spot that I'm odd.

T: So let's see . . . when you're by yourself you think you look different and people will notice this immediately. But when you're with Susan, dressed exactly the same way and acting in a pretty similar manner, you feel completely at ease. The only change seems to be that in one case you're focusing on yourself and in the other you're focusing on something else. It's amazing how that little shift of focus seems to help you.

L: I suppose so. It's to do with what you're thinking about at the time.

In this case, had the therapist said something like 'Isn't this direct evidence of your thoughts affecting your behaviour?', this would have met his schemata head-on and he would have used it as evidence of the therapist not understanding the true nature of his problem. So the indirect, quizzical approach was more effective. Likewise, it was felt better not to offer direct praise after he had successfully carried out a behavioural task (by saying, for instance, 'Well done – it was great that you walked through the park. I knew that you could do it') – this might have been met with similar resistance, and could have been seen as patronising and as further evidence that his problem had not been appreciated.

Another method used to weaken the processes maintaining the schema was *thought-challenging and the use of continua*. Statements from Luke's diaries, and from details in the sessions, revealed the following dysfunctional, global, internal and stable attributes:

- 'I am not the same as other people.'
- 'I am boring.'

When attempting to deal with such statements, the therapist needed to help Luke break down the global statements into more specific meanings. This was done with the downward-arrowing technique: for instance, with Luke it was important to determine what he actually meant by being 'different'. He answered this by saying: 'I am unlikeable; I've no social skills.' Each of these statements was then put on a continuum with extremes at the poles.

1   Test statement: 'I am unlikeable'

0+ .... +100
'I am   'I am the
the most unlikeable   most likeable
person in the world'   in the world'

2   Test statement: 'I've no social skills'

0+ .... +100
'I have no   'I am extremely
social skills'   skilled socially'

He first rated himself as 0 on each of these continua. But then through Socratic questioning he was able to explore and challenge his reasoning for such statements. For example, on examination of the first statement he was able to say that there were people whom he considered to be less likeable than he was; and, in addition, that he possessed various characteristics that he liked about himself. It was also true that he had a number of social skills that he valued, and he was able to employ many of these skills both with Susan and in the therapeutic relationship. He re-rated himself as 30 and 40 respectively. It was then determined where he would like to be: at 60–70. More dicussion led to a list of what was needed to reach these higher ratings:

• to be able to speak to people without feeling anxious;
• to be able to make good eye contact;
• to be able to present himself confidently.

The function of the schema was examined by looking at the *advantages and disadvantages* of maintaining his current ways of thinking. In addition, throughout his therapy Luke had been being trained in the use of cognitive therapy techniques – that is, identifying his basic negative automatic thoughts (NATs) and behaviours, and their relationship to his low mood, and then challenging them. Because of the rigidity of his thinking, the thought-challenging exercises were initially very difficult. For instance, he would return with diary sheets with numerous challenges to the initial NATs, but without any change in the belief rating in the original NAT or in the accompanying emotions (Table 8.5).

Table 8.5   Example of diary showing no change in affect

Negative automatic thought (NAT)	Emotion and rating	Thought-challenge	Emotion and re-rating	Belief in NAT
'People are looking at me – they can tell I'm different' Belief: 100%	Fear 90%	'They are probably looking at my new coat' Belief: 30%	fear 90%	90%

At times it appeared that he enjoyed coming back and saying: 'I tried to answer my thoughts, but it didn't change the way I felt.' The reasons for this were numerous. For instance, the thought-challenges, as in the example in Table 8.5, were not thorough enough to be convincing. Sometimes he had not assessed the real 'hot' cognitions. So now the thoughts and the challenges were reviewed in session, and he became more adept at this exercise, with concomitant improvement in his mood ratings.

It also became evident that the thoughts recorded were not addressing the true schematic issues. Once again, the downward-arrowing technique was helpful in elucidating the core dysfunctional belief. From such work the theme of being 'unlikeable' emerged again. Having elucidated this by responding to Socratic questioning, Luke was then able to construct some potent thought-challenges that specifically addressed the issue. For example:

- 'Just because they are looking at me, it does not mean that they don't like me.'
- 'You cannot decide whether or not someone is likeable until you get to know them properly.'

Another technique that Luke found somewhat helpful in challenging his thoughts was a version of Young *et al.*'s (1993) 'schema-therapy flashcard'. He kept a copy of the flashcard questions is his pocket notebook, which he carried around with him. The technique required him to ask the following questions of himself whenever he felt a low or anxious mood being triggered:

1 *Feeling* – 'How are you feeling right now? I am feeling . . . because [give reason] . . .'
2 *Identification of schema(s)* – 'This is my . . . schema being activated; this will exaggerate the degree to which . . .'
3 *Reality of situation* – 'Even though I feel . . . , the reality is . . .'
4 *Behaviour* – 'Even though I feel . . . , I could go and do . . . to help myself.'

Luke said that this technique, although it produced neither a great revelation nor an immediate change in his mood, helped to take the edge off his difficulties: 'The flashcards help me to focus on something, and think through things during some of my worst moments.'

When working with people with personality disorders it quickly becomes apparent that the therapeutic relationship is an important vehicle for change – hence, special attention needs to be given to it. Young (1990) suggests that part of the treatment should involve a 're-parenting' process. Here the therapist is attempting to provide a warm, accepting and consistent relationship to make up for deficits in the childhood environment. For Luke, re-parenting involved providing unconditional positive regard, being there when needed (for example, accepting telephone calls at unscheduled times) and giving him 'permission' to do things that he had wished his parents had allowed him to do. This meant encouraging him to 'allow himself' the weekly treat of buying a take-away meal. Previously, he had considered this as too self-indulgent.

This process was surprisingly helpful in promoting some flexibility into both his thinking and his behaviour patterns. The importance of the exercise was that he learned that previous life patterns could be changed. It also improved his socialisation skills, by promoting greater contact with other people. By the end of treatment he knew the pizza man on first-name terms.

Sessions 21–24

Luke's mother attended sessions 21 and 22 with him. This helped both to examine their relationship and to get a wider perspective of his problems. During these sessions his mother was able to provide him with some direct feedback on the influence of his behaviour on others. In addition, she was able to speak about her feelings towards Luke. She admitted, and apologised for, the ambivalence she felt towards him. She felt that this had probably been the result of having been devastated by the death of her first son: 'Although I find it very difficult to admit to myself, I was so hurt. Then Luke came along, and it was as if I was going through the motions with him.' These sessions were extremely emotional, and a debriefing was necessary after each one.

The emotions that Luke expressed in these sessions formed an important focus of discussion in the subsequent two sessions. He became tearful for the first time, and frightened. He realised that he had been frightened to acknowledge his emotions, because it might result in his being overwhelmed by them. But this had put him under an awful lot of pressure – as in the case of the poor little Dutch boy, there was an awful lot of water surging up behind his meagre plug.

The advantages and disadvantages and the consequences of sharing emotions were discussed in detail. The outcome was the realisation that his fear of being overwhelmed had resulted in his being emotionally avoidant. Unfortunately, this produced a rather distant attitude, which was often mistaken by others as lack of interest. It was agreed, after discussion, that this served to make him even more isolated, and to reinforce his sense of 'differentness'.

In the past Luke had used external coping mechanisms (drink and/or sleeping tablets) to deal with his emotions, which was clearly a matter of great concern. Hence, part of the therapeutic work explored the use of more adaptive coping strategies, and the general role and function of anxiety in his life. It was stressed that in order to overcome his current fears he would have to be prepared to experience some anxiety, and that currently the avoidance of these fears was perpetuating his dysfunctional cycle.

It is important to note that if Susan had not moved away she too would have been invited to attend, because she was an extremely important person in his life. In many ways it was she who gave him hope for the future – 'If I can make friends with her, there are probably other people who might like me.'

The use of *feedback* was seen as a crucial aspect of therapy for Luke. Because of his avoidance, he didn't know what was expected of him – 'I don't know what's normal!' (The feeding-back of information regarding behaviour, feelings and social skills is sometimes seen as part of the 'limited re-parenting' approach.) Feedback often led on to the role-playing of scenarios that he had previously found difficult.

An attempt to use imagery in order to recreate painful experiences in his childhood, at home and at school, was unsuccessful. If successful, this method would have helped evoke past painful emotions and interpretations which had played a role in moulding his early maladaptive schema. The therapist would then have helped him react to the key situations as an adult in the shoes of the child. However, Luke would not engage in this emotive approach – his avoidance was still too strong.

FINAL FORMULATION

In addition to the framework outlined in Figure 8.2, therapy emphasised two important underlying beliefs: (1) 'I'm unlikeable' – an unconditional belief; (2) 'If my emotions spiral out of control, I'll be left a wreck' – a conditional belief. The belief that he was 'unlikeable' had already become evident during previous sessions, and it was powerfully illustrated within the sessions with his mother. She had found it difficult to bond with Luke during his childhood – probably, as she had suggested, because of the impact of her first son's death in infancy. It was hypothesised that Luke might have sensed her ambivalence, and, combined with his naturally shy temperament, this might have resulted in his early childhood difficulties. These difficulties might have been further exacerbated by his father's early death, and then by the sense of further rejection when he was sent away to boarding school. Thus it appears that he internalised from his early experiences some core beliefs about being inherently 'unlovable' and 'different' – 'a reject'!

Because of such beliefs and their interaction with those described in Figure 8.2, it was evident that many of Luke's difficulties had been compounded by deficits in his social skills. In order to combat these shortcomings, social-skills training was integrated into therapy. More formal work was also done in a social skills group, in which he participated with four other patients. Despite his initial difficulties with this, he was encouraged to persevere and it proved very helpful in the long run.

OUTCOME

Psychometric scores

After the first session, Luke was required to complete a set of baseline measures, one of which was Young's schema questionnaire (YSQ) (Young, 1990). This 123-item unvalidated list was specifically designed to identify dysfunctional schemata. It comprised fifteen schema themes, as outlined in Table 8.6, and was subdivided into three meta-schema themes: autonomy, worthiness and connectedness. Young does not make any psychometric claims for this questionnaire and as yet has not produced any norms for it, although validation work is currently being carried out on the YSQ revised version (Young and Brown, 1990). The original version appears to be seen more as a therapeutic tool, to help with the assessment procedure, rather than as a diagnostic or criterion questionnaire in its own right.

Consistent with the issues highlighted in the assessment, Luke scored particularly high on issues to do with differentness, social difficulties and inadequacy. Also in line with his diagnosis of avoidant personality disorder, there was a strong feeling that his social and emotional needs were important issues but were not being met. His scores are shown in Table 8.6.

Unfortunately, Luke failed to complete the YSQ at post-

Table 8.6 Luke's scores on Young's schema questionnaire

Meta-schema			
Autonomy	*Average score*	*Worthiness*	*Average score*
• Dependence	4.7	• Defectiveness/ unlovability	5.8
• Subjugation	4.7	• Social undesirability	5.6
• Vulnerability to harm or illness	3.7	• Incompetence/failure	4.9
• Fear of losing control	3.1	• Guilt/punishment	2.6
Connectedness		• Shame/ embarrassment	5.6
• Emotional deprivation	5.7	• Unrelenting standards	4.4
• Abandonment/loss	4.2	• Entitlement/ insufficient limit	3.5
• Distrust	4.2		
• Social isolation/ alienation	5.7		

Maximum severity score: 6; minimum: 1

treatment stage, and so a measure of the impact of treatment could not be made. However, pre- and post-treatment measures were obtained on the following tests: Beck Depression Inventory (BDI) (Beck *et al.*, 1961); Hopelessness Scale (HS) (Beck *et al.*, 1974); Dysfunctional Attitude Scale (DAS) (Weissman and Beck, 1978); Automatic Thoughts Questionnaire (ATQ) (Hollon and Kendall, 1980); State-Trait Anxiety Inventory (STAI-S) (Speilberger *et al.*, 1970). For a description of the questionnaires and their norms see p. 64. The scores are presented in Figure 8.5.

Figure 8.5   Pre- and post-treatment psychometric scores

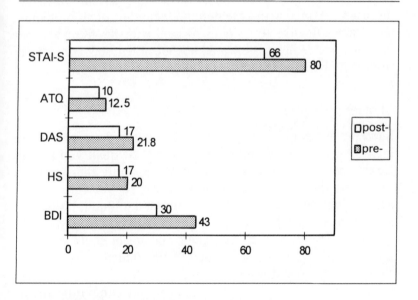

DAS and ATQ scores were reduced by a factor of 10

STAI-S   State–Trait Anxiety Inventory – State Version
ATQ   Automatic Thoughts Questionnaire
DAS   Dysfunctional Attitude Scale
HS   Hopelessness Scale
BDI   Beck Depression Inventory

As can be seen from the histogram, even after a full course of treatment Luke was still scoring high on all of the measures; especially worrying was his high score on the Hopelessness Scale – a score of 15+ is believed to indicate a high risk of suicide. Despite this rather disheartening profile, there was a clear downward trend in the data.

In addition, the high post-treatment scores may reflect some of his disappointment at being discharged: 'I don't feel that I'm ready for discharge yet – eighteen months isn't really a long time, compared to your whole life.' The issue of discharge was spoken about at length in the sessions leading up to the end of treatment. It was pointed out that cognitive therapy had clearly helped him to change the way he viewed himself, the world and his future. Armed with a greater understanding of his problems, and some effective techniques to deal with his thoughts, behaviours and feelings, he would now be able to take on greater responsibility for change.

Clinical outcome

Success with people with chronic personality disorder is often measured in terms of improvements in their quality of life. In Luke's case, this is where the most apparent changes were made. At the end of twenty-six sessions, he was able to walk around the town by himself. He continued to find it difficult to go to busy places, but he now enjoyed daily walks in the park. During therapy, as well as joining the social skills group he had started attending a fortnightly introductory course designed for pre-registration students at the local college. He had decided to study GCSE mathematics and computing in the next academic year. Another rather positive note was his successful attempt to organise, through his GP, ongoing social services support. He did this after the fifteenth session of treatment, when the issue of discharge was first broached. Social services put him in contact with a student helper organisation whose remit was to work with people 'in need' within the community. He struck up a warm relationship with one of the male helpers, and made occasional visits to the pub (at quiet times!).

When Luke was seen at six-months follow-up, it was found that his gains had been maintained. There was no evidence of any further progress, although he was hoping to take a further two GCSEs next autumn. He was due to be seen in two months' time for his twelve-months follow-up.

RELAPSE-PREVENTION

Sessions 25–26

Before he was discharged, a relapse-prevention programme was devised for Luke. Because of the lack of empirical research in this area for people with personality disorders, there was no proven relapse-prevention programme to call upon. However, the model proposed by Beck *et al.* (1990) was used because of its obvious validity. The plan involves encouraging the patient to try to establish new friendships; to deepen existing relationships; to take more responsibility; to become more assertive; to check avoidance; and to try new experiences. All these aims had been tackled during therapy, and ways of expanding on acquired gains were also discussed.

As with other relapse programmes, Luke was also encouraged to predict future problems. During the penultimate session he was asked, as part of a homework assignment, to answer a typical series of relapse questions – for example:

- What should I do if I start to avoid things again?
- What should I do if I have a setback?
- What should I do if my new friend leaves, as Susan did?

One of the important features of the relapse work, especially considering the high hopelessness scores, was an anti-suicide programme: it was based on the writings of Persons (1989) and Blackburn and Davidson (1995). Luke's programme went as follows.

1 *Production of a case formulation*   The 'wheel of misfortune' was drawn (see Figure 8.6), outlining the behaviours, feelings, events and thoughts that precipitated suicidal ideations and gestures. Spelling out these features helped to guide the relapse-prevention programme, and additionally provided Luke with a summary of main hazards.

2 *Behavioural interventions*   (a) Luke wrote a no-suicide pact; (b) he was encouraged not to stock sleeping tablets in the house; (c) he wrote an anti-suicide flashcard, which helped him to generate and test alternative solutions to his problems; (d) after extensive discussion, reasons for living and reasons for dying were listed in favour of living.

These various lists were written in Luke's pocket notebook. In addition, he agreed to contact the Cognitive Therapy Centre whenever he felt that he was at serious risk, or was experiencing significant suicidal ideations.

DISCUSSION

It cannot be said that Luke's life had been changed considerably by the end of treatment. Indeed, he was neither jumping around the park like a spring lamb, nor conversing nonchalantly with complete strangers. He was still spending up to 80–85 per cent of his time by himself. In terms of schema change (see pp. 19–20), only the lowest level had probably been reached – that is, schema camouflage. Nonetheless, significant changes had been made and, although his progress was slow, the prognostic signs were favourable. He had developed an appreciation of his dysfunctional cycles and their consequences, and was well aware of his profile of cognitive biases. He had also become more focused, and had developed the skill of breaking down previously insurmountable problems into more manageable constituent parts; and, finally, he had accepted personal responsibility for change. For what appeared to be the first time in his life he was able to tolerate anxiety, and stay with the distress, in order to learn that he could live with it. One of the major cognitive reasons for this change was the development of a

Figure 8.6   Luke's suicide formulation – his 'wheel of misfortune'

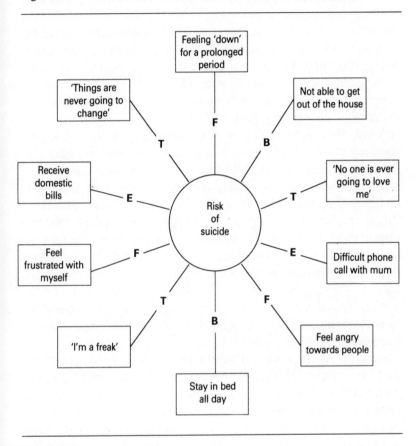

T = Thought
B = Behaviour
E = Event
F = Feeling

degree of flexibility in his thinking. The fact that he accepted that his initial thoughts (NATs) might not necessarily be correct allowed him to challenge his previously rigid perspective of the world. Hence, there had been a definite shift from an intuitive towards an inductive and deductive thinking style.

By definition, people with an avoidant personality are usually difficult to engage in treatment. So it is usually necessary for the therapist to 'play herself in' carefully. This was certainly necessary with Luke, who was sensitive to questioning techniques during the first three sessions – trust was clearly an issue. Nonetheless, he settled quite quickly thereafter, and a good rapport developed. This may have been due, in part at least, to his familiarity with the patient role.

Some therapists feel that it is important to set up a firm contract of attendance with this group of people. However, in the present case, because of Luke's extreme avoidance and high hopelessness scores the early therapeutic contract was fairly flexible. Nonetheless, after a cancellation or a failure to attend, the therapist made a point of telephoning him at the first opportunity to discuss the current problem. After the first ten sessions, a new, firmer contract was made, which stipulated that two failed appointments would result in termination of treatment. Often, his reasons for his failure to attend were on the surface trivial: for example, 'I overslept for my twelve o'clock appointment.' But it was important to acknowledge that this behaviour might have been a manifest aspect of his avoidance schemata. At such times it would have been easy to reject him, and terminate therapy – a short-term relief for both therapist and patient. However, rather than reacting in this way, the therapist chose to construe the avoidance as Luke testing her out. She saw this as an opportunity to provide him with some evidence to counteract his schematic assumption, to offer him the idea that rejection or abandonment is not an inevitable outcome of a relationship.

When working with people with personality disorders it is often easy to feel de-skilled. At such times it helped to sit down with Luke and reassess the advantages and disadvantages of his staying in therapy. This process allowed both parties to examine the progress that had been made, and to put some kind of perspective on the current difficulties. This case illustrates that perhaps the most important thing to remember, when treating patients with personality disorders, is that the sessions will be taxing for the therapist as well as for the patient; progress will be very slow, and the process often circular. With this in mind, it is vital to organise the sessions appropriately. For example, it is better to avoid weekly sessions, because this can be both threatening to the patient, particularly to someone with avoidant characteristics, and draining on the therapist.

It is also important to remember – and this is not the case for many patients with other disorders – that it is the norm for the patient's schemata to be *constantly* active within the therapeutic arena. Thus his rigid, pervasive style of thinking will often act as a barrier and at times may be actively undermining the treatment. It is also worth remembering that the patient's schemata have a tendency to activate the therapist's own schemata: here, the therapist alternated between feelings of rejection and guilt towards Luke. These feelings are often uncomfortable, but they are important in giving the therapist insight into the effect the person has on other people. For these reasons, and others, it is vital that the therapist have good peer supervision, in order to work effectively with people who have personality disorder.

Finally, the treatment goals may need to be scaled down. Indeed, it may not be possible to achieve a great shift in terms of conventional outcome measures, but one may be able to improve the person's quality of life considerably.

9

Epilogue

In this last chapter, we shall comment on the general principles that have guided us in our choice of subject-matter, on implications for training in cognitive therapy, and on future directions in practice and research.

GENERAL PRINCIPLES

In the first place, this is not an introductory book to cognitive therapy. (Several such books already exist: Beck *et al.*, 1979; Hawton *et al.*, 1989; Blackburn and Davidson, 1995; Williams, 1992.) We have assumed a certain degree of knowledge and experience in our readers.

Our intention in the first two chapters was to give to practising cognitive therapists and to trainees in cognitive therapy background information about the theory that underlies the therapy and the empirical work on which this approach is based. Although the book is primarily meant to be a demonstration of cognitive therapy in action, we believe it essential that cognitive therapists be fully cognisant with both aspects. Cognitive therapy has, right from the beginning, been empirical in its approach, and this has been its strength and appeal. Knowledge of the therapy's scientific background increases therapists' confidence in their approach, and this confidence is in turn imparted to their patients, increasing both hope and collaboration. Hope

(Frank, 1973) has rightly been considered an essential ingredient of any therapy.

The tenor of the book has been to emphasise the need for cognitive therapists to be well versed not only in cognitive theories and research but also in psychopathology, and to have the general qualities of all good therapists – namely, warmth, genuineness, empathy and understanding (Truax and Carkuff, 1967). A recurring theme has been the central role of an explicit and collaboratively elaborated formulation in therapy. This, as well described by Persons (1989), is based on general knowledge of the disorder, familiarity with the relevant theory and research, general clinical experience and extensive experience of cognitive therapy; and, importantly, on the ability to listen to the explicit and implicit communications of the patient and to make sense of his or her world.

Without such a case-formulation approach, the therapist would be like a traveller without a map or an explorer with no destination, going round in circles and perpetually distracted by immediate objects of potential interest. The formulation helps to give direction and focus to the therapy, but also to ensure that relevant work is done in a relatively short time. The cases we describe, who are all real-life cases as seen in a specialised clinic, although differing widely, improved to a marked extent within nine to twenty-six sessions. The long-term case, the one presenting with an Axis I disorder (depression) as well as with an Axis II diagnosis (avoidant personality disorder), made modest, but nonetheless remarkable changes in twenty-six sessions.

Although the style of therapy may differ somewhat across cases – indicating that cognitive therapy is not a straitjacket – between them they exemplified several important aspects of this treatment method. In addition to the cognitive conceptualisation, emphasised above, and the short-term format, stress is put on careful evaluation and assessment and on structure within and across sessions. Collaborative empiricism underlies the *modus operandi*, and is encouraged in the patient from the very beginning of therapy – through Socratic questioning, behavioural experiments and homework assignments. Above all, we have wanted to show how, while remaining within the recommended structure, style and content of cognitive therapy, the clinician can be flexible and creative.

AREAS NOT ADDRESSED IN THIS BOOK

What the case studies described in Chapters 3–8 demonstrate is the expansion of cognitive therapy from its application to depression into numerous other areas. It must be noted, though, that several important and interesting growth areas have not been addressed – for example, social phobia, the psychoses, health anxiety, psychological concomitants of physical illness (cancer, pain, dermatological disorder) and post-traumatic stress disorder; and the use of cognitive therapy with children and adolescents, with survivors of sexual abuse and with dysfunctional couples. The list could be endless, if all current areas of practice and research were included. Because of the insistence on empirical evaluation, growth in these areas is necessarily slow, but several experimental and case studies have already appeared.

Examples from two growth areas, psychosis and social phobia, will illustrate how cognitive therapy in the clinic develops from experimental work. Some of the work in delusions and hallucinations in psychotic patients was described in Chapter 2. Of interest are the experimental studies which attempt to determine the exact nature of biased reasoning in schizophrenic patients (Huq *et al.*, 1988; Bentall, 1994; Garety *et al.*, 1991). In these studies attributional biases and errors in probabilistic inferences have been identified as underlying the development and maintenance of abnormal beliefs. In therapy with psychotic patients, these biases can be directly challenged through Socratic questioning and behavioural experiments.

In social phobia, Clark and Wells (1994) report a series of experiments supporting the cognitive model, which proposes that:

1 social phobics interpret social situations in a more threatening fashion than do those who are not social phobics;

2   social phobics believe that others are evaluating them negatively because their attention is self-focused rather than other-focused;

3   relative to controls, social phobics have poorer memory of the details of recent social interactions;

4   social phobics are more aware of interoceptive information (such as heart rate) in social situations than those who are not social phobics;

5   social phobics believe that others judge them according to their own perceptions of their emotional response;

6   social phobics show an attentional bias to social-threat words;

7   social phobics conduct a post-mortem on their negative self-evaluation.

Such studies evidently help shape the model of therapy for a particular disorder, leading to specific methods of treatment which can be incorporated in the generic model of cognitive therapy.

The theoretical, experimental and treatment studies described in the first two chapters were, of necessity, selective, as each area covered would ideally require at least a chapter to itself. However, as we indicated, we refer the interested reader to more extended discussions in the numerous references (see p. 261).

TRAINING IN COGNITIVE THERAPY

The background knowledge and specific skills which the cognitive therapist must master have been underlined above and made evident in the case studies. It will be clear that specialised training and expert supervision are essential. Hence, it is a welcome development that cognitive therapy is now taught in standardised, formal courses which are university-validated and accredited as postgraduate courses by the British Psychological Society. Newcastle-upon-Tyne, Oxford and London now offer such courses to professionals from various mental health backgrounds. From our experience in Newcastle-upon-Tyne it would seem that trainees find it hard to learn cognitive therapy in its purest form, even though they may believe that they are already cognitive therapists. They usually discover that they are at the beginning of a long learning process. Usually, at the end of the year they report feeling more confident in generating cognitive formulations which they can use as the centre-point of their therapy to produce treatment strategies. They begin to be able to see the wood and not just the individual trees! Interestingly, most want to continue their supervision beyond the end of the course.

A question that is often asked is, what are the qualities of a good cognitive therapist? Can we predict at the beginning of a course who will be the best therapists? Little is known in this area. Previous research has been mostly concerned with the qualities that facilitate a good outcome in psychodynamic therapy. Lambert (1989), for example, summarised therapeutic qualities in terms of five static traits: demographics, personality patterns, attitudes and values, personal adjustment, and training orientations and experience; and in terms of three process variables: therapeutic style, techniques, and relationship attitudes. Luborsky's Rating Scale for Therapist Qualities (Luborsky *et al.*, 1985) assesses three predictive factors of good outcome: interest in helping others, the therapist's skill, and the therapist's psychological adjustment.

From our experience, the important qualities are as follows:

1   The cognitive therapist needs the ability to listen and observe in an objective but empathic way. This requires that he or she be totally other-focused and *not self-conscious*.
2   But at the same time the cognitive therapist needs to be able to be directive, enquiring and didactic. This requires that he or she ask apposite questions which will facilitate discovery; give appropriate feedback which will briefly summarise the explicit and implicit meaning of several minutes of communication, and help the patient to synthesise what may appear disparate aspects of his or her complaints.

3   A good cognitive therapist needs to enjoy the process of discovery in therapy – that is, the search for a formulation and for the change in methods that will help a particular individual.
4   The good cognitive therapist will have a sense of humour which, if used judiciously, will enhance the therapeutic relationship as well as elevating mood.
5   Importantly, the cognitive therapist needs to have a creative mind; that is, he or she needs to be able not only to adapt methods of treatment to the individual, but also to use colourful concrete images, analogies, stories and vignettes. From patients' feedback at the end of treatment it is clear that these are often what have made an impression and acted as a key turning-point.

Although the competencies of cognitive therapists are formally assessed on a validated rating scale, the Cognitive Therapy Scale (Young and Beck, 1988), it is our experience that the scale is not adequate. Competency is made up of several factors, one of which is skill in adhering to a treatment protocol. On its own, this is evidently not enough. Much more elusive and indefinable is clinical flair. Research in this area is pressingly needed.

FUTURE DIRECTIONS

In addition to expanding into new areas of psychopathology, cognitive therapy will need in the future to address specific issues. These include the prediction of response to cognitive therapy, mechanisms of change, and the prevention of onset of illness.

The prediction of response is a particularly important point for the practising clinician, given the diversity of treatment options, increasing clinical loads and the pressure of health economics. If the clinician has two or three potentially effective treatment methods in his armoury, a moot question is 'Which treatment for whom?' A temptation may be to hedge one's bets by offering a little bit of everything to everyone. But such an eclectic approach is unlikely to benefit anybody; and, far from having an additive effect, the mélange may in fact be less effective than each of its constituent parts.

Unfortunately, the results of the outcome studies described in Chapter 2 do not lead to clear predictions which would allow for decisions in the individual case. Here the least costly treatment may be indicated, which would be psychotropic medication. However, there are two qualifications to this simple solution. Psychotropic medication was found to be cheaper than cognitive therapy in the treatment of depression in the general practice only when it was prescribed by GPs. When prescribed by consultant psychiatrists who treated the patients in the practice, medication was actually more expensive than cognitive therapy (Scott and Freeman, 1992).

In addition to direct costs the indirect costs of mental disorders are extremely high (West, 1992) and, in the majority of cases, recurrence is a high risk. The prevention of relapse and/or recurrence is therefore a major factor when assessing costs in terms of both economics and human suffering. So far, as shown in studies of the long-term effects of cognitive therapy in Chapter 2, the prophylactic effect of this type of treatment appears very promising. So we would say that when there is a high risk of recurrence, cognitive therapy is highly indicated. Other instances where it would be indicated are where medication is contra-indicated or has already been shown to be ineffective, and in cases where short- or long-term compliance with medication is estimated to be low. We need, however, to do more detailed studies of predictive factors of response: by the analysis of single symptoms, as opposed to syndromes; by the analysis of the role of personality factors, of cognitive style, of psychological-mindedness and of environmental factors.

To understand the mechanisms of change in cognitive therapy would also help in the prediction of response, in that non-responders might be identified earlier on in therapy, thus saving money and effort. Such an understanding would also not only help in improving the process of therapy, but might even shorten its course. If, as described in Chapter 1, Beck *et al.*

(1990) are right in their notion that there are four levels of changing schemata – ranging from schema camouflage (lowest level), through schema reinterpretation and schema modification, to schema reconstruction (highest level) – understanding the possible mechanisms of change might also help the therapist to establish reasonable targets for individual patients. For some, only schema camouflage might be possible in the time available, while for others schema reconstruction would be a reasonable aim.

Although, as indicated in Chapter 1, there are several models of the process of change in cognitive therapy (Persons, 1993), progress is likely to come from basic research in cognitive psychology. The beginning of a welcome closer link between clinical and basic cognitive psychology is exemplified in the work of Teasdale and Barnard (1993), which promises to be fruitful. Since the role of schemata is crucial in cognitive theory and therapy, progress in the understanding of mechanisms of change is unlikely without a better methodology in the measurement and analysis of schemata. Current methodology comprises questionnaires, which are unhelpful in identifying the core self schemata of the individual patient. For progress to be made, methods inspired from basic cognitive psychology, and certainly involving idiographic instead of nomothetic approaches, are needed.

Finally, an important future direction for cognitive therapy is likely to lie in the prevention of onset of illness. Given that the therapy is psycho-educational, it is well suited for application to groups at risk. These would include pregnant women, women with young children who do not have employment outside the home, children in their final school years, general-practice patients with chronic low mood, pre-retirement people and those about to be made redundant. Cognitive therapy could be conducted in groups to teach the basic philosophy and techniques. The basic tenet of cognitive therapy – that thoughts are *not* reality – is, after all, very simple; but, unfortunately, this is not taught. Once it *is* fully grasped, the next step – to consider that there may be other views that are less painful and other behaviours that may lead to different views and different emotions – is less arduous.

In conclusion, we would like to stress that cognitive therapy has come a long way, but that it still has far to go. Some theoretical approaches, such as constructivism, are still poorly researched and await empirical validation.

The developmental history of the approach, as described in Chapter 1, indicates that middle age has now arrived, but we have to guard against the potential concomitant complacency. What we hope to have imparted in this book is that despite the confidence acquired in nearly forty years of research and practice, the pioneering attitude and the creativity of youth are needed as much as ever. Progress must be cautious, though, and at this time of growing interest in cognitive therapy we particularly have to remain anchored in our empirical tradition.

References

CHAPTER 1

Adler, A. (1936) The neurotic's picture of the world. *International Journal of Individual Psychology*, 2, 3–10.

Alloy, L. B. (1988) *Cognitive Processes in Depression*. Guilford Press, New York.

Arnkoff, B. (1981) Flexibility in practising cognitive therapy. In G. Emery, S. Hollon and R. Bedrosian (eds), *New Directions in Cognitive Therapy* (pp. 203–23). Guilford Press, New York.

Arnold, M. (1960) *Emotions and Personality* (vol. 1). Columbia University Press, New York.

Bandura, A. (1977) *Social Learning Theory*. Prentice Hall, Englewood Cliffs, NJ.

Barber, J. P., De Rubeis, R. J. (1989) On second thought: where the action is in cognitive therapy for depression. *Cognitive Therapy and Research*, 13, 441–57.

Barnard, P. J., Teasdale, J D. (1991) Interacting cognitive subsystems: a systemic approach to cognitive–affective interaction and change. *Cognition and Emotion*, 5 (1), 1–39.

Beck, A. T. (1967) *Depression: Clinical, Experimental and Theoretical Aspects*. Harper & Rowe, New York.

Beck, A. T. (1976) *Cognitive Therapy and the Emotional Disorders*. International Universities Press, Madison

Beck, A. T., Emery, G. (1985) *Anxiety Disorders and Phobias: A Cognitive Perspective*. Basic Books, New York.

Beck, A. T., Freeman, A., and associates (1990) *Cognitive Therapy of Personality Disorders*. Guilford Press, New York.

Beck, A. T., Rush, A. J., Shaw, B. F., Emery, G. (1979) *Cognitive Therapy and Depression*. Guilford Press, New York.

Beck, A. T., Young, J. (1988) *Cognitive Therapy Rating Scale*. Center for Cognitive Therapy, Philadelphia, Pa.

Blaney, P. H. (1986) Affect and memory: a review. *Psychological Bulletin*, 99, 229–46.

Bower, G. H. (1981) Mood and memory. *American Psychologist*, 36, 129–48.

Bower, G. H. (1983) Affect and Cognition. In D. E. Broadbent (ed.), *Functional Aspects of Human Memory*. London: The Royal Society, pp. 149–64.

Bowlby, J. (1969) *Attachment and Loss*. Vol. 1: *Attachment*. Basic Books, New York.

Bowlby, J. (1973) *Attachment and Loss*. Vol. 2: *Separation: Anxiety and Anger*. Basic Books, New York.

Bowlby, J. (1980) *Attachment and Loss*. Vol. 3: *Loss, Sadness and Depression*. Hogarth, London.

Campbell, R. J. (1989) *Psychiatric Dictionary*. 6th edn. Oxford University Press, New York.

Craik, F. I. M., Tulving, E. (1975) Depth of processing and the retention of words in episodic memory. *Journal of Experimental Psychology: General*, 104, 268–94.

Crowley, R. M. (1985) Cognitions in interpersonal theory and practice. In M. J. Mahoney and A. Freeman (eds), *Cognition and Psychotherapy* (pp. 291–312). Plenum Press, New York.

Davanloo, H. (1980) *Short-term Dynamic Psychotherapy*. Aronson, New York.

Dobson, K. S. (1988) The present and future of cognitive–behavioural therapies. In K. S. Dobson (ed.), *Handbook of Cognitive–behavioural Therapies* (pp. 387–414). Guilford Press, New York.

Dobson, K. S., Block, L. (1988) Historical and philosophical bases of the cognitive–behavioural therapies. In K. S. Dobson (ed.), *Handbook of Cognitive–behavioural Therapies* (pp. 3–38). Guilford Press, New York.

d'Zurilla, T. J. (1988) Problem-solving therapies. In K. S. Dobson (ed.), *Handbook of Cognitive–behavioural Therapies* (pp. 85–135). Guilford Press, New York.

Edwards, D. J. A. (1989) Cognitive restructuring through guided imagery: lessons from gestalt therapy. In A. Freeman, K. M. Simon, L. E. Beutler and H. Arkowitz (eds), *Comprehensive Handbook of Cognitive Therapy* (pp. 283–93). Plenum Press, New York.

Ellis, A. (1962) *Reason and Emotion in Psychotherapy*. Lyle Stuart, New York.

Ellis, A. (1983a) Rational–Emotive Therapy (RET). Approaches to overcoming resistance. I: common forms of resistance. *British Journal of Cognitive Therapy*, 1, 28–38.

Ellis, A. (1983b) Rational–Emotive Therapy (RET). Approaches to overcoming resistance. II: how RET disputes clients' irrational resistance-creating beliefs. *British Journal of Cognitive Therapy*, 1, 1–16.

Ellis, A. (1990) Is Rational–Emotive Therapy (RET) 'rationalist' or 'constructivist'? In L. W. Dryden (ed.), *The Essential Albert Ellis: Seminal Writings on Psychotherapy* (pp. 114–41). Springer, New York.

Ellis, A., Greiger, R. (1977) *Handbook of Rational–Emotive Therapy*. Springer, New York.

Fennell, M. J., Teasdale, J. D., Jones, S., Damlé, A. (1987) Distraction in neurotic and endogenous depression: an investigation of negative thinking in major depressive disorder. *Psychological Medicine*, 17, 441–52.

Frank, J. (1974) Therapeutic components of psychotherapy. *Journal of Nervous and Mental Disease*, 159, 325–42.

Frank, J. (1985) Therapeutic components shared by all therapies. In M. J. Mahoney and A. Freeman (eds), *Cognition and Psychotherapy* (pp. 49–80). Plenum Press, New York.

Freeman, A. (1981) Dreams and images in cognitive therapy. In G. Emery, S. D. Hollon and R. Bedrosian (eds), *New Directions in Cognitive Therapy*. Guilford Press, New York.

Freeman, A. (1992) The development of treatment conceptualizations in cognitive therapy. In A. Freeman and F. M. Dattilio (eds), *Comprehensive Casebook of Cognitive Therapy*. Plenum Press, New York.

Freeman, A., Leaf, R. (1989) Cognitive therapy of personality disorders. In A. Freeman, K. M. Simon, L. E. Beutler and H. Arkowitz (eds), *The Comprehensive Handbook of Cognitive Therapy*. Plenum Press, New York.

Freeman, A., Pretzer, J., Fleming, B., Simon, K. M. (1990) *Clinical Applications of Cognitive Therapy*. Plenum Press, New York.

Golden, W., Dryden, W. (1986) Cognitive–behavioural therapies: commonalities, divergences, and future developments. In W. Dryden and W. Golden (eds), *Cognitive–behavioral Approaches to Psychotherapy* (pp. 356–78). Harper & Row, New York.

Goldfried, M., Padawer, N., Robins, C. (1984) Social anxiety and the somatic structure of heterosocial interaction. *Journal of Abnormal Psychology*, 93, 87–97.

Greenberg, L. S., Safran, J. D. (1984) Integrating affect and cognition: a perspective on the process of therapeutic change. *Cognitive Therapy and Research*, 8, 559–78.

Greenberg, L. S., Safran, J. D. (1987) Emotion in psychotherapy. *American Psychologist*, 44, 19–29.

Guidano, V. F. (1987) *Complexity of the Self. A Developmental Approach to Psychopathology and Therapy*. Guilford Press, New York.

Guidano, V. F. (1991) *The Self in Process: Towards a Post-rationalist Psychotherapy*. Guilford Press, New York.

Guidano, V. F., Liotti, G. (1983) *Cognitive Processes and Emotional Disorders*. Guilford Press, New York.

Hamilton, E. W., Abramson, L. J. (1983) Cognitive patterns and major depressive disorder: a longitudinal study in a hospital setting. *Journal of Abnormal Psychology*, 92, 173–84.

Hollon, S., Kriss, M. (1984) Cognitive factors in clinical research and practice. *Clinical Psychology Review*, 4, 35–76.

Hollon, S. D., DeRubeis, R. J., Evans, M. D. (1987) Causal mediation of change in treatment for depression: discriminating between non-specific and non-causality. *Psychological Bulletin*, 102, 139–49.

Horney, K. (1950) *Neurosis and Human Growth: The struggle toward self-realization*. Norton: New York.

Howes, J. L., Parrott, C. A. (1991) Conceptualization and flexibility in cognitive therapy. In T. M. Vallis, J. L. Howes and P. C. Miller (eds), *The Challenge of Cognitive Therapy, Applications to Nontraditional Populations*. Plenum Press, New York.

Jack, R. L., Williams, J. M. G. (1991) Attribution and intervention in self-poisoning. *British Journal of Medical Psychology*, 64, 345–58.

Jacobson, N. S. (1989) The therapist–client relationship in cognitive behaviour therapy: implications for treating depression. *Journal of Cognitive Psychotherapy*, 3, 85–96.

Kelly, G. (1955) *The Psychology of Personal Constructs*. Norton, New York.

Kuiper, N. A., Derry, P. A. (1982) Depressed and non-depressed content self-reference in mild depressives. *Journal of Personality*, 50, 67–80.

Kuiper, N., Olinger, J. (1986) Dysfunctional attitudes and a self-worth contingency model of depression. In P. Kendall (ed.), *Advances in Cognitive–behavioural Research and Therapy* (vol. 5). Academic Press, New York.

Lambert, K. N. (1983) *Psychotherapy and Patient Relationships*. Dorsey, Homewood, Ill.

Lazarus, A. (1987) The multimodal approach with adult outpatients. In N. Jacobson (ed.), *Psychotherapists in Clinical Practice: Cognitive and Behavioral Perspectives* (pp. 286–326). Guilford Press, New York.

Lazarus, A., Fay, A. (1982) Resistance or rationalization? A cognitive–behavioural perspective. In P. Wachtel (ed.), *Resistance: Psychodynamic and Behavioral Approaches* (pp. 115–32). Plenum Press, New York.

Lazarus, R. (1966) *Psychotherapy and Patient Relationships*. McGraw-Hill, New York.

Liotti, G. (1987) The resistance to change of cognitive structures: a counterproposal to psychoanalytic metapsychology. *Journal of*

Cognitive Psychotherapy: An International Quarterly, 1, 87–104.

Liotti, G. (1991) Patterns of attachment and the assessment of inter-personal schemata: understanding and changing difficult patient–therapist relationships in cognitive psychotherapy. *Journal of Cognitive Psychotherapy*, 5, 105–14.

Louisy, H. (1989) Automatic activation of core and peripheral self-knowledge: an idiographic approach. Unpublished Masters thesis, University of Saskatchewan, Saskatoon, Canada.

Mahoney, M. J. (1974) *Cognition and Behaviour Modification*. Ballinger, Cambridge, Mass.

Mahoney, M. J. (1988) The congitive sciences and psychotherapy: patterns in a developing relationship. In E. S. Dobson (ed.), *Handbook of the Cognitive Behavioral Therapies* (pp. 357–86). Guilford Press, New York.

Mahoney, M. J. (1991) *Human Change Processes: The Scientific Foundations of Psychotherapy*. Basic Books, New York.

Malan, D. (1976) *The Frontier of Brief Psychotherapy*. Plenum Press, New York.

Mann, J. (1969) *Time-limited Psychotherapy*. Harvard University Press, Cambridge, Mass.

Mattarazzo, R., Philips, J., Weins, A., Saslow, G. (1965) Learning the art of interviewing: a study of what beginning students do and their pattern of change. *Psychotherapy: Theory, Research and Practice*, 2, 49–60.

Meichenbaum, D. (1977) *Cognitive-behavior Modification: An Integrative Approach*. Plenum Press, New York.

Meichenbaum, D. (1985) *Stress-inoculation Training*. Pergamon Press, New York.

Meichenbaum, D., Gilmore, J. B. (1982) Resistance from a cognitive–behavioral perspective. In P. Wachtel (ed.) *Resistance: Psychodynamic and Behavioural Approaches* (pp. 133–56). Plenum Press, New York.

Neimeyer, R. (1986) Personal construct therapy. In W. Dryden and W. Golden (eds.), *Cognitive–behavioral Approaches to Psychotherapy* (pp. 224–60). Harper & Row, New York.

Neimeyer, R., Twentyman, C., Prezant, D. (1985) Cognitive inter-personal group therapies for depression: a progress report. *The Cognitive Behaviorist*, 7 (1), 21–2.

Padesky, C. A. (1993) Socratic Questioning: Changing Minds or Guiding Discovery? Paper presented at the European Congress of Behavioural and Cognitive Therapies, London.

Perris, C. (1986) *Cognitive Therapy: Theory and Practice*. Natur Och Kultur, Stockholm.

Persons, J. B. (1993) The process of change in cognitive therapy: schema change or acquisition of compensatory skills? *Cognitive Therapy and Research*, 17 (2) 123–37.

Persons, J., Burns, D., Perloff, J. M. (1985) Mechanisms of action of cognitive therapy. The relative contribution of technical and interpersonal interventions. *Cognitive Therapy and Research*, 9, 539–52.

Piaget, J. (1972) *The Principles of Genetic Epistemology*. Routledge & Kegan Paul, London.

Piaget, J. (1977) *The Development of Thought*. Viking Penguin, New York.

Primakoff, L., Epstein, N., Covi, L. (1989) Homework compliance: an uncontrolled variable in cognitive therapy outcome research. In W. Dryden and P. Trower (eds), *Cognitive Psychotherapy and Stasis and Change* (pp. 175–89). Springer, New York.

Rehm, L. P. (1977) A self-control model of depression. *Behavior Therapy*, 8, 787–804.

Rendon, M. (1985) Cognitions and psychoanalysis. A Horneyman perspective. In M. J. Mahoney and A. Freeman (eds), *Cognition and Psychotherapy* (pp. 277–90). Plenum Press, New York.

Rogers, T. B., Kuiper, N. A., Kirker, W. S. (1977) Self-reference and the encoding of personal information. *Journal of Personality and Social Psychology*, 35 (9), 677–88.

Rosen, H. (1993) Developing themes in the field of Cognitive Therapy. In K. Kuehlwein and H. Rosen (eds.), *Cognitive Therapies in Action: Evolving innovative practice*. Jossey-Bass, San Francisco.

Rothstein, M. A., Robinson, P. N. (1991) The therapeutic relationship and resistance to change in cognitive therapy. In T. M. Vallis, J. L. Howes and P. C. Miller (eds), *The Challenge of Cognitive Therapy. Applications to Nontraditonal Populations*. Plenum Press, New York.

Safran, J. D. (1988) *A refinement of cognitive behavioural therapy and practice in light of interpersonal theory*. Clark Institute of Psychiatry, Toronto.

Safran, J. D. (1990) Towards a refinement of cognitive therapy in light of interpersonal theory: I. Theory. *Clinical Psychology Review*, 10, 107–21.

Safran, J. D., Greenberg, L. S. (1987) Affect and unconscious: a cognitive perspective. In R. Stern (ed.), *Theories of the Unconscious* (pp. 191–212). Analytic Press, Hillsdale, NJ.

Safran, J., Greenberg, L. (1988) Feeling, thinking and acting: a cognitive framework for psychotherapy integration. *Journal of Cognitive Psychotherapy: An International Quarterly*, 2, 109–31.

Safran, J. D., Greenberg, L. S. (1991) *Emotion, Psychotherapy and Change*. Guilford Press, New York.

Safran, J. D., Segal, Z. V. (1990) *Cognitive Therapy: An Interpersonal Process Perspective*. Basic Books, New York.

Safran, J., Vallis, T. M., Segal, Z. V., Shaw, B. F. (1986) Assessment of core cognitive processes in cognitive therapy. *Cognitive Therapy and Research*, 10, 509–26.

Schulman, B. (1985) Cognitive therapy and the individual psychology of Alfred Adler. In M. Mahoney and A. Freeman (eds), *Cognition and Psychotherapy* (pp. 243–58). Plenum Press, New York.

Segal, Z. V. (1990) Appraisal of the self-schema construct in cognitive models of depression. *Psychological Bulletin*, 103, 147–62.

Segal, Z. V., Hood, J. E., Shaw, B. F., Higgins, E. T. (1988) A structural analysis of the self-schema construct in major depression. *Cognitive Therapy and Research*, 12, 471–86.

Sifneos, P. E. (1972) *Short-term Psychotherapy and Emotional Crisis*. Harvard University Press, Cambridge, Mass.

Silverman, J. S., Silverman, J. A., Eardley, D. A. (1984) The process of change: cognitive therapy and pharmacotherapy: changes in mood and cognition. *Archives of General Psychiatry*, 43, 43–50.

Teasdale, J. D. (1983) Negative thinking in depression: cause, effect of reciprocal relationship? *Advances in Behaviour Research and Therapy*, 5, 3–25.

Teasdale, J. D. (1988) Cognitive vulnerability to persistent depression. *Cognition and Emotion*, 2, 247–74.

Teasdale, J. D. (1993). Emotion and two kinds of meaning: cognitive therapy and applied cognitive science. *Behaviour, Research and Therapy*, 31 (4), 339–54.

Teasdale, J. D., Barnard, P. J. (1993) *Affect, Cognition and Change. Re-modelling Depressive Thought*. Lawrence Erlbaum Associates, Hove.

Vallis, T. M., Shaw, B., McCabe, S. (1988) The relationship between therapist competency in cognitive therapy and general therapy skill. *Journal of Cognitive Psychotherapy: An International Quarterly*, 2, 237–50.

Weissman, A. N. (1979) The Dysfunctional Attitude Scale: a validation study. *Dissertation Abstracts International*, 40, 389–90B.

Wessler, R. L. (1993) Cognitive appraisal therapy and disorders of personality. In K. Kuehlwein and H. Rosen (eds.) *Cognitive Therapies in Action: Evolving innovative practice*. Jossey-Bass, San Francisco.

Williams, J. M. G., Watts, F. N., McLeod, C., Mathews, A. (1988) *Cognitive Psychology and Emotional Disorders*. John Wiley, London.

Young, J. E. (1990) *Cognitive Therapy for Personality Disorders: A Schema-focused Approach*. Professional Resource Exchange, Sarasota, Florida.

CHAPTER 2

Agras, W. S., Rossiter, E. M., Arnow, B., Schneider, J. A., Telch, C. F., Raeburn, S. D., Bruce, B., Perl, M., Koran, L. M. (1992) Pharmacologic and cognitive–behavioural treatment for bulimia nervosa: a controlled comparison. *American Journal of Psychiatry*, 149, 82–7.

Agras, W. S, Schneider, J. A., Arnow, B., Raeburn, S., Telch, C. F. (1989) Cognitive–behavioural and response-prevention treatments for bulimia nervosa. *Journal of Consulting and Clinical Psychology*, 57, 215–21.

Alford, B. A., Correia, C. J. (1994) Cognitive therapy of schizophrenia: theory and empirical status. *Behaviour Therapy*, 25, 17–33.

American Psychiatric Association (1987) *Diagnostic and Statistical Manual of Mental Disorders*. 3rd edn. American Psychiatric Association, Washington, DC.

American Psychiatric Association (1994) *Diagnostic and Statistical Manual of Mental Disorders*. 4th edn. American Psychiatric Association, Washington, DC.

Barlow, D. H., Cerny, J. A. (1988) *Psychological Treatment of Panic*. Guilford Press, New York.

Barlow, D. H., Cohen, A. S., Cerny, T. A., Klosko, J. (1989) Behavioural treatment of panic disorder. *Behaviour Therapy*, 20, 261–82.

Barlow, D. H., Cohen, A. S., Waddell, M. T., Vermilyea, B. B., Klosko, J. S., Blanchard, E. B., Dinardo, P. A. (1984) Panic and generalised anxiety disorders. Nature and treatment. *Behaviour Therapy*, 15, 431–49.

Barlow, D. H., Craske, M. G. (1989) *Mastery of Your Anxiety and Panic*. Graywind Publications, Albany, NY.

Barnard, P. J., Teasdale, J. D. (1991) Interacting cognitive subsystems: a systematic approach to cognitive–affective interaction and change. *Cognition and Emotion*, 5, 1–39.

Barnett, P. A., Gotlib, I. H. (1988) Psychological functioning and depression: distinguishing among antecedents, concomitants and consequences. *Psychological Bulletin*, 104, 97–126.

Bebbington, P. (1985) Three cognitive theories of depression. *Psychological Medicine*, 15, 759–69.

Beck, A. T. (1963) Thinking and depression: I. Idiosyncratic content and cognitive distortions. *Archives of General Psychiatry*, 9, 324–33.

Beck, A. T. (1967) *Depression: Clinical, Experimental and Theoretical Aspects*. Harper & Row, New York.

Beck, A. T. (1976) *Cognitive Therapy and the Emotional Disorders.* International Universities Press, New York.

Beck, A. T. (1983) Cognitive therapy and depression: new perspectives. In P. J. Clayton and J. E. Barrett (eds), *Treatment of Depression: Old Controversies and New Approaches* (pp. 265–84). Raven Press, New York.

Beck, A. T., Emery, G. (1985) *Anxiety Disorders and Phobias: A Cognitive Perspective.* Basic Books, New York.

Beck, A. T., Epstein, H., Harrison, R. (1983) Cognitions, attitudes and personality dimensions in depression. *British Journal of Cognitive Psychotherapy*, 1, 1–16.

Beck, A. T., Freeman, A. and associates (1990) *Cognitive Therapy of Personality Disorders*, Guilford Press, New York.

Beck, A. T., Hollon, S. D., Young, J. E., Betrosian, R. C., Budenz, D. (1985) treatment of depression with cognitive therapy and amitriptyline. *Archives of General Psychiatry*, 42, 142–8.

Beck, A. T., Laude, R., Bohnert, M. (1974b) Ideational components of anxiety neurosis. *Archives of General Psychiatry*, 31, 319–26.

Beck, A. T., Rush, A. J., Shaw, B. F., Emery, G. (1979) *Cognitive Therapy of Depression: A Treatment Manual.* Guilford Press, New York.

Beck, A. T., Sokol, L., Clark, D. A., Berchick, B. L., Wright, F. (1992) Focused cognitive therapy of panic disorder: a crossover design and one-year follow-up. *American Journal of Psychiatry*, 147, 778–83.

Beck, A. T., Steer, R. A. (1990) *Manual for the Beck Anxiety Inventory.* Psychological Corporation, New York.

Beck, A. T., Ward, C. H. (1961) Dreams of depressed patients: charcteristic themes in manifest content. *Archives of General Psychiatry*, 5, 462–7.

Beck, A. T., Weissman, A., Lester, D., Trexler, L. (1974a) The measurement of pessimism: the Hopelessness Scale. *Journal of Consulting and Clinical Psychology*, 42, 861–5.

Beck, J. G., Stanley, M. A., Baldwin, L. E., Deagle, E. A., Averill, P. M. (1994) Comparison of cognitive therapy and relaxation training for panic disorder. *Journal of Consulting and Clinical Psychology*, 62, 818–26.

Bentall, R. P., Kinderman, P., Kaney, S. (1994) The self-attributional processes and abnormal beliefs: towards a model of persecutory delusions. *Behaviour Research and Therapy*, 32, 331–41.

Beutler, L. E., Scogin, F., Kirkish, P., Schretlen, D., Corbishley, A., Hamblin, D., Meridith, K., Potter, R., Bamford, C. R., Levenson, A. I. (1987) Group cognitive therapy and alprazolam in the treatment of depression of older adults. *Journal of Consulting Clinical Psychology*, 55, 550–6.

Blackburn, I.-M. (1988) An appraisal of comparative trials of cognitive therapy for depression. In C. Perris, I.-M. Blackburn and H. Perris (eds), *Cognitive Psychotherapy. Theory and Practice* (pp. 160–78). Springer-Verlag, Heidelberg.

Blackburn, I.-M. (1995) The relationship between drug and psychotherapy effects. In M. Aveline and D. A. Shapiro (eds), *Research Foundations for Psychotherapy Practice* (pp. 231–45). John Wiley, London.

Blackburn, I.-M., Bishop, S., Glen, A. I. M., Whalley, L. J., Christie, J. E. (1981) The efficacy of cognitive therapy in depression: a treatment trial using cognitive therapy and pharmacotherapy, each alone and in combination. *British Journal of Psychiatry*, 139, 181–9.

Blackburn, I.-M., Davidson, K. M. (1995) *Cognitive Therapy for Depression and Anxiety*. 2nd edn. Blackwell Scientific Publications, Oxford.

Blackburn, I.-M., Eunson, K. M. (1989) A content analysis of thoughts and emotions elicited from depressed patients during cognitive therapy. *British Journal of Medical Psychology*, 62, 23–33.

Blackburn, I.-M., Eunson, K. M., Bishop, S. (1986b) A two-year naturalistic follow-up of depressed patients treated with cognitive therapy, pharmacotherapy and a combination of both. *Journal of Affective Disorders*, 10, 67–75.

Blackburn, I.-M., Jones, S., Lewin, R. J. P. (1986a) Cognitive style in depression. *British Journal of Clinical Psychology*, 25, 241–51.

Blackburn, I.-M., Roxborough, H. M., Muir, W. J., Glabus, M., Blackwood, J. D. R. (1990) Perceptual and physiological dysfunction in depression. *Psychological Medicine*, 20, 95–103.

Blaney, P. H. (1986) Affect and memory: a review. *Psychological Bulletin*, 99, 229–46.

Blowers, C., Cobb, J., Mathews, A. (1987) Generalised anxiety: a controlled treatment study. *Behaviour Research and Therapy*, 25, 493–502.

Blue, F. R., McKnight, D., Ran, B., Fulcher, R. (1987) A multidisciplinary approach to all individuals with severe ritualistic behaviour. *Psychological Reports*, 61, 407–10.

Borkovec, T. D., Costello, E. (1993) Efficacy of applied relaxation and cognitive behavioural therapy in the treatment of generalized anxiety disorder. *Journal of Consulting and Clinical Psychology*, 61, 611–19.

Borkovec, T. D., Mathews, A. (1988) Treatment of nonphobic

anxiety disorders: a comparison of nondirective, cognitive and coping desensitization therapy. *Journal of Consulting and Clinical Psychology*, 56, 877–84.

Borkovec, T. D., Mathews, A., Chambers, A., Ebraham, S., Lytler, R., Nelson, R. (1987) The effects of relaxation training with cognitive therapy or nondirective therapy and the role of relaxation-induced anxiety in the treatment of generalised anxiety. *Journal of Consulting and Clinical Psychology*, 55, 883–8.

Bower, G. H. (1981) Mood and memory. *American Psychologist*, 36, 129–48.

Bower, G. H. (1987) Commentary on mood and memory. *Behaviour Research and Therapy*, 25, 443–55.

Bradley, B. P., Mathews, A. M. (1988) Memory bias in recovered clinical depressives. *Cognition and Emotion*, 2, 235–45.

Breslow, R., Kocsis, J., Belkin, B. (1991) Contribution of the depressive perspective to memory function in depression. *American Journal of Psychiatry*, 138, 227–30.

Burgess, I. S., Jones, L. N., Robertson, S. A., Radcliffe, W. N., Emerson, E., Lawler, P., Crow, T. J. (1981) The degree of control exerted by phobic and non-phobic verbal stimuli over the recognition behaviour of phobic and non-phobic subjects. *Behaviour Research and Therapy*, 19, 223–34.

Burns, D. D., Nolen-Hoeksema, S. (1992) Therapeutic empathy and recovery from depression in cognitive-behavioural therapy: a structural equation model. *Journal of Consulting and Clinical Psychology*, 60, 441–9.

Butler, G., Cullington, D., Hibbert, G., Kumes, I., Gelder, M. (1987) Anxiety management for persistent generalised anxiety. *British Journal of Psychiatry*, 151, 535–42.

Butler, G., Fennell, M., Robson, P., Gelder, M. (1991) Comparison of behaviour therapy and cognitive behaviour therapy in the treatment of generalised anxiety disorders. *Journal of Consulting and Clinical Psychology*, 59, 167–75.

Butler, G., Mathews, A. (1983) Cognitive processes in anxiety. *Advances in Behaviour Research and Therapy*, 5, 51–62.

Carney, M. W. P., Roth, M., Garside, R. F. (1965) The diagnosis of depressive syndromes and the prediction of ECT response. *British Journal of Psychiatry*, 111, 659–74.

Carter, C. S., Maddock, R. J., Magliozzi, J. (1992) Patterns of abnormal processing of emotional information in panic disorder and major depression. *Psychopathology*, 25, 65–70.

Chadwick, P. D. J., Birchwood, M. (1994) The omnipotence of voices. A cognitive approach to auditory hallucinations. *British Journal of Psychiatry*, 164, 190–201.

Chadwick, P. D. J., Lowe, C. F. (1990) Measurement and modification of delusional beliefs. *Journal of Consulting and Clinical Psychology*, 58, 225–32.

Chadwick, P. D. J., Lowe, C. F. (1994) A cognitive approach to measuring and modifying delusions. *Behaviour Research and Therapy*, 32, 355–62.

Chambless, D. L., Gillis, M. M. (1993) Cognitive therapy of anxiety disorders. *Journal of Consulting and Clinical Psychology*, 61, 248–60.

Clark, D. A., Beck, A. T. (1991) Personality factors in dysphoria: a psychometric refinement of Beck's sociotropy-autonomy scale. *Journal of Psychopathology and Behavioral Assessment*, 13, 369–88.

Clark, D. A., Beck, A. T., Brown, G. K. (1992) Sociotropy, autonomy and life-event perspectives in dysphoric and non-dysphoric individuals. *Cognitive Therapy and Research*, 16, 635–52.

Clark, D. A., Steer, R. A., Beck, A. T., Ross, L. (1995) Psychometric characteristics of revised sociotropy and autonomy scales in college students. *Behaviour Research and Therapy*, 33, 325–34.

Clark, D. M. (1986) A cognitive approach to panic. *Behaviour Research and Therapy*, 24, 461–70.

Clark, D. M. (1989) Anxiety states: panic and generalised anxiety. In K. Hawton, P. Salkovskis, J. Kirk, D. Clark (eds), *Cognitive Behaviour Therapy for Psychiatric Problems: A Practical Guide* (pp. 52–96). Oxford University Press, Oxford.

Clark, D. M., Salkovskis, P. M., Chalkey, A. J. (1985) Respiratory control as a treatment for panic attacks. *Journal of Behaviour Therapy and Experimental Psychiatry* 16, 23–30.

Clark, D. M., Salkovskis, P. M., Hackmann, A., Middleton, H., Anastasiades, P., Gelder, M. (1994) A comparison of cognitive therapy, applied relaxation and imipramine in the treatment of panic disorder. *British Journal of Psychiatry*, 164, 759–69.

Clark, D. M., Teasdale, J. D. (1982) Diurnal variation in clinical depression and accessibility of memories of positive and negative experiences. *Journal of Abnormal Psychology*, 91, 87–95.

Clifford, P. I., Hemsley, D. R. (1987) The influence of depression on the processing of personal attributes. *British Journal of Psychiatry*, 150, 95–193.

Cottraux, J., Mollard, E., Bouvard, M., Marks, I., Sluys, M., Nury, A. M., Douge, R., Ciadella, P. (1990) A controlled study of fluoxamine and exposure in obsessive–compulsive disorders. *International Journal of Clinical Pharmacotherapy*, 5, 17–30.

Covi, L., Lipman, R. S. (1987) Cognitive behavioural group psychotherapy combined with imipramine in major depression. *Psychopharmacological Bulletin*, 23, 173–6.

Coyne, J., Gotlib, I (1983) The role of cognition in depression: a critical appraisal. *Psychological Bulletin*, 94, 472–505.

Craighead, L. W., Agras, W. S. (1991) Mechanisms of action in cognitive–behavioural and pharmacological interventions for obesity and bulimia nervosa. *Journal of Consulting and Clinical Psychology*, 59, 115–25.

Crandell, C. J., Chambless, D. L. (1986) The validation of an inventory for measuring depressive thoughts: the Crandell Cognitions Inventory. *Behavior Research and Therapy*, 24, 403–11.

Craske, M. G., Brown, T. A., Barlow, D. H. (1991) Behavioural treatment of panic disorder: a two-year follow-up study. *Behaviour Therapy*, 22, 289–304.

Dalgleish, T., Watts, F. N. (1990) Biases of attention and memory in disorders of anxiety and depression. *Clinical Psychology Review*, 10, 589–604.

Dattilo, F. M., Freeman, A. (eds) (1994) *Cognitive–Behavioural Strategies in Crisis Intervention*. Guilford Press, New York.

Derry, P. A., Kuiper, N. A. (1981) Schematic processing and self-reference in clinical depression. *Journal of Abnormal Psychology*, 90, 286–97.

DeRubeis, R. J., Evans, M. D., Hollon, S. D., Garvey, M. J., Grove, W. M., Tuason, V. B. (1990) How does cognitive therapy work? Cognitive change and symptom change in cognitive therapy and pharmacotherapy for depression. *Journal of Consulting and Clinical Psychology*, 58, 862–9.

Dobson, K. (1989) A meta-analysis of the efficiency of cognitive therapy for depression. *Journal of Consulting and Clinical Psychology*, 57, 414–19.

Dobson, K. S., Shaw, B. F. (1987) Specificity and stability of self-referent encoding in clinical depression. *Journal of Abnormal Psychology*, 96, 34–40.

Dohr, K. B., Rush, A. T., Bernstein, I. J. (1989) Cognitive biases and depression. *Journal of Abnormal Psychology*, 98, 263–7.

Dunn, R. J. (1979) Cognitive modification with depression-prone psychiatric patients. *Cognitive Therapy and Research*, 3, 307–17.

Dupont, S. (1992) A case of a worried well obsessional (or an 8-month one-night stand) *Behavioural Psychotherapy*, 20, 287–90.

Durham, R. C., Allan, T. (1993) Psychological treatment of generalised anxiety disorder. A review of the clinical significance of results in outcome studies since 1980. *British Journal of Psychiatry*, 163, 19–26.

Durham, R. C., Murphy, I. J. C., Allan, T., Richard, K., Treliving, L. R., Fenton, G. W. (1994) A comparison of cognitive therapy, analytic psychotherapy and anxiety management training in the treatment of generalised anxiety disorder. *British Journal of Psychiatry*, 165, 315–23.

Durham, R. C., Turvey, A. A. (1987) Cognitive therapy vs behaviour therapy in the treatment of chronic general anxiety. *Behaviour Research and Therapy*, 25, 229–35.

Eaves, G., Rush, A. J. (1984) Cognitive patterns in symptomatic and remitted unipolar major depression. *Journal of Abnormal Psychology* 93, 31–40.

Elkin, I., Shea, M. T., Watkins, J. T., Imber, S. D., Sotsky, S. M., Collins, J. F., Glass, D. R., Pilkoniz, P. A., Leber, W. R., Docherty, J. P., Fiester, S. J., Parloff, M. B. (1989) NIMH treatment of depression collaborative research program: general effectiveness of treatments. *Archives of General Psychiatry*, 46, 971–82.

Ellis, A. (1987) Integrative development in rational-emotive therapy. *Journal of Integrative and Eclectic Psychotherapy*, 6, 470–9.

Emmelkamp, P. M., Beens, H. (1991) Cognitive therapy with obsessive–compulsive disorder: a comparative evaluation. *Behaviour Research and Therapy*, 29, 293–300.

Emmelkamp, P. M., Van der Helm, M., Van Zainten, B. L., Ploghg, I. (1980) treatment of obsessive–compulsive patients: the contribution of self-instructional training to the effectiveness of exposure. *Behaviour Research and Therapy*, 18, 61–6.

Emmelkamp, P. M., Visser, S., Hoekstra, R. J. (1988) Cognitive therapy vs exposure *in vivo* in the treatment of obsessive–compulsives. *Cognitive Therapy and Research*, 12, 103–14.

Endicott, J., Spitzer, R. L., Fleiss, J. Z., Cohen, J. (1976) The Global Assessment Scale: a procedure measuring overall severity of psychiatric disturbance. *Archives of General Psychiatry*, 33, 766–71.

Enright, S. T. (1991) Group treatment for obsessive–compulsive disorder: an evaluation. *Behavioural Psychotherapy*, 19, 183–92.

Evans, M. D., Hollon, S. D., DeRubeis, R. J., Piasecki, J. M., Grove, W. M., Garvey, M. J., Tuason, V. B. (1992) Differential relapse following cognitive therapy and pharmacotherapy for depression. *Archives of General Psychiatry*, 49, 802–8.

Fairburn, C. G. (1985) Cognitive–behavioural treatment for bulimia. In D. M. Garner and P. E. Garfinkel (eds), *Handbook of Psychotherapy for Anorexia Nervosa and Bulimia*. Guilford Press, New York.

Fairburn, C. G. (1988) The current status of psychological treatments for bulimia nervosa. *Journal of Psychosomatic research*, 32, 635–45.

Fairburn, C. G., Cooper, P. J. (1989) Eating disorders. In K. Hawton, P. Salkovskis, J. Kirk, D. M. Clark (eds), *Cognitive Behaviour Therapy for Psychiatric Problems. A Practical Guide*. Oxford University Press, Oxford.

Fairburn, C. G., Jones, R., Peveler, R., Carr, S., Hope, R., O'Connor, M. E. (1993) Psychotherapy and bulimia nervosa: longer-term effects of interpersonal psychotherapy, behaviour therapy and cognitive therapy. *Archives of General Psychiatry*, 50, 419–28.

Fairburn, C. G., Jones, R., Peveler, R., Carr, S., Solomon, R., O'Connor, M. E., Hope, R. E. (1991) Three psychological treatments for bulimia nervosa: a comparative trial. *Archives of General Psychiatry*, 48, 463–9.

Fairburn, C. G., Kirk, J., O'Connor, M., Cooper, P. J. (1986) A comparison of two psychological treatments for bulimia nervosa. *Behaviour Research and Therapy*, 24, 629–43.

Fairburn, C. G., Norman, P. A., Welch, S. L., O'Connor, M. G., Doll, H. A., Peveler, R. C. (1995) A prospective study of outcome in bulimia nervosa and the long-term effects of three psychological treatments. *Archives of General Psychiatry*, 52, 304–11.

Foa, E. B. (1979) Failure on treating obsessive–compulsives. *Behaviour Research and Therapy*, 17, 169–76.

Fowler, D., Morley, S. (1989) The cognitive–behavioural treatment of hallucinations and delusions: a preliminary study. *Behavioural Psychotherapy* 17, 267–82.

Frank, E., Kupfer, D. J., Perel, J. M., Cornes, C., Jarrett, D. B., Mallinger, A. G., Thase, M. E., McEachran, A. B., Grocholinski, V. J. (1990) Three-year outcome for maintenance therapies in recurrent depression. *Archives of General Psychiatry*, 47, 1093–9.

Freedman, D. X. (1989) Editorial note (especially for the media). *Archives of General Psychiatry*, 46, 983.

Freeman, A., Dattilo, F. M. (eds) (1992) *Comprehensive Casebook of Cognitive Therapy*. Plenum Press, New York.

Freeman, C. P. L., Barry, F., Dunkeld, D., Turnbull, J., Henderson, A. (1988) Controlled trial of psychotherapy for bulimia nervosa. *British Medical Journal*, 296, 521–5.

Gallagher, D. E., Thompson, L. W. (1982) Treatment of major affective disorder in older adult out-patients with brief psychotherapies. *Psychotherapy, Theory, Research and Practice*, 19, 482–90.

Gandev, P. S. (1992) A cognitive–behavioural approach for the treatment of obsession with an aggressive theme. *Journal of Cognitive Psychotherapy*, 6, 155–91.

Gandev, P. S. (1993) Cognitive–behavioural treatment of compulsive water-drinking: a case report. *Journal of Cognitive Psychotherapy*, 7, 63–8.

Garety, P. A. (1991) Reasoning and delusions. *British Journal of Psychiatry*, 159 (supplement), 14–18.

Garety, P. A., Kuipers, L., Fowler, D., Chamberlain, F., Dunn, D. (1994) Cognitive–behavioural therapy for drug-resistant psychosis. *British Journal of Medical Psychology*, 67, 259–71.

Garner, D. M., Rockert, W., Davis, R., Gasker, M. W., Olmsted, M. P., Eagle, M. (1993) A comparison between CBT and supportive expressive therapy for bulimia nervosa. *American Journal of Psychiatry*, 150, 37–46.

Gelder, M. G. (1990) Psychological treatment for depressive disorder. *British Medical Journal*, 300, 1087–8.

Gelder, M. G., Clark, D. M., Salkovskis, P. M. (1993) Cognitive treatment for panic disorder. *Journal of Psychiatric Research*, 27, 171–8.

Gilbert, P., Reynolds, S. (1990) The relationship between the Eysenck Personality Questionnaire and Beck's concepts of sociotropy and autonomy. *British Journal of Clinical Psychology*, 29, 319–25.

Glen, A. I. M., Johnson, A. L., Shepherd, M. (1984) Continuation therapy with lithium and amitriptyline in unipolar depressive illness: a randomized, double-blind, controlled trial. *Psychological Medicine*, 14, 37–50.

Haaga, D. A., Dyck, M. J., Ernst, D. (1991) Empirical status of cognitive theory of depression. *Psychological Bulletin*, 110, 215–36.

Hamilton, E. W., Abramson, L. Y. (1983) Cognitive patterns and major depressive disorder: a longitudinal study in a hospital setting. *Journal of Abnormal Psychology*, 92, 173–84.

Hamilton, M. (1959) The assessment of anxiety states by rating. *British Journal of Medical Psychology*, 32, 50–5.

Hamilton, M. A. (1960) A rating scale for depression. *Journal of Neurological and Neurosurgical Psychiatry*, 23, 56–62.

Hammen, C., Dyck, M. J., Miklowitz, D. J. (1986) Stability and severity parameters of depressive self-schema responding. *Journal of Social and Clinical Psychology*, 4, 23–43.

Hammen, C., Ellicott, A., Gitlin, M., Jamison, K. R. (1989) Sociotropy/autonomy and vulnerability to specific life events in patients with unipolar depression and bipolar disorders. *Journal of Abnormal Psychology*, 98, 154–60.

Hartmann, A., Herzog, T., Drinkman, A. (1992) Psychotherapy of bulimia nervosa: What is effective? A meta-analysis. *Journal of Psychosomatic Research*, 2, 159–67.

Hibbert, G. A. (1984) Ideational components of anxiety: their origin and content. *British Journal of Psychiatry*, 144, 618–24.

Hollon, S. D. (1982) Cognitive–behavioural treatment of drug-induced pansituational anxiety states. In G. Emery, S. D. Hollon and R. C. Bedrosian (eds), *New Directions in Cognitive Therapy: A Casebook* (pp. 120–38). Raven Press, New York.

Hollon, S. D., Beck, A. T. (1994) Cognitive and cognitive–behavioral therapies. In A. E. Bergin and S. L. Garfield (eds), *Handbook of Psychotherapy and Behaviour Change*. 44th edn. Wiley, New York.

Hollon, S. D., DeRubeis, R. J., Evans, M. D., Wiemer, M. J., Garvey, M. J., Grove, W. M., Tuason, V. B. (1992) Cognitive therapy and pharmacotherapy for depression. Singly and in combination. *Archives of General Psychiatry*, 49, 774–81.

Hollon, S. D., Kendall, P. C. (1980) Cognitive self-statement in depression: development of an automatic thoughts questionnaire. *Cognitive Therapy and Research*, 4, 383–95.

Hollon, S. D., Kendall, P. C., Lumry, A. (1986) Specificity of depressotypic cognitions in clinical depression. *Journal of Abnormal Psychology*, 95, 52–9.

Hollon, S. D., Shelton, R. C., Davis, D. D. (1993) Cognitive therapy for depression: conceptual issues and clinical efficiency. *Journal of Consulting and Clinical Psychology*, 61, 270–5.

Ingram, R. E., Lumry, A. E., Cruet, D., Sieber, W. (1987) Attentional processes in depressive disorders. *Cognitive Therapy and Research*, 11, 351–60.

Isen, A. M., Shalker, T. E., Clark, M., Karp, L. (1978) Affect, accessibility of material in memory and behaviour: a cognitive loop? Journal of Personality and Social Psychology, 36, 1–12.

James, I. A., Blackburn, I.-M. (1995) Cognitive therapy with obsessive–compulsive disorder. *British Journal of Psychiatry*, 166, 444–50.

Jaremko, M. E. (1982) Cognitive restructuring-assistance in the clinical extinction of fear and avoidance. *Scandinavian Journal of Behaviour Therapy*, 11, 175–82.

Kearney, C., Silverman, W. K. (1990) Treatment of an adolescent with obsessive–compulsive disorder by alternating response prevention and cognitive therapy: an empirical analysis. *Journal of Behaviour Therapy and Experimental Psychiatry*, 21, 39–47.

Kingdon, D. G., Turkington, D. (1991) The use of cognitive behaviour therapy with a normalising rationalise in schizophrenia. *Journal of Nervous Disease Rationale*, 179, 201–11.

Klein, D. F. (1989) Review of American psychiatric press review of psychiatry (vol. 7). *American Journal of Psychiatry*, 146, 263–4.

Klosko, J. S., Barlow, D. H., Tassinari, R., Cerny, J. A. (1990) A comparison of alprazolam and behaviour therapy in the treatment of panic disorder. *Journal of Consulting and Clinical Psychology*, 58, 77–84.

Kovacs, M., Beck, A. T. (1978) Maladaptive cognitive structures in depression. *American Journal of Psychiatry*, 135, 525–33.

Kovacs, M., Rush, A. J., Beck, A. T., Hollon, S. D. (1981) Depressed out-patients treated with cognitive therapy and pharmacotherapy. A one-year follow-up. *Archives of General Psychiatry*, 38, 33–9.

Kupfer, D. J., Frank. E., Perel, J. M., Cornes, C., Mallinger, A. G., Thase, M. E., McEachran, A. S. B., Grocholinski, V. J. (1992) Five-year outcome for maintenance therapies in recurrent depression. *Archives of General Psychiatry*, 49, 769–73.

Lam, D. H., Brewins, C. R., Woods, R. T., Bebbington, P. E. (1987) Cognition and social adversity in the depressed elderly. *Journal of Abnormal Psychology*, 96, 23–6.

Last, C., Barlow, D. H., O'Brien, G. T. (1983) Comparison of two cognitive strategies in treatment of a patient with generalised anxiety disorder. *Psychological Reports*, 53, 19–26.

Layden, M. A., Newman, C. F., Freeman, A., Morse, S. B. (1993) *Cognitive Therapy of Borderline Personality Disorder*. Allyn & Bacon, Boston.

Lee, N. F., Rush, A. J. (1986) Cognitive–behavioural group therapy for bulimia. *International Journal of Eating Disorders*, 5, 599–615.

Leitenberg, H., Rosen, J., Gross, J., Nudelman, S., Vara, L. S. (1988) Exposure plus response prevention treatment of bulimia nervosa. *Journal of Consulting and Clinical Psychology*, 56, 535–41.

Lewinsohn, P. M., Steinmetz, J. L., Larson, D. W., Franklin, J. (1981) Depression-related cognitions: antecedent or consequence? *Journal of Abnormal Psychology*, 90, 147–62.

Lindsay, W. R., Gamsu, C. V., McLaughlin, E., Hood, E. M., Epsie, C. A. (1987) A controlled trial of treatments for generalised anxiety. *British Journal of Clinical Psychology*, 26, 3–15.

Linehan, M. M. (1993a) *Cognitive–behavioural Treatment of Borderline Personality Disorders*. Guilford Press, New York.

Linehan, M. M. (1993b) *Skills Training Manual for Treating Borderline Personality Disorders*. Guilford Press, New York.

Linehan, M. M., Armstrong, H. E., Suarez A., Allmon, D., Heard, H. (1991) Cognitive–behavioural treatment of chronically para-suicidal borderline patients. *Archives of General Psychiatry*, 48, 1060–4.

Linehan, M. M., Heard, H., Armstrong, H. E. (1993) Naturalistic follow-up of a behavioural treatment for chronically parasuicidal borderline patients. *Archives of General Psychiatry*, 50, 971–4.

Lloyd, G. G., Lishman, W. A. (1975) Effect of depression on the speed of recall of pleasant and unpleasant experiences. *Psychological Medicine*, 5, 173–80.

Luka, L., Agras, W. S., Schneider, J. A. (1986) Thirty-month follow-up of cognitive behavioural group therapy for bulimia. *British Journal of Psychiatry*, 148, 614–15.

MacLeod, C. (1990) Mood disorders and cognition. In M. W. Eysenck (ed.), *Cognitive Psychology: An International Review* (pp. 9–56). Wiley, Chichester.

MacLeod, C. (1991) Clinical anxiety and the selective encoding of threatening information. *International Review of Psychiatry*, 3, 279–92.

MacLeod, C., Mathews, A. M. (1991) Cognitive experimental approaches to the emotional disorders. In P. R. Martin (ed.), *Handbook of Behaviour Therapy and Psychological Science: An Integrative Approach* (pp. 116–50). Pergamon Press, New York.

MacLeod, C., Mathews, A., Tata, P. (1986) Attentional bias in emotional disorders. *Journal of Abnormal Psychology*, 95, 15–20.

MacLeod, C., McLaughlin, K. (1995) Implicit and explicit memory bias in anxiety: a conceptual replication. *Behaviour Research and Therapy*, 33, 1–14.

Mathews, A. M., MacLeod, C. (1985) Selective processing of threat cues in anxiety states. *Behaviour Research and Therapy*, 23, 563–9.

Mathews, A. M., MacLeod, C. (1986) Discrimination of threat cues without awareness in anxiety states. *Journal of Abnormal Psychology*, 95, 131–8.

Mathews, A. M., Mogg, K., May, J., Eysenck, M. W. (1989) Implicit and explicit memory bias in anxiety. *Journal of Abnormal Psychology*, 98, 236–40.

McDowell, J. (1984) Recall of pleasant and unpleasant words in depressed subjects. *Journal of Abnormal Psychology*, 93, 401–7.

McLean, P. D., Hakstian, A. R. (1979) Clinical depression: comparative efficacy of out-patient treatments. *Journal of Consulting Clinical Psychology*, 47, 818–36.

McLean, P., Taylor, S. (1992) Severity of unipolar depression and choice of treatment. *Behaviour Research and Therapy*, 30, 443–51.

Meterissian, G. B., Bradwejn, J. (1989) Comparative studies on the efficiency of psychotherapy, pharmacotherapy, and their combination in depression: Was adequate pharmacology provided? *Journal of Clinical Psychopharmacology*, 9, 334–9.

Miller, I. W., Bishop, S. D., Norman, W. H., Keitner, G. I. (1985) Cognitive–behavioural therapy and pharmacotherapy with chronic drug-refractory depressed in-patients: a note of optimism. *Behavioural Psychotherapy*, 13, 320–7.

Miller, I. W., Norman, W. H., Keitner, G. I. (1989) Cognitive behavioural treatment of depressed in-patients: six- and twelve-month follow-up. *American Journal of Psychiatry*, 145, 1274–9.

Mineka, S. (1992) Evolutionary memories, emotional processing, and the emotional disorders. In D. Medlin (ed.), The Psychology of Learning and Motivation (vol. 28). Academic Press, New York.

Miranda, J., Persons, J. B. (1988) Dysfunctional attitudes are mood state dependent. *Journal of Abnormal Psychology*, 97, 76–9.

Mitchell, J. E. (1991) A review of controlled trials of psychotherapy for bulimia nervosa. *Journal of Psychosomatic Research*, 35, 23–31.

Mitchell, J. E., Pyle, R. L., Eckert, E. D., Hatsukami, D., Pomeroy, C., Zimmermann, R. (1990) A comparison study of antidepressants and structured intensive group psychotherapy in the treatment of bulimia nervosa. *Archives of General Psychiatry*, 47, 149–57.

Mogg, K., Bradley, B. P., Williams, R. (1995) Attentional bias in anxiety and depression. *British Journal of Clinical Psychology*, 34, 17–36.

Mogg, K., Mathews, A., May, J., Grove, M., Eysenck, M., Weinman, J. (1991) Assessment of cognitive bias in anxiety and depression using a colour-perception task. *Cognition and Emotion*, 5, 221–38.

Mogg, K., Mathews, A. M., Weinman, J. (1987) Memory bias in clinical anxiety. *Journal of Abnormal Psychology*, 96, 94–8.

Moore, K., Burrows, G. D. (1991) Hypnosis in the treatment of obsessive–compulsive disorders. *Australian Journal of Clinical and Experimental Hypnosis*, 19, 63–75.

Moore, R. G., Blackburn, I.-M. (1994) The relationship of sociotropy and autonomy to symptoms, cognition and personality in depressed patients. *Journal of Affective Disorders*, 32, 239–45.

Moore, R. G., Blackburn, I.-M. (in press) The stability of sociotropy and autonomy in depressed patients undergoing treatment. *Cognitive Therapy and Research*.

Murphy, G. E., Simons, A. D., Wetzel, R. D., Lustman, P. J. (1984) Cognitive therapy and pharmacotherapy, singly and together in the treatment of depression. *Archives of General Psychiatry*, 41, 33–41.

Nekanda-Trepka, C. J. S., Bishop, S., Blackburn, I.-M. (1983) Hopelessness and depression. *British Journal of Clinical Psychology*, 22, 49–60.

Ordman, A. M., Kirschenbaum, D. S. (1985) Cognitive–behavioural therapy for bulimia: an initial outcome study. *Journal of Consulting and Clinical Psychology*, 53, 305–13.

Ost, L. B. (1987) Applied relaxation: description of a coping technique and review of controlled studies. *Behaviour Research and Therapy*, 25, 397–410.

Ownby, R. (1983) A cognitive–behavioural intervention for compulsive handwashing with a thirteen-year-old boy. *Psychology in School*, 20, 219–22.

Parkinson, L. A., Rachman, S. (1981) Intrusive thoughts: the effects of an uncontrived stress. *Advances in Behaviour Research and Therapy*, 3, 111–18.

Perris, C., Skagerlind, L. (1994) Cognitive therapy with schizophrenic patients. *Acta Psychiatrica Scandinavica*, 89 (supplement 382), 65–70.

Peselow, E. D., Robins, C., Block, P., Barouche, F., Fieve, R. R. (1990) Dysfunctional attitudes in depressed patients before and after clinical treatment and in normal control subjects. *American Journal of Psychiatry*, 147, 439–44.

Power, K. G., Jerrom, D. W. A., Simpson, R. J., Mitchell, M. J., Swanson, V. (1989) A controlled comparison of cognitive behaviour therapy, diazepam and placebo in the management of generalised anxiety. *Behavioural Psychotherapy*, 17, 1–14.

Power, K. G., Simpson, R. J., Swanson, V., Wallace, L. A,. Feistner, A. T. C., Sharp, D. (1990) A controlled comparison of cognitive behaviour therapy, diazepam and placebo, alone and in combination for the treatment of generalised anxiety disorder. *Journal of Anxiety Disorders*, 4, 267–92.

Pretzer, J., Fleming, B. (1989) Cognitive–behavioural treatment of personality disorders. *The Behaviour Therapist*, 12, 105–9.

Prien, R. F., Kupfer, D. J., Mansky, P. A., Small, J. G., Tuason, V. B., Voss, C. B., Johnson, W. E. (1984) Drug therapy in the prevention of recurrences in unipolar and bipolar affective disorders. *Archives of General Psychiatry*, 41, 1096–1104.

Rachman, S. (1981) The primacy of affect: some theoretical implications. *Behaviour Research and Therapy*, 19, 279–96.

Rachman, S. (1984) A reassessment of the 'primacy of affect'. *Cognitive Therapy and Research*, 8, 579–84.

Rachman, S. J., Hodgson, R. J. (1980) *Obsessions and Compulsions*. Prentice Hall, New York.

Ray, C. (1979) Examination stress and performance on a colour-word interference test. *Perceptual and Motor Skills*, 4, 400–2.

Reda, M. A., Carpiniello, B., Secchiaroli, L., Blanco, S. (1985) Thinking, depression and antidepressants; modified and unmodified depressive beliefs during treatment with amitriptyline. *Cognitive Therapy and Research*, 9, 135–43.

Richards, A., French, C. (1991) Effects of encoding and anxiety on implicit and explicit memory performance. *Personality and Individual Differences*, 12, 131–9.

Robins, C. J. (1990) Congruence of personality and life events in depression. *Journal of Abnormal Psychology*, 99, 393–7.

Robins, C. J., Block, P. (1988) Personal vulnerability, life events, and depression symptoms: a test of a specific interactional model. *Journal of Personality and Social Psychology*, 54, 847–52.

Robinson, L. A., Berman, J. S., Neimeyer R. A. (1990) Psychotherapy for the treatment of depression: a comprehensive review of controlled outcome research. *Psychological Bulletin*, 108, 30–49.

Ross, M., Scott, M. (1985) An evaluation of the effectiveness of individual and group cognitive therapy in the treatment of depressed patients in an inner-city health centre. *Journal of the Royal College of General Practitioners*, 35, 239–42.

Rush, A. J., Beck, A. T., Kovacs, M., Hollon, S. (1977) Comparative efficacy of cognitive therapy and imipramine in the treatment of depressed patients. *Cognitive Therapy and Research*, 1, 17–31.

Rush, A. J., Watkins, J. T. (1981) Group versus individual cognitive therapy: a pilot study. *Cognitive Therapy and Research*, 5, 221–9.

Rush, A. J., Weissenberger, A. J., Eaves, G. (1986) Do thinking patterns predict depression symptoms? *Cognitive Therapy and Research*, 10, 225–36.

Salkovskis, P. M. (1985) Obsessional–compulsive problems: a cognitive–behavioural analysis. *Behaviour Research and Therapy*, 23, 521–83.

Salkovskis, P. M., Jones, D. R., Clark, D. M. (1986) Respiratory control in the treatment of panic attacks: replication and extension with concurrent measurement of behaviour and pC02. *British Journal of Psychiatry*, 148, 526–32.

Salkovskis, P. M., Warwick, H. M. (1985) Cognitive therapy of obsessive–compulsive disorder – treating treatment failures. *Behavioural Psychotherapy*, 13, 243–55.

Schwartz, R. M. (1986) The internal dialogue: on asymmetry between positive and negative coping thoughts. *Cognitive Therapy and Research*, 6, 591–605.

Scott, A. I. F., Freeman, C. L. (1992) Edinburgh primary care depression study: treatment outcome, patient satisfaction and cost after 16 weeks. *British Medical Journal*, 8304, 883–7.

Segal, Z. V. (1988) Appraisal of the self-schema construct in major depression. *Psychological Bulletins*, 103, 147–62.

Segal, Z. V., Shaw, B. F., Vella, D. D. (1989) Life stress and depression: a test of the congruency hypothesis for life event content and depressive sub-type. *Canadian Journal of Behavioural Science*, 21, 389–400.

Shaw, B. F. (1977) Comparison of cognitive therapy and behaviour therapy in the treatment of depression. *Journal of Consulting and Clinical Psychology*, 45, 543–51.

Shea, M. T., Elkin, I., Imber, S. D., Sotsky, S. M., Watkins, J. T., Collins, J. F., Pilkonis, P. A., Beckham, E., Glass, D. R., Dolan, R. T., Parloff, M. B. (1992) Course of depressive symptoms over follow-up. *Archives of General Psychiatry*, 49, 782–7.

Shea, M. T., Pilkonis, P. A., Beckham, E., Collins, J. F., Elkin, I., Solsky, S. M., Docherty, J. P. (1990) Personality disorders and treatment outcome in the NIMH Treatment of Depression Collaborative Research Program. *American Journal of Psychiatry*, 147, 711–18.

Shear, M. K., Fyer, A. J., Ball, G., Josephson, S., Fitzpatrick, M., Gorman, J., Liebowitz, M., Klein, D. F., Frances, A. J. (1991) Vulnerability to sodium lactate in panic disorder patients given cognitive behaviour therapy. *American Journal of Psychiatry*, 148, 795–7.

Shear, M. K., Pilkonis, P. A., Cloitre, M., Leon, A. C. (1994) Cognitive–behavioural treatment compared with nonprescriptive treatment of panic disorders. *Archives of General Psychiatry*, 51, 395–401.

Shipley, C. R., Fazio, A. F. (1973) Pilot study of a treatment for psychological depression. *Journal of Abnormal Psychology*, 82, 372–6.

Sifford, L. A., Raeburn, S. D. (1993) Group cognitive–behavioural therapy and group interpersonal psychotherapy for the non-purging bulimic individual: a controlled comparison. *Journal of Consulting and Clinical Psychology*, 61, 296–303.

Simons, A. D., Garfield, S. L., Murphy, G. E. (1984) The process of change in cognitive therapy and pharmacotherapy for depression: changes in mood and cognition. *Archives of General Psychiatry*, 41, 45–51.

Simons, A. D., Murphy, G. E., Levine, J. L., Wetzel, R. D. (1986) Cognitive therapy and pharmacotherapy for depression: sustained improvement over one year. *Archives of General Psychiatry*, 43, 43–8.

Spitzer, R., Endicott, J., Robins, E. (1978) Research diagnostic criteria: rationale and reliability. *Archives of General Psychiatry*, 35, 773–82.

Steuer, J. L., Mintz, J., Mammen, C. L., Hill, M. A., Jarvik, L. F., McCarley, T., Motoike, P., Rosen, R. (1984) Cognitive–behavioural and psychodynamic group therapy in treatment of geriatric depression. *Journal of Consulting and Clinical Psychology*, 55, 180–9.

Stravynski, R., Greenberg, D. (1992) The psychological management of depression. *Acta Psychiatrica Scandinavica*, 85, 407–14.

Sullivan, P. F., Joyce, P. R., Mulder, R. T. (1994). Borderline personality disorder in major depression. *Journal of Nervous and Mental Disorders*, 182, 508–16.

Tarrier, N., Beckett, R., Harwood, S., Baker, A., Yusupoff, L., Ugarterburn, I. (1993a) A trial of two cognitive–behavioural methods of treating drug-resistant residual psychotic symptoms in schizophrenic patients: I. Outcome. *British Journal of Psychiatry*, 162, 524–32.

Tarrier, N., Sharpe, L., Beckett, R. (1993b) A trial of two cognitive–behavioural methods of treating drug-resistant residual psychotic symptoms in schizophrenic patients: II. Treatment-specific changes in coping and problem-solving skills. *Social Psychiatry and Psychiatric Epidemiology*, 28, 5–10.

Taylor, F. G., Marshall, W. L. (1977) Experimental analysis of cognitive–behavioural therapy for depression. *Cognitive Therapy and Research*, 1, 59–72.

Teasdale, J. D. (1988) Cognitive volunerability to persistent depression. *Cognition and Emotion*, 2, 247–74.

Teasdale, J. D., Barnard, P. J. (1993) *Affect, Cognition and Change. Re-modelling Depressive Thought*. Lawrence Erlbaum Associates Ltd, Hove, UK.

Teasdale, J. D., Dent, J. (1987) Cognitive vulnerability to depression: an investigation of two hypotheses. *British Journal of Clinical Psychology*, 26, 113–26.

Teasdale, J. D., Fennell, M. J. V., Hibbert, G. A., Amies, P. L. (1984) Cognitive therapy for major depressive disorders in primary care. *British Journal of Psychiatry*, 144, 400–6.

Teasdale, J. D., Fogarty, S. J. (1979) Differential effects of induced mood on retrieval of pleasant and unpleasant events from episodic memory. *Journal of Abnormal Psychology*, 88, 248–57.

Teasdale, J. D., Russell, M. L. (1983) Differential effects of induced mood on the recall of positive, negative and neutral words. *British Journal of Clinical Psychology*, 22, 163–71.

Teasdale, J. D., Segal, Z., Williams, J. M. G. (1995) How does cognitive therapy prevent depressive relapse and why should additional control (mindfulness) training help? *Behaviour Research and Therapy*, 33, 25–39.

Teasdale, J. D., Taylor, R. (1981) Induced mood and accessibility of memories: an effect of mood state or of induction procedure? *British Journal of Clinical Psychology*, 20, 39–48.

Teasdale, J. D., Taylor, R., Fogarty, S. J. (1980) Effects of induced elation–depression on the accessibility of memories of happy and unhappy experiences. *Behaviour Research and Therapy*, 18, 339–46.

Thase, M. E., Simons, A. D., Cahalance, J., McGreary, J., Harden, T. (1991) Severity of depression and response to cognitive behavior therapy. *American Journal of Psychiatry*, 148, 784–9.

Thompson, L. W., Gallagher, D., Breckenridge, J. S. (1987) Comparative effectiveness of psychotherapies for depressed elders. *Journal of Consulting and Clinical Psychology*, 55, 385–90.

Thoren, P., Asberg, M., Cronholm, B., Jornestedt, L., Traskman, L. (1980) Clomipramine treatment of obsessive–compulsive disorders: a clinical controlled trial. *Archives of General Psychiatry*, 37, 1281–5.

Turkat, I. D., Carlson, C. R. (1984) Data-based versus symptomatic formulation of treatment. The case of a dependent personality. *Journal of Behaviour Therapy and Experimental Psychiatry*, 15, 153–60.

Turkat, I. D., Levin, R. A. (1984) Formulation of personality disorders. In H. E. Adamson and P. B. Sutker (eds), *Comprehensive Handbook of Psychotherapy*. Plenum Press, New York.

Turkat, I. D., Maisto, S. A. (1985) Personality disorders: application of the experimental method to the formulation and modification of personality disorders. In D. H. Barlow (ed.), *Clinical Handbook of Psychological Disorders*. Guilford Press, New York.

Tyrer, P., Merson, S., Onyett, S., Johnson, T. (1994) The effect of personality disorder on clinical outcome, social networks and adjustment – a controlled clinical trial of psychiatric emergencies. *Psychological Medicine*, 24, 731–40.

van Oppen, P., Arutz, A. (1994) Cognitive therapy for obsessive–compulsive disorders. *Behaviour Research and Therapy*, 32, 70–87.

van Oppen, P., de Haan, E., Van Balkom, A. T., Spinhoven, P., Hoogduin, K., Van Dyck, R. (1995) Cognitive therapy and exposure *in vivo* in the treatment of obsessive–compulsive disorder. *Behaviour Research and Therapy*, 33, 379–90.

Waddell, M. T., Barlow, D. H., O'Brien, G. T. (1984) A preliminary investigation of cognitive and relaxation treatment of panic disorder: effects on intense anxiety vs background anxiety. *Behaviour Research and Therapy*, 22, 393–402.

Watts, F. M., McKenna, F. P., Sharrock, R., Tresize, L. (1986a) Colour-naming of phobia-related words. *British Journal of Psychology*, 77, 97–108.

Watts, F. M., Tresize, L., Sharrock, R. (1986b) Processing of phobic stimuli. *British Journal of Clinical Psychology*, 25, 253–61.

Weissman, A. N., Beck, A. T. (1978) Development and validation of the Dysfunctional Attitude Scale. Paper presented at the annual meeting of the Association for the Advancement of Behaviour Therapy, Chicago.

Welkowitz, L. A., Papp, L. A., Cloitre, M., Liebowitz, M. R., Martin, L. Y., Gorman, J. M. (1991) Cognitive–behaviour therapy for panic disorders delivered by psychopharmacologically oriented clinicians. *Journal of Nervous and Mental Disease*, 179, 473–7.

West, R. (1992) *Depression*. London: Office of Health Economics.

Whisman, M. A. (1993) Mediators and moderators of change in

cognitive therapy of depression. *Psychological Bulletin*, 114, 248–65.

Wilfrey, D. E., Agras, W. S., Telch, C. F., Rossiter, E. M., Schneider, J. A., Golomb, A. G., Sifforch, L. A., Raeburn, S. D. (1993) Group cognitive–behavioural therapy and group inter-personal psychotherapy for the non-purging bulimic individual: a controlled comparison. *Journal of Consulting and Clinical Psychology*, 61, 296–303.

Williams, J. M. G. (1992) *The Psychological Treatment of Depression.* 2nd edn. Routledge, London.

Williams, J. M. G., Watts, F. N., MacLeod, C., Mathews, A. (1988) *Cognitive Psychology and Emotional Disorders.* Wiley, Chichester.

Willmuth, M. E. (1988) Cognitive–behavioural and insight-oriented psychotherapy of an eleven-year-old boy with obsessive–compulsive disorder. *American Journal of Psychotherapy*, 42, 472–8.

Wilson, G. T., Fairburn, C. G. (1993) Cognitive treatment for eating disorders. *Journal of Consulting and Clinical Psychology*, 61, 261–9.

Wilson, G. T., Rossiter, E. M., Kleifield, E. I., Landholm, L. (1986) Cognitive–behavioural treatment of bulimia nervosa: a controlled evaluation. *Behaviour Research and Therapy*, 24, 277–88.

Wilson, P. H., Goldin, J. C., Charbonneau-Powis, M. (1983) Comparative efficacy of behavioural and cognitive treatments of depression. *Cognitive Therapy and Research*, 7, 111–24.

Woody, G. E., McLellan, T., Luborsky, L., O'Brien, C. P. (1985) Sociopathy and psychotherapy outcome. *Archives of General Psychiatry*, 179, 188–93.

Young, J. E. (1990) *Cognitive Therapy for Personality Disorders: A Schema-focused Approach.* Professional Resource Press, Sarasoto, Florida.

Zajonc, R. B. (1980) Feeling and thinking: preferences need no inferences. *American Psychologist*, 35, 151–75.

Zeiss, A. M., Lewinsohn, P. M., Munoz, R. F. (1979) Non-specific improvement effects in depression using interpersonal, cognitive and pleasant events focused treatments. *Journal of Consulting and Clnical Psychology*, 47, 427–39.

Zeitlin, S., McNally, R. (1991) Implicit and explicit memory bias for threat in post-traumatic stress disorder. *Behaviour Research and Therapy*, 29, 451–7.

Zuroff, D. C., Colussy, S. A., Wielgus, M. S. (1983) Selective memory and depression: a cautionary note concerning response bias. *Cognitive Therapy and Research*, 7, 223–32.

CHAPTER 3

Alloy, L. B., Abramson, L. Y. (1988) Depressive realism. Four theoretical perspectives. In L. B. Alloy (ed.), *Cognitive Processes in Depression* (pp. 223–65). Guilford Press, New York.

American Psychiatric Association (1994) *Diagnostic and Statistical Manual of Mental Disorders*. 4th edn. American Psychiatric Association, Washington, DC.

Beck, A. T. (1967) *Depression: Clinical, Experimental and Theoretical Aspects*. Harper & Row, New York.

Beck, A. T. (1976) *Cognitive Therapy and the Emotional Disorders*. International Universities Press, New York.

Beck, A. T. (1983) Cognitive therapy of depression: new perspectives. In P. J. Clayton and J. E. Barrett (eds.) *Treatment of Depression: Old controversies and new approaches*. Raven Press, New York.

Beck, A. T., Rush, A. J., Shaw, B. F., Emery, G. (1979) *Cognitive Therapy of Depression*. Guilford Press, New York.

Beck, A. T., Ward, C. H., Mendelson, M., Mock, J. E., Erbaugh, J. K. (1961) An inventory for measuring depression. *Archives of General Psychiatry*, 4, 561–71.

Beck, A. T., Weissman, A., Lester, D., Trexler, L. (1974) The measurement of pessimism: the Hopelessness Scale. *Journal of Consulting and Clinical Psychology*, 42, 861–5.

Blackburn, I.-M. (1987) *Coping with Depression*. Chambers, Edinburgh.

Blackburn, I.-M., Davidson, K. M. (1995) *Cognitive Therapy for Depression and Anxiety*. 2nd edn. Blackwell Scientific Publications, Oxford.

Blackburn, I.-M., Jones, S., Lewin, R. J. P. (1986) Cognitive style in depression. *British Journal of Clinical Psychology*, 25, 241–51.

Blacker, C. V. R., Clare, A. W. (1987) Depressive disorder in primary care. *British Journal of Psychiatry*, 150, 737–51.

Burns, D. (1980) *Feeling Good: The New Mood Therapy*. William Morrow, New York.

Clinical Resource and Audit Group, the Scottish Office (1993) *Depressive Illness. A Critical Review of Current Practice and the Way Ahead*. Scottish Office, Edinburgh.

Fennell, M. J. V. (1989) Depression. In K. Hawton, P. M. Salkovskis, J. Kirk, D. M. Clark (eds), *Cognitive Behaviour Therapy for Psychiatric Problems. A Practical Guide* (pp. 169–234). Oxford University Press, Oxford.

Freeling, P. R., Tylee, A. (1992) Depression in general practice. In E. S. Pankel (ed.), *Handbook of Affective Disorders*. Churchill Livingstone, Edinburgh.

Hamilton, M. (1960) A rating scale for depression. *Journal for Neuro-logical and Neurosurgical Psychiatry*, 23, 59–61.

Hollon, S. D., Kendall, P. C. (1980) Cognitive self-statements in depression: development of an automatic thoughts questionnaire. *Cognitive Therapy and Research*, 4, 383–95.

Isacsson, G., Boethius, G., Bergman, U. (1992) Low level of anti-depressant prescription for people who later commit suicide: 15 years of experience from a population-based drug database in Sweden. *Acta Psychiatrica Scandinavica*, 85, 444–8.

Kahneman, D., Slovic, P., Tversky, A. (eds) (1982) *Judgement under Uncertainty: Heuristics and Biases*. Cambridge University Press, Cambridge.

Nisbett, R. E., Ross, L. (1980) *Human Inference Strategies and Shortcomings of Social Judgement*. Prentice-Hall, Englewood Cliffs, NJ.

Safran, J. D., Segal, Z. V. (1990) *Interpersonal Process in Cognitive Therapy*. Appendix II. Basic Books, New York.

Schou, M., Weeke, A. (1988) Did manic–depressive patients who committed suicide receive prophylactic or continuation treatment at the same time? *British Journal of Psychiatry*, 153, 324–7.

Speilberger, C., Gorsuch, R., Lushene, R. (1970) *Manual for the State-Trait Anxiety Inventory*. Consulting Psychologists Press, Palo Alto, California.

Weissman, A. N., Beck, A. T. (1978) Development and validation of the Dysfunctional Attitude Scale. Paper presented at the annual meeting of the Association for the Advancement of Behaviour Therapy, Chicago, Illinois.

West, R. (1992) *Depression*. London: Office of Health Economics.

Wilkinson, D. G. (1989) *Depression: Recognition and Treatment in General Practice*. Radcliffe Medical Press, Oxford.

Williams, J. M. G. (1992) *The Psychological Treatment of Depression*. 2nd edn. Routledge, London.

World Health Organisation (1993) *The ICD-10 Classification of Mental and Behavioural Disorder. Diagnostic Criteria for Research*. WHO, Geneva.

CHAPTER 4

American Psychiatric Association (1994) *Diagnostic and Statistical Manual of Mental Disorders*. 4th edn. American Psychiatric Association, Washington.

Angst, J., Doblar-Mikola, A., Schbeindegger, P. (1985) The Zurich study: anxiety and phobia in young adults. *European Archives of Psychiatric and Neurological Sciences*, 235, 171–8.

Barlow, D. H. (1988) *Anxiety and Its Disorders: The Nature and Treatment of Anxiety and Panic*. Guilford Press, New York.

Beck, A. T. (1976) *Cognitive Therapy and the Emotional Disorders*. International Universities Press, New York.

Beck, A. T. (1988) *Love Is Never Enough*. Penguin, London.

Beck, A. T., Emery, G., Greenberg, R. L. (1985) *Anxiety Disorders and Phobias: A Cognitive Perspective*. Basic Books, New York.

Beck, A. T., Steer, R. A. (1990) *Manual for the Beck Anxiety Inventory*. Psychological Corporation, New York.

Beck, A. T., Ward, C. H., Mendelson, M., Mock, J. E., Erbaugh, J. K. (1961) An inventory for measuring depression. *Archives of General Psychiatry*, 4, 561–71.

Beck, A. T., Weissman, A., Lester, D., Trexler, L. (1974) The measurement of pessimism: the Hopelessness Scale. *Journal of Consulting and Clinical Psychology*, 42, 861–5.

Blackburn, I.-M., Davidson, K. (1990) *Cognitive Therapy for Depression and Anxiety*. Blackwell Scientific Publications, Oxford.

Blazer, D. G., Hughes, D., George, L. K., Swartz, M., Boyer, R. (1991) Generalised anxiety disorder. In L. N. Robins, D. A. Regier (eds), *Psychiatric Disorders in America: The Epidemiological Catchment Area Study*. Free Press, New York.

Borkovec, T. D., Costello, E. (1993) Efficacy of applied relaxation and cognitive–behavioural therapy in the treatment of generalized anxiety disorder. *Journal of Consulting and Clinical Psychology*, 61, 611–19.

Borkovec, T. D., Inz, J. (1990) The nature of worry in generalised anxiety disorder. A predominance of thought activity. *Behaviour, Research and Therapy*, 2, 153–8.

Breslau, N., Davis, G. C. (1985) *DSM*-III generalised anxiety disorder: an empirical investigation of more stringent criteria. *Psychiatry Research*, 14, 231–8.

Butler, G. (1992) Personal communication.

Dean, C., Surtees, P. G., Sashisharan, S. P. (1983) Comparison of research diagnostic systems in an Edinburgh community sample. *British Journal of Psychiatry*, 142, 247–56.

Hamilton, M. A. (1960) A rating scale for depression. *Journal of Neurological and Neurosurgical Psychiatry*, 23, 56–62.

Safran, J. D., Segal, Z. V. (1990) *Interpersonal Process in Cognitive Therapy*. Appendix II. Basic Books, New York.

Salkovskis, P. M. (1989) Cognitive–behavioural factors and the persistence of intrusive thoughts in obsessional problems. *Behaviour Research and Therapy*, 27, 677–82.

Salkovskis, P. M., Kirk, J. (1989) Obsessional disorders. In K. Hawton, P. Salkovskis, J. Kirk, D. M. Clark (eds), *Cognitive*

Behaviour Therapy for Psychiatric Problems. A Practical Guide (pp. 129–68). Oxford University Press, Oxford.

Uhlenhuth, E. H., Balter, M. B., Mellinger, G. D., Cisin, I. H., Clinthorne, J. (1983) Symptom checklist syndromes in the general population: correlations with psychotherapeutic drug use. *Archives of General Psychiatry*, 40, 1167–72.

Weissman, A. M., Beck, A. T. (1978) *Development and Validation of the Dysfunctional Attitude Scale*. Paper presented at the annual meeting of the Association for the Advancement of Behaviour Therapy, Chicago.

CHAPTER 5

American Psychiatric Association (1987) *Diagnostic and Statistical Manual of Mental Disorders*. 3rd edn. American Psychiatric Association, Washington, DC.

American Psychiatric Association (1994) *Diagnostic and Statistical Manual of Mental Disorders*. 4th edn. American Psychiatric Association, Washington, DC.

Barlow, D. H., Craske, M. G. (1989) *Mastery of Your Anxiety and Panic*. Graywind Publications, Albany, NY.

Beck, A. T., Emery, G., Greenberg, R. L. (1985). *Anxiety Disorders and Phobias*. Basic Books, New York.

Beck, A. T., Steer, R. A. (1990) *Manual for the Beck Anxiety Inventory*. Psychological Corporation, New York.

Beck, A. T., Ward, C. H., Mendelson, M., Mock, J. E., Erbaugh, J. K. (1961) An inventory for measuring depression. *Archives of General Psychiatry*, 4, 561–71.

Bernstein, D. A., Borkovec, T. D. (1976) *Progressive Relaxation Training: A Manual for the Helping Professionals*. Research Press, Champaign, Ill.

Chambless, D. L., Caputo, G. C., Bright, P., Gallagher, R. (1984) Assessment of fear in agoraphobics: the body sensations questionnaire and the agoraphobic cognitions questionnaire. *Journal of Consulting and Clinical Psychology*, 52, 1090–7.

Clark, D. M. (1986) A cognitive approach to panic. *Behaviour Research and Therapy*, 24, 461–70.

Clark, D. M. (1989) Anxiety states: panic and generalised anxiety. In K. Hawton, P. Salkovskis, J. Kirk and D. M. Clark (eds), *Cognitive Behaviour Therapy for Psychiatric Problems: A Practical Guide*. Oxford Medical Publications, Oxford.

Clark, D. M., Ehlers, A. (1993) An overview of the cognitive treatment of panic disorder. *Applied and Preventive Psychology*, 2, 131–9.

Clark, D. M., Salkovskis, P. M., Gelder, M., Koehler, K., Martin, M., Anastasiades, P., Hackmann, A., Middleton, H., Jeavons, A. (1988) Tests of a cognitive theory of panic. In I. Hand and H. Wittchen (eds), *Panic and Phobias* (vol. 2). Springer-Verlag, New York.

Clark, D. M., Salkovskis, P. M., Hackmann, A., Middleton, H., Anastasiades, P., Gelder, M. (1994) A comparison of cognitive therapy, applied relaxation and imipramine in the treatment of panic disorder. *British Journal of Psychiatry*, 164, 759–69.

Foa, E. B. (1988) What cognitions differentiate panic disorder from other anxiety disorders? In I. Hand and H. Wittchen (eds), *Panic and Phobias* (vol. 2). Springer-Verlag, New York.

Hamilton, M. A. (1960) A rating scale for depression. *Journal of Neurological and Neurosurgical Psychiatry*, 23, 56–62.

Marshall, S. L. (1978) *Men against Fire*. Peter Smith Publications, Gloucester.

McNally, R. (1991) Psychological approaches to panic disorder: a review. *Psychological Bulletin*, 108, 403–19.

Michelson, L., Marchione, K. (1989) Cognitive, behavioural, and physiological-based treatments of agoraphobia: a comparative outcome study. Paper presented at American Association of Behaviour Therapy, November, Washington, DC.

Norton, G. R., Harrison, B., Haunch, J., Rhodes, L. (1985) Characteristics of people with infrequent panic attacks. *Journal of Abnormal Psychology*, 94, 216–21.

Reich, J. H. (1986) The epidemiology of anxiety. *Journal of Nervous and Mental Disorders*, 174, 129–36.

Robins, L. N., Regier, D. A. (1991) *Psychiatric Disorders in America: The Epidemiological Catchment Area Study*. Free Press, New York.

Roth, A., Fonagy, P. (1995) *Research on the Efficacy and Effectiveness of the Psychotherapies*. Department of Health Report, London.

Safran, J. D., Segal, Z. V. (1990) *Interpersonal Process in Cognitive Therapy*. Appendix II. Basic Books, New York.

Salkovskis, P. M. (1988) Phenomenology, assessment and cognitive model of panic. In S. Rachman and j. Maser (eds), *Panic: Psychological Perspectives*. Erlbaum, Hillsdale, NJ.

Salkovskis, P. M., Clark, D. M. (1991) Cognitive therapy for panic disorder. *Journal of Cognitive Psychotherapy*, 5, 215–26.

Speilberger, C., Gorsuch, R., Lushene, R. (1970) *Manual for the State-Trait Anxiety Inventory*. Consulting Psychologists Press, Palo Alto, California.

CHAPTER 6

American Psychiatric Association (1994) *Diagnostic and Statistical Manual of Mental Disorders*. 4th edn. American Psychiatric Association, Washington, DC.

Beech, H. R., Liddel, A. (1974) Decision-making, mood states and ritualistic behaviour among obsessional patients. In H. R. Beech (ed.), *Obsessional States*. Methuen, London.

Emmelkamp, P. M. (1987) Recent developments in the treatment of phobic and obsessive–compulsive disorders. In W. Huber (ed.), *Progress in Psychotherapy Research* (pp. 161–87). University of Louvain Press, Louvain.

Guidano, V. F., Liotti, G. (1983) *Cognitive Processes and Emotional Disorders: A Structural Approach to Psychotherapy*. Guilford Press, New York.

James, I. A., Blackburn, I.-M. (1995) Cognitive therapy with obsessive–compulsive disorder. *British Journal of Psychiatry*, 166, 444–50.

Rachman, S. J., DeSilva, P. (1978) Abnormal and normal obsessions. *Behaviour Research and Therapy*, 16, 233–8.

Rachman, S. J., DeSilva, P., Roper, G. (1976) The spontaneous decay of compulsive urges. *Behaviour Research and Therapy*, 14, 445–53.

Roper, G., Rachman, S. J. (1975) Obsessional–compulsive checking: replication and development. *Behaviour Research and Therapy*, 13, 25–32.

Roper, G., Rachman, S. J., Hodgson, R. (1973) An experiment on obsessional checking. *Behaviour Research and Therapy*, 11, 271–7.

Safran, J. D., Segal, Z. V. (1990) *Interpersonal Process in Cognitive Therapy*. Appendix II. Basic Books, New York.

Salkovskis, P. M. (1985) Obsessional–compulsive problems: a cognitive–behavioural analysis. *Behaviour Research and Therapy*, 25, 571–83.

Salkovskis, P. M. (1988) Intrusive thoughts and obsessional disorders. In D. Glasgow and N. Eisenberg (eds), *Current Issues in Clinical Psychology*. Gower, London.

Salkovskis, P. M. (1989) Obsessions and compulsions. In J. Scott, J. M. G. Williams, A. T. Beck (eds), *Cognitive Therapy in Clinical Practice* (pp. 50–77). Routledge, London.

Salkovskis, P. M., Harrison, J. (1984) Abnormal and normal obsession: a replication. *Behaviour Research and Therapy*, 22, 549–52.

Salkovskis, P. M., Warwick, H. M. C. (1988) Cognitive therapy of obsessive–compulsive disorder. In C. Perris, I.-M. Blackburn and H. Perris (eds), *The Theory and Practice of Cognitive Therapy*. Springer, Heidelberg.

CHAPTER 7

American Psychiatric Association (1994) *Diagnostic and Statistical Manual of Mental Disorders*. 4th edn. American Psychiatric Association, Washington, DC.

Beck, A. T. (1976) *Cognitive Therapy and the Emotional Disorders*. Penguin, London.

Beck, A. T., Ward, C. H., Mendelson, M., Mock, J. G., Erbaugh, J. K. (1961) An inventory for measuring depression. *Archives of General Psychiatry*, 4, 561–71.

Beck, A. T., Weissman, A., Lester, D., Trexler, L. (1974) The measurement of pessimism: the Hopelessness Scale. *Journal of Consulting and Clinical Psychology*, 42, 861–5.

Chernin, K. (1983) *Womansize. The Tyranny of Slenderness*. Women's Press, London.

Fairburn, C. G. (1992) Personal communication.

Fairburn, C. G., Beglin, S. J. (1990) Studies of the epidemiology of bulimia nervosa. *American Journal of Psychology*, 167, 401–8.

Fairburn, C. G., Cooper, P. J. (1989a) Eating disorders. In D. M. Garner and P. E. Garfinkel (eds), *Handbook of Psychotherapy for Anorexia Nervosa and Bulimia*. Guilford Press, New York.

Fairburn, C. G., Cooper, P. J. (1989b) Eating disorders. In K. Hawton, P. Salkovskis, J. Kirk, D. Clark (eds), *Cognitive Behaviour Therapy for Psychiatric Problems: A Practical Guide* (ch. 8). Oxford University Press, Oxford.

Fennell, M. J. V. (1992) Personal communication.

Fleming, J. (1992) *Never Give Up*. Penguin, London.

Garner, D. M., Garfinkel, P. E. (1979) The eating attitudes test: an index of symptoms of anorexia nervosa. *Psychological Medicine*, 9, 273–9.

Garner, D. M., Garfinkel, P. E. (1985) *Handbook of Psychotherapy for Anorexia Nervosa and Bulimia Nervosa*. Guilford Press, New York.

Gilbert, S. (1989) *Tomorrow I'll Be Slim: The Psychology of Dieting*. Routledge, London.

Hamilton, M. A. (1960) A rating scale for depression. *Journal of Neurological and Neurosurgical Psychiatry*, 23, 56–62.

Harrison, G. B. (1950) *A Book of English Poetry*. (Sonnet CXXX, William Shakespeare.) Penguin, London.

Henderson, M., Freeman, C. P. L. (1987) A self-rating scale for bulimia. The 'BITE'. *British Journal of Psychiatry*, 150, 18–24.

Herzog, D. B., Keller, M. B., Lavori, P. W., Sacks, N. R. (1991) The course and outcome of bulimia nervosa. *Journal of Clinical Psychiatry*, 52 (supplement 10), 4–8.

Lees, S. (1993) *Sugar and Spice, Sexuality and Adolescent Girls.* Penguin Women's Studies, London.

Safran, J. D., Segal, Z. V. (1990) *Interpersonal Processes in Cognitive Therapy.* Basic Books, New York.

Weissman, A. N., Beck, A. T. (1978) Development and validation of the Dysfunctional Attitude Scale. Paper presented at the annual meeting of the Association for the Advancement of Behaviour Therapy, Chicago.

Wolf, N. (1990) *The Beauty Myth.* Vintage, London.

CHAPTER 8

American Psychiatric Association (1994) *Diagnostic and Statistical Manual of Mental Disorders (DSM–IV).* American Psychiatric Association, Washington, DC.

Beck, A. T., Freeman, A., and associates (1990) *Cognitive Therapy of Personality Disorders,* Guilford Press, New York.

Beck, A. T., Ward, C. H., Mendelson, M., Mock, J. E., Erbaugh, J. K. (1961) An inventory for measuring depression. *Archives of General Psychiatry,* 4, 561–71.

Beck, A. T., Weissman, A., Lester, D., Trexler, L. (1974) The measurement of pessimism: the Hopelessness Scale. *Journal of Consulting and Clinical Psychology,* 42, 861–5.

Blackburn, I.—M., Davidson, K. M. (1995) *Cognitive Therapy for Depression and Anxiety.* 2nd edition. Blackwell Scientific Publications, Oxford.

Elkin, I., Shea, M. T., Watkins, J. T., Imber, S. D., Sotsky, S. M., Collins, J. F., Glass, D. R., Pilkoniz, P. A., Leber, W. R., Docherty, J. P., Fiester, S. J., Parloff, M. B. (1989) NIMH Treatment of Depression Collaborative Research Program: general effectiveness of treatments. *Archives of General Psychiatry,* 46, 971–82.

Hollson, S. D., Kendall, P. C. (1980) Cognitive self-statements in depression: development of an automatic thoughts questionnaire. *Cognitive Therapy and Research,* 4, 383–95.

Ingram, R. E., Hollon, S. D. (1986) Cognitive therapy for depression from an information-processing perspective. In R. E. Ingram (ed.), *Information–processing Approaches to Clinical Psychology.* Academic Press, New York.

Layden, M. A., Newman, C. F., Freeman, A., Morse, S. B. (1993) *Cognitive Therapy of Borderline Personality Disorder.* Allyn & Bacon, Boston.

Linehan, M. M. (1993a) *Cognitive–Behavioural Treatment of Borderline Personality Disorder.* Guilford Press, New York.

Linehan, M. M. (1993b) *Skills Training Manual for Treating Border-line Personality Disorder*. Guilford Press, New York.

Mays, D. T., Franks, C. M. (1975) Negative outcome: what to do about it. In D. T. Mays and C. M. Franks (eds), *Negative Outcome in Psychotherapy and What to do about It*. Springer, New York.

Padesky, C. A. (1990) Schema as self-prejudice. *International Cognitive Therapy Newsletter*, 6, 22–3.

Persons, J. B. (1989) *Cognitive Therapy in Practice. A Case Formulation Approach*. Norton, New York.

Rush, A., Shaw, B. F. (1983) Failure in treating depression by cognitive therapy. In E. B. Foa and P. G. M. Emmelkamp (eds), *Failures in Behaviour Therapy*. Wiley, New York.

Rutter, M. (1987) Temperament, personality and personality disorder. *British Journal of Psychiatry*, 150, 443–58.

Safran, J. D., Segal, Z. V. (1990) *Interpersonal Process in Cognitive Therapy*. Appendix II. Basic Books, New York.

Shea, M. T., Pilkonis, P. A., Beckham, E., Collins, J. F., Elkin, I., Solsky, S. M., Docherty, J. P. (1990) Personality disorders and treatment outcome in the NIMH Treatment of Depression Collaborative Research Program. *American Journal of Psychiatry*, 147, 711–18.

Speilberger, C., Gorsuch, R., Lushene, R. (1970) *Manual for the State-Trait Anxiety Inventory*. Consulting Psychologists Press, Palo Alto, California.

Swartz, M., Blazer, D., Winfield, I. (1990) Estimating the prevalence of borderline personality in the community. *Journal of Personality Disorders*, 4, 257–67.

Turkat, I. D., Maisto, S. A. (1985) Personality disorders: application of the experimental method to the formulation and modification of personality disorders. In D. H. Barlow (ed.), *Clinical Handbook of Psychological Disorders*. Guilford Press, New York.

Tyrer, P., Sievewright, N., Ferguson, B., Murphy, S., Johnson, A. L. (1993) The Nottingham study of neurotic disorder: effect of personality status on response to drug treatment, cognitive therapy and self-help over two years. *British Journal of Psychiatry*, 162, 219–26.

Weissman, A. N., Beck, A. T., (1978) Development and validation of the Dysfunctional Attitude Scale. Paper presented at the annual meeting of the Association for the Advancement of Behaviour Therapy, Chicago, Ill.

Weissman, M. M. (1993) The epidemiology of personality disorders. In R. Michels (ed.), *Psychiatry*. J. B. Lippincott, Philadelphia, Pa.

Young, J. E. (1990) *Cognitive Therapy for Personality Disorders: A Schema-focused Approach*. Professional Resource Press, Sarasoto, Florida.

Young, J. E., Brown, G. (1990) *Schema Questionnaire*. 2nd ed. Cognitive Therapy Center of New York, New York.

Young, J. E., Klosko, J. S. (1993) *Reinventing Your Life*. Penguin Books, New York.

Young, J. E. Wattenmaker, D., Wattenmaker, R. (1993) *Schema Therapy Flashcard*. Cognitive Therapy Center of New York, New York.

CHAPTER 9

Beck, A. T., Freeman, A. and associates (1990) *Cognitive Therapy of Personality Disorders*, Guilford Press, New York.

Beck, A. T., Rush, A. J., Shaw, B. F., Emery, G. (1979) *Cognitive Therapy of Depression: A Treatment Manual*. Guilford Press, New York.

Bentall, R. P. (1994) Cognitive biases and abnormal beliefs: towards a model of persecutory delusions. In A. S. David and J. Cutting (eds), *The Neuropsychology of Schizophrenia* (pp. 337–60). Erlbaum, London.

Blackburn, I.–M., Davidson, K. M. (1995) *Cognitive Therapy for Depression and Anxiety*. 2nd ed. Blackwell Scientific Publications, Oxford.

Clark, D. M., Wells, A. (1994) A Cognitive Model of Social Phobia. In R. G. Heimberg, M. Liebowitz, D. Hope and F. Schneir (eds), *Social Phobia: Diagnosis, Assessment and Treatment*. Guilford Press, New York.

Frank, F. O. (1973) *Persuasion and Healing*. 2nd edn. Johns Hopkins University Press, Baltimore, Md.

Garety, P. A., Hemsley, D. R., Wesseley, S. (1991) Reasoning in deluded schizophrenic and paranoid patients. Biases in performance on a probabilistic inference task. *Journal of Nervous and Mental Diseases*, 179, 194–201.

Hawton, K., Salkovskis, P. M., Kirk, J., Clark, P. M. (1989) *Cognitive Behaviour Therapy for Psychiatric Problems. A Practical Guide*. Oxford University Press, Oxford.

Huq, S. F., Garety, P. A., Hemsley, D. R. (1988) Probabilistic judgements in deluded and non-deluded subjects. *Quarterly Journal of Experimental Psychology*, 40A, 801–2.

Lambert, M. J. (1989) The individual therapist contribution to psychotherapy process and outcome. *Clinical Psychology Review*, 9, 469–85.

Luborsky, L., McLellan, A., Woody, G., O'Brien, C., Auerbach, A. (1985) Therapist success and its determinants. *Archives of General Psychiatry*, 42, 602–11.

Persons, J. B. (1989) *Cognitive Therapy in Practice. A Case Formulation Approach*. Norton, New York.

Persons, J. B. (1993) The process of change in cognitive therapy: schema change or acquisition of compensatory skills? *Cognitive Therapy and Research*, 17, 123–37.

Scott, A. I. F., Freeman, C. L. (1992) Edinburgh primary care depression study: treatment outcome, patient satisfaction and cost after 16 weeks. *British Medical Journal*, 8304, 883–7.

Teasdale, J. D., Barnard, P. J. (1993) *Affect, Cognition and Change. Re-modelling Depressive Thought*. Lawrence Erlbaum Associates, Hove, UK.

Truax, C. B., Carkuff, R. R. (1967) *Toward Effective Counselling Psychotherapy: Training and Practice*. Aldine, Chicago, Ill.

West, R. (1992) *Depression*. London: Office of Health Economics.

Williams, J. M. G. (1992) *The Psychological Treatment of Depression*. 2nd edn. Routledge, London.

Young, J. E., Beck, A. T. (1988) *Cognitive Therapy Scale*. Unpublished manuscript, University of Pennsylvania, Philadelphia, Pa.

Index of Subjects

accommodation, 20
achievement, 156, 172
activation–deactivation, 20
activity scheduling, 196, 198
anxiety (content of thought), 24
anxiogenic triad, 25
assessment, 64–9, 92–7, 126, 129, 180–7, 221–5
attachment, 10, 13, 14
attentional bias, 25
attitude, 28
attributional style, 4
automatic thoughts, 4, 156, 159; *see also* negative automatic thoughts
autonomy, 30–2
avoidance: *see* emotional avoidance

basic assumptions, 30
behavioural experiment, 138–42, 200, 205, 253
behavioural tasks, 77
behavioural test, 102, 109, 116, 120
behavioural therapy, 150, 153, 154
beliefs, 28; *see also* conditional beliefs, underlying beliefs
binge eating, 177–8, 180, 184, 196–8, 200, 202–3
bodily sensations, 124
body image, 182, 192
body mass index, 182
bulimia nervosa:
    activity scheduling, 196, 198
    assessment, 180–7
    behavioural experiment, 200, 205
    binge eating, 177–8, 180, 184, 196–8, 200, 202–3
    body image, 182, 192
    body mass index, 182
    case study, 176–212
    conditional assumptions, 192, 202, 209
    core schemata, 186, 192, 202
    diagnostic criteria, 176–7
    epidemiology, 176
    formulation, 189, 190, 199, 208
    guided discovery, 194–6, 201
    low self-esteem, 180, 184, 203, 206
    outcome studies, 48–51
    psychometric measures, 180, 182–3, 207
    purging behaviours, 178, 180, 182, 184, 202, 203
    relapse-prevention, 203, 207, 210
    self-monitoring, 189
    sociocultural factors, 177–9, 211
    suitability for short-term cognitive therapy, 187–9

camouflage: *see* schematic camouflage
case studies: *see* bulimia nervosa, depression, generalised anxiety disorder, long-term problems, obsessional-compulsive disorder, panic disorder
case-formulation approach, 253
catastrophic interpretations, 133–8
change process, 19
cognitive conceptualisation, 6, 9
cognitive diathesis, 4
cognitive model, 59–62, 216–20
cognitive triad, 24
collaborative empiricism, 7, 253; *see also* empiricism
compensatory skills, 20
compulsions, rituals, 149–50, 157, 164, 172
conditional assumptions, 114, 115, 192, 202, 209
conditional beliefs: *see* beliefs
constructivist–rationalist continuum, 12
constructivist/constructivism, 10–13, 18

contamination, contaminated, 149, 154, 164, 166
content-based models, 3
continuum method, 83, 238
coping skills model, 19
core schemata, 108, 114–15, 119, 186, 192, 202; see also schemata

decentring, 153
depression:
  assessment, 64–9
  behavioural tasks, 77
  case study, 57–87
  cognitive model, 59–62
  continuum method, 83
  definition, 58
  diagnostic criteria, 59
  dysfunctional automatic thoughts, 80
  outcome measures, 84
  outcome studies, 33–41
  relapse-prevention, 85
  self-schema, 82
  suitability for short-term cognitive therapy, 69
  treatment plan, 72
  weekly activity schedule, 73
developmental theory, 11
diagnostic criteria, 59, 88–9, 94, 123, 176–7, 215
dialectical behaviour therapy, 219, 220
differential activation hypothesis, 5, 29
distancing, 153, 164
downward arrow, 166
Dysfunctional Attitude Scale (DAS), 29
dysfunctional automatic thoughts, 80

Early Maladaptive Schemata (EMS), 32, 219, 231
efficacy (controlled outcome studies), 33–55
egodystonic, 149
egosyntonic, 149
emotional avoidance, 156–8, 161, 169
empirical approach, 252
empiricism, 9; see also collaborative empiricism
epidemiology, 88, 123, 176, 213
experimental studies, 22

formulation, 92, 100–2, 105, 107–8, 115–17, 189, 190, 199, 208

General Anxiety Disorder (GAD):
  assessment, 92–7
  behavioural test, 102, 109, 116, 120
  case study, 88–121
  conditional assumptions, 114, 115
  core schemata, 108, 114–15, 119
  diagnostic criteria, 88–9, 94
  epidemiology, 88
  formulation, 92, 100–2, 105, 107–8, 115–17
  imagery, 91–3, 103, 108
  outcome studies, 41–3
  psychometric measures, 92, 95, 116–17
  reassurance-seeking, 89, 95–7, 102–3
  relapse-prevention, 118–19
  Socratic questioning, 113–14
  subtle avoidance, 89, 93, 96
  suitability for short-term cognitive therapy, 98–100
  treatment plan, 100
  worry, 89–93, 96
guided discovery, 8, 194–6, 201

historical roots, 1
historical text, 234
homework, 9
hopelessness, 24
hypothesis-testing, 12

imagery, 91–3, 103, 108
induced mood, 26–7
information-processing, 4, 15, 23, 25, 28
interpersonal theory, interpersonal perspective, 10, 15
intrusion, intrusive thoughts, 149, 151, 163, 167, 170

lateral linkaging, 161, 165
long-term problems:
  assessment, 221–5
  case study, 213–51
  cognitive model, 216–20
  continuum method, 238
  definition, 214
  diagnostic criteria, 215
  dialectical behaviour therapy, 219, 220
  Early Maladaptive Schemata (EMS), 219, 231
  epidemiology, 213
  historical text, 234
  negative automatic thoughts, 239
  outcome measures, 243–6

long-term problems – *cont.*
  outcome studies (personality
    disorders), 53–5
  outcome studies (psychoses), 51–3
  personality disorder, 213–21, 225,
    253
  principles of treatment, 230
  relapse-prevention, 247
  re-parenting, 241
  schema-therapy flashcard, 240
  Socratic questioning, 231
  suicide formulation, 249
  suitability for short-term cognitive
    therapy, 225
  treatment plan, 228
low self-esteem, 180, 184, 203, 206

mechanisms of change, 258
memory, 26–8
metacognition, 10
methodological assumptions, 6
modification: *see* schematic modification

negative automatic thoughts, 239; *see
  also* automatic thoughts
neuroticism, 30
neutralising behaviour, 148–9, 151–2,
  154

objective relativism, 11
obsessional-compulsive disorder:
  achievement, 156, 172
  automatic thoughts, 156, 159
  behavioural therapy, 150, 153, 154
  case study, 148–75
  compulsions, rituals, 149–50, 157, 164,
    172
  contamination, contaminated, 149,
    154, 164, 166
  decentring, 153
  distancing, 153, 164
  downward arrow, 166
  egodystonic, 149
  egosyntonic, 149
  emotional avoidance, 156–8, 161, 169
  intrusion, intrusive thoughts, 149, 151,
    163, 167, 170
  lateral linkaging, 161, 165
  neutralising behaviour, 148–9, 151–2,
    154
  outcome studies, 46–8
  perfectionism, perfectionistic, 152,
    153

  problem-solving, 151
  reassurance, 162
  relapse-prevention, 161
  responsibility, 151, 152, 159, 162,
    170–1
  ruminations, 150
  symptom diary, 163
  therapeutic relationship, 153, 161
  underlying beliefs, 151
  vertical linkaging, 161, 166, 168
onset, prevention of, 259
outcome measures, 84, 243–6
outcome studies, 33–41, 41–3, 44–6,
  46–8, 48–51, 51–3, 53–5

panic cycle, 125
panic disorder (content of thought),
  24
panic disorder:
  assessment, 126, 129
  behavioural experiments, 138–42
  bodily sensations, 124
  case study, 122–47
  catastrophic interpretations, 133–8
  diagnostic criteria, 123
  epidemiology, 123
  outcome studies, 44–6
  panic cycle, 125
  relapse-prevention, 145
  safety behaviours, 138
  suitability for short-term cognitive
    therapy, 130
  treatment plan, 131
perfectionism, perfectionistic, 152, 153
personal constructs, 2
personality disorder, 53–5, 213–21, 225,
  253
phenomenology, 6, 7
problem-solving, 151
psychometric measures, 92, 95, 116–17,
  180, 182–3, 207
purging behaviours, 178, 180, 182, 184,
  202, 203

Rational–Emotive Therapy, 2, 12
reassurance, 89, 95–7, 102–3
relapse-prevention, 20, 85, 118–19, 145,
  161, 162, 203, 207, 210, 247, 258
reinterpretation: *see* schematic
  reinterpretation
re-parenting, 241
resistance, 18, 19
response, prediction of, 257–8

responsibility, 151, 152, 159, 162, 170–1
ruminations, 150

safety behaviours, 138
scales (content of thought), 23
schema-therapy flashcard, 240
schemata, 4, 10, 13, 16, 28; *see also* core
    schemata
schematic camouflage, 19, 259
schematic modification, 19, 259
schematic reinterpretation, 19, 259
schizophrenia, 254
self-schema, 82
short-term format, 253
Social Learning Theory, 2
social phobia, 254
sociocultural factors, 177–9, 211
sociotropy, 30–2
Socratic questioning, 8, 9, 17, 113–14,
    231, 253
structural models, 11
subtle avoidance, 89, 93, 96
suicide formulation, 249

suitability for short-term cognitive
    therapy, 69, 98–100, 130, 187–9,
    225
supervision, 255
symptom diary, 163
system process-orientated model, 13

therapeutic relationship, 12, 16, 18, 153,
    161
therapist characteristics, 7, 16, 253
therapist competency, 8, 256, 257
training, 255
transference, 7
treatment plan, 72, 100, 131, 228
tripartite models, 3

unconscious, 10, 15
underlying beliefs, 151; *see also* beliefs

vertical linkaging, 161, 166, 168

weekly activity schedule, 73
worry, 89–93, 96

Index of Authors

Abramson, L. J., 5, 29
Abramson, L. Y., 61
Adler, A., 2, 216
Agras, W. S., 49, 50
Alfrod, B. A., 52
Allan, T., 41
Alloy, L. B., 4, 61
American Psychiatric Association, 48, 53, 58, 88, 123, 127, 148, 176, 215, 221
Angst, J., 88
Arnkoff, B., 16
Arnold, M., 2
Arutz, A., 46

Bandura, A., 2
Barber, J. P., 20
Barlow, D. H., 44, 45, 89, 90, 91, 94, 126
Barnard, P. J., 10, 14, 23, 26, 28, 259
Barnett, P. A., 31
Bebbington, P. 24
Beck, A. T., xi, xiii, 2, 3, 4, 5, 6, 7, 8, 12, 14, 15, 16, 18, 19, 20, 23, 24, 25, 28, 29, 30, 31, 32, 33, 34, 37, 40, 43, 44, 45, 46, 47, 53, 59, 60, 64, 82, 90, 94, 95, 100, 116, 123, 142, 143, 144, 183, 189, 200, 207, 216, 218, 219, 220, 228, 245, 247, 252, 257, 258
Beech, H. R., 150
Beens, H., 47
Beglin, S. J., 176
Bentall, R. P., 51, 254
Bernstein, D. A., 136
Beutler, L. E., 34
Birchwood, M., 52
Blackburn, I., x, xi, xiii, 23, 24, 29, 31, 32, 33, 34, 36, 40, 41, 47, 59, 62, 64, 90, 91, 151, 247, 252
Blacker, C. V. R., 57

Blaney, P. H., 5, 26
Blazer, D. G., 88
Block, L., 8
Block, P., 31
Blowers, C., 42, 43
Blue, F. R., 47
Borkovec, T. D., 41, 42, 43, 89, 90, 92, 136
Bower, G. H., 5, 10, 25, 28
Bowlby, J., 10, 13
Bradley, B. P., 27
Bradwejn, J., 36
Breslau, N., 88
Breslow, R., 27
British Psychological Society, 255
Brown, G., 244
Burgess, I. S., 25
Burns, D. D., 54, 61
Burrows, G. D., 47
Butler, G., 24, 42, 43, 90, 91

Campbell, R. J., 5
Carkuff, R. R., 253
Carlson, C. R., 54
Carney, M. W. P., 36
Carter, C. S., 25
Cerny, J. A., 44
Chadwick, P. D. J., 51, 52
Chambless, D. L., 23, 41, 43, 125
Chernin, K., 206
Clare, A. W., 57
Clark, D. M., 27, 31, 32, 44, 45, 123, 124, 125, 126, 130, 136, 137, 143, 146, 147, 254
Clifford, P. I., 23
Clinical Resource and Audit Group, Scottish Office, 57
Cooper, P. J., 48, 50, 178, 182, 189
Correia, C. J., 52
Costello, E., 42, 43, 90

Cottraux, J., 46
Covi, L., 34
Coyne, J., 26
Craighead, L. W., 50
Craik, F. I. M., 3
Crandell, C. J., 23
Craske, M. G., 44, 45, 46, 126

Dalgleish, T., 25
Dattilo, F. M., 54
Davis, G. C., 88
Davidson, K. M., 41, 59, 90, 91, 247, 252
Dean, C., 88
Dent, J., 30
Derry, P. A., 6, 23
DeRubeis, R. J., 20, 39
DeSilva, P., 150, 151
Dobson, K. S., 8, 23, 33, 36
Dohr, K. B., 23
Dunn, R. J., 34
Dupont, S., 47
Durham, R. C., 41, 42, 43
D'Zurilla, T. J., 7

Eaves, G., 23, 29
Edwards, D. J. A., 14
Ehlers, A., 125
Elkin, I., 34, 35, 36, 213
Ellis, A., 2, 3, 4, 12, 13, 18, 33, 47
Emery, G., 3, 7, 8, 24, 28, 44
Emmelkamp, P. M., 47, 151
Enright, S. T., 47
Eunson, K. M., 24
Evans, M. D., 39, 40

Fairburn, C. G., 48, 49, 50, 51, 176, 178, 182, 188, 189
Fay, A., 18
Fazio, A. F., 38
Fennell, M. J. V., 5, 59, 203
Fleming, B., 53
Fleming, J., 206
Foa, E. B., 46, 125
Fogarty, S. J., 26
Fonagy, P. 123
Fowler, D., 52
Frank, E., 39
Frank, F. O., 253
Franks, C. M., 214
Freedman, D. X., 35
Freeling, P. R., 57
Freeman, A., 5, 15, 19, 54

Freeman, C. P. L., 35, 38, 49, 50, 183, 258
French, C., 28

Gallagher, D. E., 38, 39
Galvin, S., xi
Gandev, P. S., 47
Garety, P. A., 51, 52, 254
Garfinkel, P. E., 176, 183
Garland, A., x, xiii
Garner, D. M., 49, 176, 183
Gelder, M. G., 35, 44
Gilbert, P. 31
Gilbert, S., 206
Gillis, M. M., 41, 43
Glen, A. I. M., 38, 39
Goldfried, M., 3
Gotlib, I., 26, 31
Greenberg, D., 33
Greenberg, L. S., 14, 15
Greiger, R., 3, 4
Guidano, V. F., 10, 13, 16, 152, 170

Haaga, D. A., 23
Hakstian, A. R., 34
Hamilton, E. W., 5, 29
Hamilton, M. A., 30, 43, 64, 82, 95, 143, 144, 183, 207
Hammen, C., 27, 31
Harrison, G. B., 211
Harrison, J., 151
Hartmann, A., 50
Hawton, K., 252
Helmsley, D. R., 23
Henderson, M., 183
Herzog, D. B., 176
Hibbert, G. A., 24
Hodgson, R. J., 46, 151
Hollon, S. D., 10, 20, 23, 35, 36, 41, 43, 64, 216, 245
Horney, K., 2, 216
Huq, S. F., 254

Ingram, R. E., 26, 216
Inz, J., 89, 92
Isacsson, G., 58
Isen, A. M., 27

Jack, R. L., 18
Jacobson, N. S., 15, 16
James, I., x, xiii, 47, 151
Jaremko, M. E., 47
Joyce, L., xiii

Kahneman, D., 61
Kearney, C., 47
Kelly, G., 2, 7, 10
Kendall, P. C., 23, 64, 245
Kingdon, D. G., 52
Kirk, J., 102
Kirschenbaum, D. S., 49
Klein, D. F., 36
Klosko, J. S., 45, 219
Kovacs, M., 28, 40
Kriss, M., 10
Kuiper, N. A., 6, 10, 23, 38
Kupfer, D. J., 39

Lam, D. H., 23
Lambert, K. N., 16
Lambert, M. J., 256
Last, C., 41
Layden, M. A., 53, 220
Lazarus, R., 2, 18
Leaf, R., 19
Lee, N. F., 49
Lees, S., 206
Leitenberg, H., 49
Levin, R. A., 54
Lewinsohn, P. M., 29
Liddel, A., 150
Lindsay, W. R., 42
Linehan, M. M., 53, 54, 219
Liotti, G., 10, 13, 14, 16, 18, 152, 170
Lipman, R. S., 34
Lishman, W. A., 26
Lloyd, G. G., 26
Lowe, C. F., 51, 52
Luborsky, L., 256
Luka, L., 50

MacLeod, C., 25, 27, 28
Mahoney, M. J., 2, 10, 11, 13
Maisto, S. A., 54, 213
Marchione, K., 133
Marshall, S. L., 122
Marshall, W. L., 38
Mathews, A., 24, 25, 27, 28, 42
Mattarazzo, R., 8
Mays, D. T., 214
McDowell, J., 27
McLaughlin, K., 27, 28
McLean, P. D., 34, 35
McNally, R., 28, 125
Meichenbaum, D., 2, 3, 4, 7
Meterissian, G. B., 36
Michelson, L., 131

Miller, I. W., 33, 36, 41
Mineka, S., 27
Miranda, J., 19, 39
Mitchell, J. E., 50
Mogg, K., 25, 26, 27
Moore, K., 47
Moore, R. G., 31, 32
Morley, S., 52
Murphy, G. E., 34, 36

Neimeyer, R., 10, 18
Nekanda-Trepka, C. J. S., 24
Newcastle Cognitive Therapy Centre, ix, x
Nisbet, R. E., 61
Nolen-Hoeksema, S., 54
Norton, G. R., 123

Olinger, J., 10
Ordman, A. M., 49
Ost, L. B., 45
Ownby, R., 47

Padesky, C. A., 17, 230
Parkinson, L. A., 25
Perris, C., 52
Persons, J. B., 10, 19, 20, 39, 247, 253, 259
Peselow, E. D., 29
Piaget, J., 2, 11, 13
Power, K. G., 42
Pretzer, J., 15, 53
Prien, R. F., 38, 39
Primakoff, L., 10

Rachman, S. J., 23, 25, 46, 150, 151
Ray, C., 25
Reda, M. A., 29
Regier, D. A., 123
Rehm, L. P., 7
Reich, J. H., 123
Reichelt, K., xiii
Reynolds, S., 31
Richards, A., 28
Robins, C. J., 31
Robins, L. N., 123
Robinson, L. A., 33
Robinson, P. N., 8
Roper, G., 151
Rosen, H., 10
Ross, L., 61
Ross, M., 34
Roth, A., 123

Rothenstein, M. A., 8
Rush, A. J., 23, 29, 33, 34, 35, 49, 214
Russell, M. L., 27
Rutter, M., 215, 216

Safran, J. D., 10, 11, 14, 15, 17, 69, 98, 131, 145, 157, 187, 226
Salkovskis, P. M., 44, 46, 47, 102, 109, 123, 126, 150, 151, 152, 170
Schou, M., 58
Schwartz, R. M., 23
Scott, A., 35, 38, 258
Scott, J., xi
Scott, M., 34
Segal, Z. V., 6, 10, 11, 14, 15, 17, 29, 31, 39, 69, 98, 131, 145, 157, 187, 226
Shaw, B. F., 23, 38, 214
Shea, M. T., 40, 213
Shear, M. K., 44, 45
Shipley, C. R., 38
Silverman, J. S., 5
Silverman, W. K., 47
Simons, A. D., 29, 40
Skagerlind, L., 52
Speilberger, C., 64, 143, 245
Spitzer, R., 36
Steer, R. A., 43, 95, 142
Steuer, J. L., 38
Stravynski, R., 33
Sullivan, P. F., 54, 216
Swartz, M., 214

Tarrier, N., 52
Taylor, F. G., 38
Taylor, R., 26
Taylor, S., 35
Teasdale, J. D., 5, 6, 10, 13, 14, 23, 26, 27, 28, 29, 30, 34, 36, 39, 259
Thase, M. E., 35
Thompson, L. W., 38, 39
Thoren, P., 46
Truax, C. B., 253
Tulving, E., 3
Turkat, I. D., 54, 213

Turkington, D., 52
Turvey, A. A., 42
Twaddle, V., x, xiii
Tylee, A., 57
Tyrer, P., 54, 214

Uhlenhuth, E. H., 88
US National Institute of Mental Health, 123

Vallia, T. M., 8
van Oppen, P., 46, 47

Waddell, M. T., 41
Ward, D. C. H., 23
Wardle, E., xiii
Warwick, H. M., 47, 151
Watkins, J. T., 34
Watts, F. N., 25, 27
Weeke, A., 58
Weissman, A. N., 5, 29, 64, 95, 245
Weissman, M. M., 214
Welkowitz, L. A., 44
Wells, A., 254
Wessler, R. L., 15
West, R., 39, 58, 258
Whisman, M. A., 39, 56
Wilfrey, D. E., 49
Wilkinson, D. G., 58
Williams, J. M. G., 2, 10, 18, 25, 26, 27, 33, 39, 59, 252
Willmuth, M. E., 47
Wilson, G. T., 49, 50
Wilson, P. H., 38
Wolf, N., 206
Woody, G. E., 54
World Health Organisation, 58

Young, J. E., 14, 15, 16, 32, 53, 219, 220, 231, 240, 243, 244, 257

Zajonc, R. B., 23
Zeiss, A. M., 38
Zeitlin, S., 28
Zuroff, D. C., 27